My River Speaks

THE HISTORY AND LORE OF THE MAGOTHY RIVER

by Marianne Taylor

Bay Media, Inc. Publisher

ARNOLD, MARYLAND

Photographs throughout the book by Michael A. Dulisse are reproduced with permission.

Photographs and illustrations throughout the book by Joan B. Machinchick are reproduced with permission.

The photograph on page 175 is reproduced with permission of the Maryland State Archives from SPECIAL COLLECTIONS (M. E. Warren Collection) Buy boats on the Magothy River, 1969 [33-11-3].

The portrait of Charles Carroll of Carrollton on page 52 is by James Barton Longacre, 1794-1869, after a painting by Field and is reproduced with permission of the National Portrait Gallery, Smithsonian Institution.

The quotations in chapter 10, excerpted from "Turning the Tide, Saving the Chesapeake Bay" by Tom Horton and William M. Eichbaum, are reproduced with permission of Island Press, Washington, DC and Covelo, CA © 1991.

Published by Bay Media, Inc., 1244 Ritchie Highway, Suite 6, Arnold, Maryland 21012

Sponsored by Energy Recovery Corp.

Printed in the United States of America

Library of Congress Catalog Card Number: 98-73314:
    Taylor, Marianne M.
    My River Speaks: The History and Lore of the Magothy River
        Includes maps, illustrations
        Ancient History • Indian • to 1970s
        River lore

ISBN 0-9665239-0-3

Cover photograph by Michael A. Dulisse

For my husband, Robert,
who brought me to the river,
and for all my daughters,
Lauren, Kimberly, Deborah and Rachel,
children of the river.

ACKNOWLEDGEMENTS

I wish to thank graphic designer and illustrator, Joan Machinchick, whose precision, artistic sense of detail, and tenacity have propelled me forward during difficult moments. Without her expertise and loyalty, the book would have been impossible to complete. Much appreciation goes to Michael Dulisse for countless hours spent photographing. I thank Melvin Bender and the Magothy River Land Trust for encouragement and support through a grant, as well as the Magothy River Association for their interest, ongoing newsletter reports, and connections into the community. Much gratitude goes to Pat Troy, publisher, and her staff at Bay Media, Inc. for their vision and expertise and to Kymberly Taylor-Haywood and Helene Becker, editors.

Organizations, trusts, and libraries have contributed greatly to my research with full cooperation and high interest. Among these are researchers at the Natural History Society of Maryland, the Maryland Historical Trust, Kuethe Library, Enoch Pratt Library, the Gibson Island Historical Society, the Museum of Industry and Science, Maryland State Archives and the Ann Arrundell County Historical Society. Much thanks to Tyrone R. Stinson of the Maryland Department of Natural Resources Boating Administration, Dr. Al Luckenbach,

Anne Arundel County archaeologist, Dr. Dennis Jorde of the National Biological Service, U.S. Department of the Interior, and Peter Bergstrom of the U.S. Fish and Wildlife Service for ongoing reports of water quality and wildlife statistics on the Magothy; also helpful was Dr. Paul Hundley, underwater archaeologist, Anne Arundel County. A special thanks to the Gibson Island Historical Society for access to the historical collections and for many hours of patience, especially to Lavinia Peltosaolo, Nancy Bartlett, and William Gilbert. Assiduous readers of the text were Edward Covert and William Gilbert. My thanks to Richard Henderson for information on the Gibson Island Yacht Squadron.

Countless Magothy people have invited me into their homes, and have provided their stories, family records and pictures, contributing abundantly to this endeavor. Milton and Carol Rickets inspired me to start on the project. Among others are the late Natalie Wood Leach, who was my first interviewee; Nellie Watson, Dot Banner, Howard Schindler, Milton T. Oler, Beverly Luper, Howard W. Hammerbacher, Richard Buek, Christian Zeichner, and Marie Angel Durner. A special thanks to Colby Rucker for his help with mills of the Magothy and name origins; Dr. Stephen Hittle for records of the Old Stone House; Sara Anne Stinchcomb for digging out old diaries, which led me into the history of the south side of the Magothy; Peg Howard for her detailed collection of memorabilia on the Persimmon Point House and her ghost stories, to Bob Johnson for his permission to use his invaluable collection of river stories and history of the south side. My appreciation extends to Mr. and Mrs. John Gass who provided historic photographs of Camp Milbur and to Phil Beigel wo led me into the research of the Grachur Club. Many thanks to Kathleen Giddings Hankins, Maxine Councill, Franklin Fick, and all those unnamed people, lovers of the Magothy, who have contributed their lore and enthusiasm to the project.

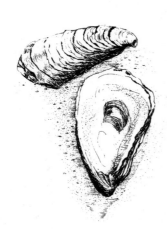

We are a river people, a bay people, tidal and estuarine, whose moods reflect its shores, inlets, coves and beaches. We recognize in each other the draw of energy which the water gives. At the water's edge we experience a source of life, primal and complex, even mysterious.

As lovers of rivers, we know the river as connector between its waters and its people. River enters our souls, joins our families and friends, and provides work and play. River probes the brain and carries the heart to quiet waters. River forms the focus for family gatherings; it offers escape from the ordinary; it backdrops a time remembered that lives beyond a person's life time.

Quickly vanishing along with its quiet waters and sheltered coves are river-remembrances, haunting its creeks and marshes, whispering myriad stories and tales. The once clear, blue-green waters are gone; the quiet days of the soft paddling canoe and of a lone wind-ruffling sail; the old river families paddling across the waters to deliver party invitations; the farms, the mills, the vegetable and lumber landings, the windmills—physically absent now, yet still alive in some memories.

Trying to recapture some of this river's beginnings, I began to search archival records in a quest for early settlers of the region. I searched through general writ-

ten histories, ancient maps, land grants, early land plats and old pictures. The oral history of the region provided invaluable clues to the past. I thank the countless elder citizens who shared their time with me, residents who taxed their memories, and proudly brought forth family albums showing riverside gatherings. A fierce sense of pride of heritage did not cover the fine tears of nostalgia for those once blue-green waters and open sandy shores, synonymous with carefree afternoons and escape from city life. Riverscape and memory produced a stronghold of cherished times for elder citizens.

My initial curiosity was replaced by a passion to recall the ancient and historic peoples who could speak to us of a time less complicated, of a time when the waters were sparkling and unpolluted. I was drawn to the historical Indians who left their artifacts on these shores; their spirit seemed always present.

Pieces of a giant puzzle began to shift into a brightly colored kaleidoscope of Magothy tradition and rich memories. I attempted to correlate the existent Magothy artifacts with the general lifestyle of the Western Shore Indians. In the layers of Magothy clay and mud, Indian pottery, spearheads, scraping tools and pounding tools speak of a particular life—a river existence unlike our own, in some ways; yet in others, it provides a strong bond of connection.

Driving my research were key questions. How did the prehistoric and historic Western Shore peoples react personally to the terrain and respond to the new land opening before them? How did they live and interact with the waters? What characterized their quality of life? Finally, what did their stories reveal about them?

I found that the present moment on the Magothy River contains all past moments; in fact, its history provides a prologue for the future. The treasured stories of elderly citizens integrate into who we are now and transform into the people we will become. Perhaps a look at the past can revive the spirit, refresh the soul and transform into a future vision for reclaiming a river's natural buoyancy and life.

For, speaking quietly to us are the river's remaining natural resources. Among its wild and marshy coves are endangered plants and birds, waterfowl whose very existence depends upon the Magothy's continued life cycles. These endangered species still haunt the river, their unique presence a small miracle of life.

I found that the history of the Magothy River connects richly with the evolving history of the entire Western Shore. I would hope to show through this book that the Magothy's uniqueness lies in its geographical placement, its geology, its topographical configuration, and in its types of early settlers. The responsibility and hope of reclaiming its ecological balance lies with us. In the revelation of its stories, personal lore, and special "tall tales," the Magothy takes its place among the estuaries and tributaries of value which comprise the great Chesapeake Bay. Just as its historical peoples informed its life, its present peoples now shall hold and shape its future.

Marianne Taylor
Ferry Point, 1997

CONTENTS

PART I

Early Peoples
of the Magothy

Ancient river Indians watch the sun go down into the thick groves of pine and oak which rise up along the water's edge

CHAPTER 1

The Ancient Peoples of the Magothy

Prehistoric time is not a time remembered. It is a time when the only memory "chips" lie in the artifacts and fossils of an age long past. Contemporary river people can only imagine this past and try to get a sense of what riverfront life was like so long ago. From 11,000 B.C. to 1600 A.D. a people we cannot actually come to know wandered along the Western Shores of the Chesapeake. Imagining such an early riverine time period can conjure only vague, distant shapes and fragments of what life could have been like during ancient times. In the mind's eye, a primordial scene emerges, a flickering of early life-forms: ancient river Indians watch the sun go down into the thick groves of pine and oak which rise up from the river banks.

Curiosity catapults backwards into origins, to the sources of history, the fundamentals of one's longing for the past. These ancient Indians of the Chesapeake Bay left fragments of a lifestyle which continued through later Indian cultures of the 1600s. Of the prehistoric artifacts found on the Magothy, only a few Paleoindian artifacts (11,000 to 8000 B.C.) have been unearthed; nevertheless these are the actual remnants of the early seasonal encampments within the Magothy environs. Other artifacts found here date from 8000 to 1000 B.C, a time known as the Archaic Period; following this period, plentiful amounts of artifacts have been found which date from 1000 B.C. to 1600 A.D. This is known as the Woodland Period. All of these periods of Indian culture constitute what archaeologists call *prehistory*.

Thousands of years ago this area was covered by a coastal plain, and the Chesapeake Bay did not exist. Originally, during the Pleistocene period, a vast time frame dating from 700,000 to approximately 10,000 years before the present, this area was a freshwater river valley dominated by tundra and spruce forest. Later, as the waters merged with the ocean, the brackish water developed and gradually permeated the land mass due to the melting of the Pleistocene glaciers.

From 12,000 B.C. to 8000 B.C., the ancient Susquehanna River cut a gorge through the area that today forms the central part of the Bay and joined the sea some 657 feet below today's sea level. Slowly, growths of pine forest and oak developed and formed a mosaic of fluctuating landscape with large areas of marshlands and grassland along the edges of the water.

What details are known of early forms of life on these shores? Who were these people? How did they live? What did they do with their time? Archaeologists draw models of the Paleo-hunter life from archaeological evidence found in Northern Pennsylvania, where the huge ancient ice sheets of

that region helped to preserve Paleoindian remnants. They also use evidence from the upper Delaware Valley and from settlement models of Virginia's Shenandoah Valley to create a fuller picture of how ancient peoples lived. Among these forested edges of the Chesapeake the ancient Indians subsisted in a wild, rugged environment, filled with plenteous natural resources. Probably, no person "of any current civilized society could have lasted a year in any of these environments despite their richness of food sources," asserts Louis A. Brennan.[1]

4

In the Mid-Atlantic region, as the Indians ventured to tributary shores such as those of the Magothy, they would set up miniscule hunting and gathering communities. These "hunting parties" would follow the seasonal hunting and fishing cycles, searching for sustenance.[2]

This early race of prehistoric people was characterized as cunning, swift, and lithe as they moved gracefully among the dense pine and oak forests. They followed the herd patterns of animals now extinct. Expert at maximizing all the natural resources which could keep them alive, they subsisted on nuts, fish and whatever wild animals they could hunt down. The Paleoindians learned to cope with fundamental obstacles. They were careful and wary of danger. Perhaps around the corner, a cougar or a wild boar would pounce; shadowy mammoths or mastodons might lurk behind trees. Giant armadillos scuttled around the trees. Grey wolves would howl in the night, and bears and bison roamed the forests. Gradually, as these large mammals became extinct, along with the Pleistocene big brown bat, smaller animals provided sustenance. Between 8000 and 1000 B.C., during the Archaic Period, some of the smaller animals of the hunt were the grey wolf, bear, elk, white-tailed deer, weasel, fox, caribou, otter, shrew and mole. Mink, rabbit, turkey, grouse, and quail were also plentiful.

Keenly, the Indians would plot strategies for hunting and gathering. Local group size had to be adjusted so as not to exhaust the available resources of the local area. Social groups had to change locations with strategic timing to coincide with the availability of certain critical resources that may have varied according to season. They developed perceptive judgment so as to have enough resources when they finally did make small outer encampments away from the primary lithic tool source-camps. These were the sites where they quarried the stone for their implements. Out of this framework of prehistoric life, emerges the Magothy River, a small, significant tributary of the Chesapeake Bay.

The Magothy River

To its north, the Susquehanna and the Patapsco Rivers flow into the great Chesapeake Bay. To its south lies the lovely Severn River, center of yachting on the East Coast, where historic Annapolis sits upon its banks. Tucked into the center of these more popularized rivers, the Magothy seems almost forgotten at times. Paradoxically, it is one of the most heavily used rivers for recreational boating in Maryland. How did this proliferation of life evolve? Where are its own earliest beginnings, its ancient roots which now lie hidden within its archaeological remains?

The Magothy River, one tidal estuary in the complex Chesapeake Bay system, is 6.8 miles long and has a water area of 8.7 square miles. Its hidden coves and shorelines reveal rich sources of historic and archaeological finds which bring forth the spirit of an ancient people. Its ancestors are the aboriginal Indians, later to be followed by Woodland Indians, and the indentured servants, slaves and immigrants, as well as wealthy land owners of the colonial past.

The whisper of this word, "Magothy," is an invitation to fling open the door to a time when these waters were clear and unpolluted, when oysters, fish and fowl were plentiful. Magothy speaks of the haunting days of wild duck calls piercing the stillness, the days of eagles soaring above blue-green waters, of the fish leaping in great bunches, and of the long, still summer afternoons out on the river's edge.

In fact, the name "Magothy," according to Dr. Hamil Kenny, stems from an Indian word, "megä, pi-meguke," meaning "without timber, a wide plain." The root of this word, "mäkw-axkyä" means "great earth."[3] Quite often rivers were named according to their moods, their flow, or their surrounding topography. This implies that, supposedly, wide, spacious lands surrounded at least the mouth of the Magothy. Dr. Kenny notes that the literal meaning of Magothy does not suit its present topography. One explanation for this interpretation could be that at different times during the evolution of Indian land use surrounding the Bay, the lands were known to have been burned for hunting purposes or for seasonal agricultural plots. Known as "barrens," they were common in Tidewater Maryland. It would be safe to say that there was indeed a wide gap between the two land-masses of the Magothy, north and south, and that this configuration played a role in its Indian root name.

A later English translation of its earliest spelling, "Magoty," was "full of Maggots." This was no doubt, the English, colonial version of this translation which Dr. Kenny disclaims. Colby Rucker, noted historian of the Severn, informs that the word "maggot" as defined by Webster, originally meant a "fantastic notion or caprice." He adds that these definitions thus speak of a "capricious or changeable river, on possessed of subtle, elusive moods."[4] Anyone who lives on the Magothy can vouch for that part of its name.

Historically, the spelling of the word has varied over the years. When Captain John Smith mapped the area in 1608, he did not include the Magothy in his *Map of Virginia, 1612.* The earliest citation of the word occurred in 1663 as *Magoty (Magotty) River* (MHM XXVI). It appeared as *Magoty River* (Archives XI, for 1776). On Griffith's Map (Md. 1795) it was titled *"Magothy R."* On the G. M. Hopkins Map (1878), it was titled *"Magothy River."* Interestingly, the *Little Magothy Creek* , now known as the Little Magothy River, was noted as *(Lit. Magothy Cr.)* on the *Martenet Map of Anne Arundel County, Maryland, 1795.*[5]

Just glimpsing into its plethora of meanings and its various spellings, we begin to realize that even the name, "Magothy" evokes a mystery. A definite conclusion can be made that the word is Indian in origin including the notion of a wide, expanse between open lands. What we experience as the beauty and the magic of the Magothy, its unknowable quality and elusiveness are woven into her name.

An Overview of Magothy River Prehistoric Artifacts

The specific archaeological finds of the Magothy, including both the north and the south sides, are palpable connectors into the past, reminders in stone, granite, ceramic and bone of a culture other than our own. Only a few found artifacts date back as far as 11,000 B.C; clusters of archaic artifacts dating from 8000 to 1000 B.C. were also present. Generally, most of the finds dated from 1000 B.C. to 1600 A.D., but are considered a part of Maryland's "prehistory," since at this time "aboriginal population densities reached their apex." Archaeologists relate that during this time, settlements "became more oriented towards riverine environments."[6] (More lifestyle details of this Woodland Indian follow in Chapter 2.)

Various artifacts found along riverbanks and shores of the Magothy are classified into types—lithic, debitage, ceramics, floral or faunal remains and fossilized fragments. The presence, for example, of plentiful amounts of *lithic remains* on the Magothy leads us into the mysterious life of the ancient Indian. (In general, this term refers to all stone artifacts, used functionally by the Indians in various ways, depending upon the structure and stylistic variations of the artifact.) These include such items as *stone drills,* artifacts which have a shaft element and a long, narrow, often extensively retouched blade. Upon further investigation of the region, archaeologists found such artifacts as *chipped stone tools* which have been "manufactured" by shaping the side of the stone into various shapes for different functions. Some of these are shaped into *points.* These include items such as *unifaces, bifaces,* and *projectile points,* whose shape determined their functions.

Countless projectile points or *spearheads* can still be discovered along the Magothy shores. The Indians, both ancient and historical, utilized these stone tools "in much the same way that we use metal tools today." Some of the points were used as weapons in killing game; others were used as knives or re-fashioned into tools, called *scrapers,* for scraping hides to dry . Other types of manufactured tools include special types of *biface knives* for butchering animals. These were also utilized for the manufacture of other tools.[7]

Other findings include what is known as *debitage* or the by-products of the manufacture of chipped stone tools. These include all *cores* defined as fragments or nodules of lithic material from which flakes have been removed, without evidence of retouch or use-wear. In the Magothy region, several *flakes* or sharp tools were discovered. These were used for working bone or hide, once an animal was killed, and are characterized by the striking platform with a few chipping scars on the dorsal face and an acute angle between the platform and ventral face. Also unearthed were *ground stone tools,* manufactured by grinding cobbles of quartzite into a desired shape. These artifacts reveal the abrading on one or more faces of the stone. Several axes and celts (stone "hatchets" or hand adzes), manufactured from granite or greenstone, were tools used for heavy chopping and cutting tasks. Besides stone tools made of chert or jasper, quartz-like in nature, miscellaneous items of Paleoindian origin such as *fossilized shark teeth* and *fossilized barnacles* were found. *Ceramics*, or sherds of pottery found along Magothy shores, form viable reminders of its long history.

Other late Woodland pieces discovered were several *gorgets* or stone orna- ments worn around the neck, dating approximately to 1600 A.D. Large sources of *quartz* and *quartzite* used for tool-making as well as for cooking vessels were also found. Several *bannerstones* were also discovered on various Magothy sites. These were a kind of weight, characterized with a center-groove, and used at the end of a "spear" for the hunt.

Tools found, such as *hammerstones* for grinding herbs or medicinal plants, date later into the historic period from 1000 B.C. to approximately 1600 A.D. Also, a few *ironstone* and *rhyolite tools* for the hunt have been discovered at various Magothy River sites. One important prehistoric site, near the headwaters of the Magothy River, termed "The Magothy Quartzite Site," revealed several large deposits of stone artifacts of various types, including materials of quartzite and sandstone. A possible *rockshelter* was located beneath one of the outcroppings. Even though only a random surface collection had been conducted to date at that site, several artifacts were recovered, indicating the presence of very ancient Indians in this area, dating from about 5000 to 4200 B. C. or perhaps even earli- er. At that site, Dr. Al Luckenbach, Anne Arundel County archeologist and Wayne Clark, Director of the Jefferson Patterson Park and Museum, have done preliminary studies and have found a *Morrow Mountain Point* which dates from 5000 to 4200 B.C. or earlier. These were the hunting tools of the Archaic Indian. This type of hunting point was notched and often serrated, differing from the fluted projectile point of the very ancient Paleoindian. This spearhead is made of a lithic or stone material similar to the quartzite found at the quarry site nearby.[8]

A few prehistoric artifacts were discovered along Forked Creek as well. An

Morrow Mountain Point (Mid-Archaic Period)

Artifacts found on the west bank of Forked Creek, including:

pottery sherds:
#1,2,4 & 7 cord impressed, beach sand tempered;
#3 & 6:incised, shell tempered
#5: fabric marked, quartz tempered

arrowpoints:
#8-12: stemmed and triangular
#17: antler

#13-16: bone awls
#18: gorget, black slate
#19: abrading stone, red sandstone with 2 grooves for smoothing arrow-shafts
(The Natural History Society of Maryland)

isolated *quartz utilized flake* was found, as well as four Accokeek ceramic sherds made of crushed quartz temper and cord-marked, dating to 700 B.C. Others found there "had fit together" and were made of coil construction with paddle-malleated surfaces, dating from 500 B.C. to 900 A.D. This prehistoric site, found at an isolated place along Forked Creek, connects perhaps with the other more plentiful Woodland Indian campsites found there.

Even though the scope of actual Paleoindian finds along the Magothy and its creeks had been scarce, many artifacts came from the later Woodland Period. Countless Indian shell deposits were discovered on Forked Creek. A huge storm in l934, which lasted three days, washed away much of the shoreline which faces a large stretch of water. At that time a long section of the shell deposit exposed rich sources of artifacts. A ceramic pot was found lying on the beach; others were still in place at the bottom of the shell deposit. The vessel had been restored, revealing its basketry marks on the pottery. Ten or twelve cooking and storage vessels were pieced together from almost 200 sherds which had been washed out of the shell deposit. These were impressed with cords and contain beach sand as tempering material. Others found there were marked with fabric, and the ceramic was made with crushed quartz as tempering material.

Accokeek cord-marked pot shown with a cord-wrapped stick, used to impress a border design.

Included among these artifacts were thirty arrowpoints, consisting of both stemmed and triangular types. Other stone objects recovered were a broken grooved axe, a small celt, two fragments of a steatite vessel, a pitted stone, two abrading stones, and a black slate gorget. In another area of Forked Creek, artifacts dating from the mid-eighteenthth to the mid-nineteenth century such as earthenware sherds, some English porcelain, stoneware, refined earthenware, ironstone, redware, pearlware, and yellowware date to the late colonial period.

On Gibson Island, *Buffalo Point Rhyolite,* a prehistoric stone material used for making weapons and tools, was discovered,

Steatite bowl

Gorget - a stone ornament worn around the neck.

as well as a few remnants of *prehistoric pits* used for cooking and for storage. Another unusual find there, which dates far back into early Magothy history was a *corner-notched pentagonal point* which dates to 500 A.D. Other finds include *cryptocrystalline chert* (a flint-like quartz), and points of *jaspers*, materials that were easily tempered into tools.[9]

Along the south side of the river near Dividing Creek, extensive prehistoric shell-midden heaps were found. These are remains of ossified oysters. At other sites situated between Mill and Forked Creek, one small prehistoric heap was located near South Ferry Point where a Woodland period site was unearthed, which included *tempered sherds, quartz debitage, fire cracked rock, faunal remains,* an *awl fragment,* a *Potomac Creek cord impressed pipe* and a *bi-pitted hammerstone.*

From areas along the south side of the Magothy, especially around Ulmstead Point, late woodland pieces (1400 to 1600 A.D.) such as *steatite bowls* (soapstone) used as cooking vessels or for storage, were unearthed. Also discovered were four grooved axes, five celts and one grooved adz, plus pitted hammerstones, rubbing stones and broken gorgets.[10] These represent a more "settled" way of life, an evolutionary phenomenon which occurred during the later Woodland period, as the Indians became relatively more sedentary.

Ancient Indian Modes of River Camp Life

Using these artifacts to interpret ancient Indian cultures in Maryland, archaeologists have devised various "models" of reconstructed life-cultures as well as living patterns of sustenance. Dr. Al Luckenbach has noted that these ancient Indians were seasonal hunters and gatherers, not as entirely nomadic as was previously thought. Supporting this view, state archaeologists of Maryland discovered the existence of what could have been a base camp in an area near the Magothy. This indicates that social groups of a semi-permanent nature were formed in which there would be one permanent campsite with several satellite camps for going forth to hunt, to fish, and to gather special herbs, plants and roots. Central to these campsites would be a lithic or stone quarry, a source for the raw material of Indian weapons and tools. One such source was the "Magothy Quartzite Quarry." Theoretically, this site could have been one of the sources for the base camp located near the environs of what is now the Baltimore-Washington International Airport, playing an essential role in the pattern of movement between the quarry site, the primary base camp, and the seasonal waterside camp. One can assume, based on these archaeological findings, the Magothy River was a satellite for small hunter groups in search of food, a place away from the hub.

blackberry

wild grape

sedge

hackberry

Even though the Indians would hunt in various locations as the season provided, they would still form semi-permanent communities around specific satellite camps. During the archaic era, approximately between 8,000 to 1000 B.C., with the creation of the Chesapeake Bay as we know it, additional resources such as shellfish, anadromous fish, and migratory waterfowl developed in the area. Dr. Luckenbach states that seasonally, the Indians "would follow the fish runs, for example, down near the Patuxent." On the Magothy, the Woodland Indians hunted water-fowl, geese and ducks, and gathered oysters, since these resources were so prolific on the Magothy River, as well as throughout the larger bay.[11]

Louis A. Brennan claims that, "We can conjecture about the nature of such groups. One theory holds that a large band would break up according to family clans, with each family subsisting as a unit, venturing to shoreline sites, such as the Magothy River, for hunting and fishing. At certain times of the year, these family units would gather at a base camp to share resources."[12] Once supplies were exhausted, they ventured forth to places where they could replenish their food stock.

Although specialized plant food processing tools are not usually found in typical Paleoindian assemblages, archaeologists concede that plant foods probably played some role in the ancient Indian diet (Griffen, 1977). Communities of Aboriginal and Woodland Indians gathered around the fire in groups to cook, eat, hone their tools, and to communicate. Plant remains such as wild grape, amaranth, silene, blackberry, lactula, smartweed, physalis, ragweed, sedge, hackberry and hawthorne plum, have been found along the coastal plain area which includes the Magothy River and the entire Chesapeake Bay.[13]

smartweed

The Hunt

Spearpoints or darts central to the hunt were found in great numbers on both the north and south sides of the Magothy. What significance does such a tool have in our understanding of the Magothy River? Why should a single tool such as this captivate our imagination and spur archaeologists into further excavation?

Brennan asserts that ". . . they made their kills with a weapon of their own invention, the [stone] projectile point. It was this invention that made them what they were—self-reliant nomads who could go where the game was afoot and make a living. With his weapon in hand—it probably never left his hand except for sleep—the spearman was as much a hunter by instinct as any carnivore alive."[14]

Thus, this small spearhead represents a people who lived closely connected with nature's cycle of seasons and larger ecosystems; it controlled their activity and increased their mobility. It centralized their lives and extended into their communities. After the major kill, the women and children hauled, cleaned and scraped the game, creating little waste. They cooked with herbs and berries, with the innards of the animals and with the meat itself; they sewed with the hides which had been dried by river sun on high ridges of the Magothy. Native Americans used natural materials to create a life lived in harmony with the land, their "Great Giver."

The projectile point was joined with a simple wooden shaft, its fire-hardened point or a javelin tipped with either stone, antler, or bone. These tool kits accompanied the paleo-hunters everywhere they went and were as essential to their character as is the modern saw and hammer today to the carpenter. The *hide-scraper*, the *flint knives*, the *chopper*, a heavy-edged stone like a hand ax, and the *cutting-edged flakes*—these were the implements of flesh eaters. For it took something as sharp as glass and as hard as steel to puncture the hides of the large sabre-toothed cat, the dire wolf and the bison, the providers of meat for their meals and hides for shelter and clothing.

Brennan interprets some of the details of the hunt: ". . . the propulsive power was the human arm only." Although none of the paleo-hunter sites of the

Magothy yield evidence of the *atlatl* or spear-throwing stick, it nevertheless existed, since the *bannerstones*, the spear-throwing weights, were discovered both at

Gibson Island and near Ulmstead Point. This would add power to a hunter's thrust, but the projectile point itself had to be honed sharply.

The wound inflicted perhaps would be to a vital organ, and eventually could be mortal, but "hunt-to-hunt" success must have depended upon setting two or three shafts deeply enough in the quarry to cause quick and heavy bleeding after which, if the animal ran, one only had to follow him until he dropped. Other tools, such as flakes and bi-faced knives, were used for butchering and skinning the hide.[15]

Bannerstone, showing its use on a spear as a weight to propel the spear further by keeping the point higher.

Primordial life of the Western Shore rivers involved not only the ritual of the hunt, but also the search for the raw materials. Archaeologists relate the fine points of that prehistoric hunt: it comprised a structured style of life which began first with finding the lithic or stone material at the quarry site, then creating the tools such as hammerstones, projectiles, or bifaces. The actual hunting was done in bands with teamwork, and the aerobic run, chasing of the wounded animal, would gain speed as Paleoindians spurred each other on. Brennan gives us a modern equivalent: "one would imagine that a good mammoth hunter was like a .300 hitter in baseball who can also reach the outfield fence."[16]

Paleoindians and Archaic Indians, as well as the historic Woodland Indians, would

Travel Routes

be willing to go to far-flung sites for specific stone quarry material for their tool kits. Historical evidence reveals that they were known to travel from the Susquehanna areas to the Patapsco and to the Patuxent. In turn, and according to season, they travelled to the Magothy Region; they also rafted to the areas around the Severn River. Archaeological finds scattered throughout the general area of the Western Shore rivers attest to this presence. Rivers such as the South and the West Rivers also bear large traces of Indian travel. In fact, the Indians were known to have bartered from as far away as

Frederick, Maryland, based on spearpoints found on Ulmstead Point and Gibson Island made of rhyolite, a Catoctin Mountain material.

During the late Woodland Period, Indians used the trade routes of the Bay for barter between tribes and different peoples. This offered variety and even a form of social life. Luckenbach notes, "They [the Woodland Indians, 1000 B.C. to 1600 A.D.] traded to create social relationships even though the items probably weren't needed."[17]

Although the Indians of the Colonial Era between 1600 and 1800 A.D. used dug-out canoes for water travel, the question arises as to whether the Paleoindian used the waterways for transportation. Common among anthropologists was the concept that "Paleoindians could only travel overland." Counter to that theory, however, is the hypothesis that "various Paleoindians were using rafts both for river crossings and for coastwise travel in very early times."[18] For the ancient Indian as well as the colonial-era Indian, travel by water would prove to be pragmatic and convenient. The Chesapeake Bay formed a core of life, an excellent source of food, and the primary pathway to major resources. Through trade routes of the Bay, the Indians could be mobile and benefit from other tribal circulation. Offering protective coves and inlets from rival tribes, the Magothy campsites indeed were important to these early peoples.

Tracing early Indian pathways in and among the tributaries of the western shores of the Chesapeake Bay, one necessarily must alter the mental images of Native Americans as a band of ragged and scruffy nomads. Cunningly, they had to plan strategies for travel, food, the hunt and for the making of small societies. They were a competitive group of people who had a preoccupation with status, iconography, water control, and the accumulation of luxury goods.[19] Even though their "luxury items of various wood ornaments, decorative baskets, and wood carvings, have not survived the span of time, they serve as reminders of a complex people."[20] These people of the fluted projectile point were Magothy's early inhabitants, men of action and women of strong constitution—magnificent.

Towards the end of this prehistoric epochal past, during the late *Archaic Period,* scientists relate that the lifestyle began to tend toward increased sedentary patterns. People remained longer in one place and formed more stable communities. For proof, the tool kit spoke for itself. For on the Magothy, residents and archaeologists have found the old stone axes, used for clearing settlement areas and soapstone (steatite) bowls, remnants of relatively non-portable cooking vessels. Also a plethora of notched and stemmed projectile points, drills, scrapers, and winged bannerstones from this later era of the Archaic period were found.

The ancient peoples left a legacy of a life lived for survival. As the larger mammals of the region grew extinct, gradually this way of life shifted from a primordial one of subsistence in the wild to life in a more complex world. The Indians of the late Woodland Period lived in a more confrontational world of inter-tribal "wars" and skirmishes than did their forebears. The mode of life thus became more pragmatic and competitive when they interfaced with the colonials in the 1600s.

1. Louis A. Brennan, "American Dawn, A New Model of American Prehistory." p. 208.

2. Ibid. p. 19.

3. Hamil Kenny, *The Origin and Meaning of the Indian Place Names of Maryland* (Baltimore; Waverly Press; 1961) pp. 82-83.

4. Colby Rucker, in personal correspondence with the author, Nov. 1992.

5. H. Kenny, P. 83.

6. Dennis C. Curry and Norma A. B. Wagner, *Maryland Prehistory*, This is a summary of Maryland prehistory and "Some Characteristic Artifacts of Indian Cultures in Maryland." (Maryland: Division of Archaeology, Maryland Geological Survey, 1976, 1980).

7. Richard E. Stearns, "Village Sites of the Magothy River, Anne Arundel County," *Some Indian Village Sites of Tidewater Maryland, Proceeding No. 9*, pp. 20-23. (Baltimore: Natural History Society of Maryland. July, 1943).

8. "Magothy Quartzite Quarry Archaeological Site," USDI/NPS NRHP, NPS Form 10-900-a, sec. E, p. 3.

9. R. E. Stearns, "Village Sites of the Magothy River," *Proceeding No. 9*. pp. 20-23.

10. *Phase I Archaeological Testing at Jamestown on the Magothy*. (Anne Arundel County, Maryland, submitted to Mandrin Construction Company, Inc., Pasadena, Maryland. March 1989), p. 10. [Most of these artifacts can be viewed at the Anne Arundel County Historical Society, the Natural History Society of Maryland and at the Gibson Island Historical Society. Some remain in private collections.]

11. Dr. Al Luckenbach, archaeologist, Anne Arundel County, per phone conversation with the author, Oct. 1992.

12. L. A. Brennan, "American Dawn," p. 19.

13. United States Department of the Interior/National Park Service, (OMB no. 1024-0018,) pp. 3-5.

14. L. A. Brennan, "American Dawn," p. 19.

15. Ibid. p. 23.

16. Ibid.

17. Dr. Al Luckenbach, related per phone conversation, Mar. 1994.

18. "Readings from Scientific American," *New World Archaeology*, with introduction by Ezra B. W. Zubrow, M. C. Fritz, John Fritz. (San Francisco, W.H. Freeman & Company, 1948), p. 62.

19. Jay F. Custer, *Delaware Prehistoric Archaeology: an Ecological Approach.* (Delaware: Associated University Presses), pp. 51-65.

20. Kent V. Flannery, "Archaeological Systems Theory and Early Mesoamerica," *Contemporary Archaeology,* ed. Mack P. Leone, p. 222.

CHAPTER 2

Indian Pathways: Mindfulness and Passion

A tableau of life in historical river-time between 1 and 1600 A.D. and the period between 1600 and 1700 A.D. slowly emerges, like a lighthouse throwing out its yellow beams in the fog. On one of those clear nights on the Magothy when the stars gleam their light upon the darkened waters and the moon makes clear each ripple in the breeze, one can almost hear the chanting, the singing of historical Native American peoples. In the imagination one conjures a picture of the dances and rituals, the prayers and the songs, piercing the still of night. But the real archaeological finds along the Magothy River provide palpable concrete testimony of a lifestyle which lends a rich layer of meaning to one's own contemporary existence in the search for the continuity of history.

A recent manuscript entitled "American Indians in the Baltimore Area," by Louise E. Akerson, synthesizes in great detail the specific archaeological and historical information of the Baltimore area after John Smith's initial contact in 1608.[1] Much of this information can apply to the Magothy because of its proximity to the Patapsco, taking into account that these Indians proved to be highly mobile in their patterns of travel for food sources and tools. Delving more deeply into Native American existence, one finds it difficult to name the specific tribes who

On one of those clear nights on the Magothy when the stars gleam their light upon the darkened waters and the moon makes clear each ripple in the breeze, one can almost hear the chanting, the singing of Native American peoples.

may have encamped on these shores. Ms. Akerson points out that Captain John Smith in 1608, on his second voyage to "'finish discovering the bay,'" states that "Thirty leagues Northward is a river not inhabited, yet navigable; for the red earth or clay resembling bole Amoniak, the English called it Bolus (Arber 1967)."[2] Later that river assumed its original Indian name, "Patapsco." He sailed right by a "creeke of little significance" [the Magothy River] in pursuit of the larger ports of call such as the "bolus" or Patapsco River and the large bay at Baltimore. He recorded that he encountered the Susquehannock Indians near the Patapsco and the reaches of the Susquehanna River, noting that they were a very aggressive tribe who made war with neighboring tribes. Initially, Indian relationships with Captain John Smith and the early English colonists were congenial and sharing. But they did not remain that way because of greed, corruption and the quiet dawning upon the Indian spirit that land use by the colonists differed greatly from their concept of the land as sacred.

Obviously, Smith passed right by the Magothy on his way up the Bay and came to the same conclusion that the area was "uninhabited" as well. But this report by John Smith seems to contradict further evidence of a "king's house, labeled Cepewig," which existed at the head of the Gunpowder River dating to the same time frame of the 1600s. Akerson offers the explanation for Smith's oversight of any habitation of these areas in a further study of his diaries. She found that as he continues his search of this area, Smith "encounters" the people of those "countries" [Native Americans]. Later, Captain Smith writes of a fierce tribe of Indians called Massawomecks, an Iroquois-speaking group of the region, who were enemies of the native groups living in the Chesapeake Bay area, especially bothersome to the Susquehannocks of the North. Smith describes them:

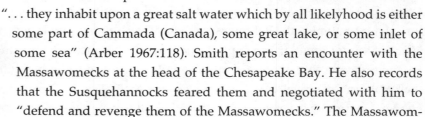

brown jasper chipped
implement found near
Ulmstead Point

". . . they inhabit upon a great salt water which by all likelyhood is either some part of Cammada (Canada), some great lake, or some inlet of some sea" (Arber 1967:118). Smith reports an encounter with the Massawomecks at the head of the Chesapeake Bay. He also records that the Susquehannocks feared them and negotiated with him to "defend and revenge them of the Massawomecks." The Massawomecks frequently conducted war on the various groups of the region and either killed or kidnapped them. [3]

Akerson concludes that such reports, however valuable, as those of Captain John Smith, contain some contradictions or, in this case "omissions," since there were indeed traces of Indians all over the area under study. She concludes that in referring to other primary sources, which relate primarily to St. Mary's City; Kent Island; and Kittamaquindi (Piscattaway) the "metropolis of the Pascatoe," the Algonkian-speaking groups predominated in those areas. Later evidence from significant studies affirms the existence of elaborate trade routes from the Baltimore area and areas all over the Chesapeake Bay.

She states that "a picture emerges of several native groups living in the Chesapeake Bay area at the time of European contact until at least 1666. Most of the area was inhabited by Algonkian-speaking groups (Powhatan, Piscataway, Patuxent, Nanticoke, Tockwogh); however, the upper Chesapeake Bay area was dominated by Iroquois-speaking groups (Susquehannocks and Massawomecks)."[4]

Thus, the possibility exists that some of these Iroquois-speaking tribes camped transitionally along the Magothy, as did the Algonquians. Adding to the understanding of the Indians of the Baltimore area, Akerson relates that the Piscataway were acknowledged as one of three ruling powers in the 1630s by the province of Maryland and were situated on the Potomac River. It was reported by Captain Henry Fleet in his *Journal of 1631-1632* that the "poore number of natives which are in Patomack and places adjacent, were not above five thousand per and the "Piscatowies" suffered a "great slaughter formerly to the number of one thousand persons in my time . . . by the Massamacks." Akerson concludes that "this bit of evidence would seem to support the theory that groups in the Baltimore area were slaughtered by the Massowomecks during the early 1600s."[5]

To date, however, no complete synthesis has been made as to precisely what travel routes between the Patapsco, the

Grooved ax found near Ulmstead Point

Magothy, and the Severn, these disputing tribes may have had. But with all of the artifacts and heaps of shell-midden found on the Magothy, one can assume that perhaps some of these disputing groups used the Magothy strategically for both cover from hostile tribes and for sources of fish and fowl.

A Look Into Indian Lifestyle

Like their Paleoindian predecessors, the Indians from 1000 B.C. to 1600 A.D, known as the Woodland Indians, had continued an existence of hunting, gathering and fishing. More complex social systems, much trading, and a plethora of native life-customs became evident as the Native American tribes such as the Piscataway and Nanticoke were encountered by the first Europeans of Maryland. They recorded in diaries and letters how the Native American Indian considered that animals, the trees, their own bodies, all of their activities including hunting, travelling, trading, planting and gathering of crops—connected with ritual.

Clearly, the Indian lifestyle was made visible through symbols and decorations on their pottery, some of which has been located upon Magothy shores. Small semi-permanent Indian settlements reveal many clues to the ways of life lived on Western Shore rivers. Sherds or pieces of pottery were discovered, which added to the basic understanding of how these Native Americans lived. A significant innovation of the basic tool kit, these fragments were pieced together by archaeologists to reveal cooking and storage vessels made from local clays. Gradually, these clay pots replaced the heavy, cumbersome soapstone bowls used by earlier tribes and were supplemented by fragile basketry and animal-skin containers.

The hunting styles of the later historical Woodland Indian evolved from those of the Paleoindian. But a new form of the hunt evolved, considered a significant leap of Indian technology—the bow and arrow. Developed by 800 A.D., this invention began to change the style of hunting in the woods and glades near the Chesapeake. The Western Shore woods abounded with the swift quiet sound of the arrow finding its mark in the deer, wild turkey or other small game which proliferated. Because this technique of the hunt was more efficient, the Indians could kill more game.

Wide-ranging networks for food and trade became intensified as the Woodland Indian of the 1600s rafted throughout the Western Shore riverine complex to hunt fowl. Also, he blazed elaborate trails through the hemlock and pine forests bordering the rivers.

Centralized villages were established inland, not too far from seasonal village river camp sites; thus friendly, as well as hostile communication among various-speaking tribes developed. Inter-tribal quarrels were fought for the acquisition of larger tribal territories. For example, the Susquehannocks, a fierce Iroquois-speaking tribe who had migrated from the upper Delaware Valley and camped along the Susquehanna River area and the Patapsco, were known to have had territorial "disputes" with the gentler Algonquians who had migrated gradually from the Eastern Shore of the Chesapeake to the Western Shore. A recent study reveals that these groups, reportedly cannibalistic, warred with the peaceful Piscataway over territorial and hunting rights.[6]

Gradually, during the middle of the 1600s, as the Indians became more sedentary and thus more established in territorial acquisitions, they needed to defend territorial tribal rights. During this period small seasonal encampments became more popular along the shores of the Severn, Magothy, Patapsco, Susquehanna, South and West Rivers. Here the Indians would travel to fish and to hunt, migrating from their established encampments or villages inland to many Chesapeake river points and inlets.

The Algonquians

The difficulty of prying into the life of the Western Shore Indians from fragments and artifacts dug into the clay and mud of river banks is somewhat lightened by several diary entries of the early 1600s. Such questions as, "How did the Indians live on river-banks?," "Did they band into cohesive communities?," "What unique contributions did they make?," can be only partially answered. A vague, thin picture emerges as we try to penetrate the mystery of a way of life which no longer exists.

Most experts agree that primarily the Algonkian-speaking tribes inhabited the western shores of the Chesapeake. These peoples belonged to the large group of Algonquians which were made up of independent tribes, speaking related languages who occupied much of northeastern North America. Within this large range of tribes, the Piscataway or Conoy and the Nanticoke tribes settled on the Eastern Shore in large numbers, as did the Powhatan, the Patuxent, and the Tockwogh. Gradually, some of these tribes travelled to more western shores.

Early descriptions from diaries provide fascinating details of Native American dress and deportment of a people who once inhabited the lands surrounding the tributaries, coves and inlets of the Chesapeake. By the year 1600, Indians were seen in Maryland and in Virginia and were documented by Father Andrew White, a Jesuit who had the foresight to record in his diaries all of his experiences when he came over with the first Maryland settlers to St. Clements Island in Southern Maryland in February, 1634. Most likely, his first hand account of an Algonquian can accurately be applied to the Indian who set up seasonal camps along the shores of the Magothy. Father White wrote in his journals:

The natives of person be very proper and tall men, by nature swarthy, but much more by art, painting themselves with colours in oile a darke read, especially about the head, which they doe to keep away the knats. . . their faces they use sometimes other colours, as blew from the nose downeward, and read upward, and sometimes contrary wise with great variety, and in gastly manner. They have noe bearde till they be very old, but instead thereof sometimes draw long lines with colours from the sides of their mouth to their eares. They weare their [hair] diversly some haveing it cut all short, one halfe of the head, and long on the other; others have it all long, but generally they weare all a locke at the left eare, and sometimes at both eares which they fold up with a string of wampampeake or roanoake about it. Some of their Caucorouses as they terme them, or great men, weare the forme of a fish of Copper in their foreheads. They all weare beade about their neckes, men and women, with otherwhiles a haukes bill or the talents of an eagles or the teethe of beasts, or sometimes a pare of great eagles wings linked together and much more of the like. Their apparell is deere skins and other furrs, which they weare loose like mantles, under which all their women, and those which are come to mans stature weare perizomata of skins, which keep them decently covered from all offence of sharpe eies. All the rest are naked, and sometimes the men of the younger sort weare nothing at all. [7]

Perhaps Magothy and Severn River secret coves and creeks offered protection and hiding places for migrating Algonquians, tracking territory for their survival and peace. Allowing one's imagination to fly, one might visualize a Weroan or chieftan making his way to these shores with a group of his followers. Cunningly and swiftly, he sets up an encampment to fish the waters and to hunt the woods. What does he look like? The Weroan, or great lord, of the Algonquians has been described by Thomas Harriot in a colonial report:

Such great and well proportioned men, are seldom seene, for they seemed like giants to the English . . . yet seemed of an honest and simple disposition. . . for their language it may well beseme their porportions, wounding from them, as it were a great voice in a vault, or ca[v]e. as an eccho. Their attire is the skinnes of Bears heades and Wooltes, some have Cassacks made of Bears heades and skinnes that a mans necke goes through the skinnes neck, behind, the nose and teeth hanging downe his breast, ane at the end of the nose hung a Beares Pawe: . . . One had the head of a Woofe hanging in a chaine for a Iewell: His Tobacco pipe 3 quarters of a yard long, prettily carved with a Bird, a Beare, a Deare, or some such devise at the great end, sufficient to beat out the braines of a man: with bowes, and arrowes, and clubs, su[i]table to their greatness and conditions. [8]

A Susquehannock Indian depicted by Captain John Smith on his map of Virginia, which included the entire Chesapeake Bay, 1608 [1612]. (John Work Garrett Library, the Johns Hopkins University, Md HR G 1213-257)

Whether the Magothy Indian was a Weroan or just a person of the tribal community, these men and women used every raw natural material of the immediate locale as a part of their lives. Adornments reflected the natural world, and everyday objects—weaponry, cooking vessels, storage pots, jewelry—all bore the stamp of personalized decoration.

Characterizing more particularly the spirit and inner life of the Algonquian, experts relate that they were known to be a gentle, kindly people. Tribal life predominated. All territory which was occupied and used belonged to everyone; it came to them from the "Great Spirit" and was returned to the Spirit when they moved away from it. An animal was asked permission, through religious chant and ceremony, before the kill. These Indians killed only what they needed and used every part of the animal for either food, clothing, housing or ornamentation. From Father Andrew White's journals comes this description of their basic disposition:

The naturall wit of these men is good, conceiveing a thing quick to. They excell in smell and taste, and have farre sharper sight than we have. . . . They are very temperate from wines and hote waters, and will hardly taste them, save those whome our English have corrupted. For chastity I never see any action in a man or woman tending to sow much as levity, and yet the poor soules are daily with us and bring us turkie, partridge, oisters, squirells as good as any rabbit, bread and the like, running to us with smileing countenance and will help us in fishing, fouling, hunting what we please.

• • •

They hold it lawful to have many wives, but all [women] keep the rigour of conjugal faith to their husbands.The very aspect of the women is modest and grave' they are generally so noble, as you can doe them noe favour, but they will returne....[9]

Although settling near waters and rivers such as the Magothy provided the Indians with transportation utilized extensively by means of dugout log canoes, land use surrounding the waters was mindful. Land, considered sacred, was used carefully in the spirit of conservation. William B. Marye, historian of Indian life writes:

Many [trails] follow[ed] streams and rivers, but also on land especially when they (the Indians) ran into snags, freshets, or opened onto the shore. Indians marched single file; therefore the trails were usually no more than 18 inches wide and became well packed over generations. Trails were generally along high ground and where there were the fewest and shallowest streams to be crossed. . . . Indian roads usually crossed a stream at the mouth of a tributary because at such places there were nearly always bars. The Indian never blazed his roads.[10]

Marye continues to inform that there were four types of roads: those used for hunting, war, portage, and trade routes, each being only as wide as was necessary.

Co-equal sharing systems were common. All members of the tribe shared equal rights of land usage. To clear the forest for planting, the Indians would

constructing a log canoe

either build fires around the trunks of the trees or cut a groove around the trunks with a stone axe, several of which have been found on the banks of the Magothy. Gradually the trees would die; the leaves would fall off, allowing sunlight to reach the ground. Gardens would then be planted beneath the dead trees. In a few years, the trees would fall, or the Indians would bring them down complete-ly. Later the colonists referred to these clearings as Indian Fields or Barrens.

Women and children were responsible for tending the crops. First the women would prepare the soil with crooked tree limbs or hoes made of stone, shell, or bone. After the soil was loosened, they planted seeds of maize (corn), beans, squash, pumpkin, sunflowers and tobacco. The younger children were responsible for weeding the gardens and acting as "live scarecrows," climbing high on sheltered platforms built in the middle of a field. Here young boys perched, screeching loud noises to scare the birds away.

These small plots of land, which were the early farms of the Magothy, dotted the river banks. They were not large farms as we know them; rather, they were temporary clearings used seasonally for providing particular needs such as corn for drying and pounding into meal, and beans for sustenance. Prudently, the river Indians used plant and animal resources connected with their immediate surroundings, depending upon the season. The women and children gathered various edible wild plants, roots, bird eggs, berries and nuts such as acorn, chestnuts, hickory nuts and walnuts. Assiduously, they would make the campfires and create the cooking utensils; they would dry the hides of animals for their shelters as well as for clothing. With their mortars and pestles, found near Magothy banks, the women and children would pound the corn for breads and bake them in charcoal pits.

Grooved axhead, (handle modern). Found at Gibson Island By Jimmy Wolfe. Courtesy Gibson Island Historical Society.
(photo by Michael A. Dulisse)

The men hunted aggressively, using their bows and arrows to get squirrel, raccoon, opossum, deer and bear. Father Andrew White describes their weapons:

Their weapons are a bow and a bundle of arrowes, an ell long, feathered with turkies feathers, and headed with points of deereshornes, peeces of glasse, or flints, which they make fast with an excellent glew which they have for that purpose. The shaft is a small cane or sticke, wherewith I have seene them kill at 20 yards distance, little birds of the bignesse of sparrows, and they use to practise themselves by casting up small stickes in the aire, and meeting it with an arrow before it come to ground. Their bow is but weake and shoots level but a little way. They daily catch partridge, deere, turkies, squirrels, and the like of which there is wonderfull [plenty?], but as yet we dare not venture ourselves in the woods to seeke them, nor have we leasure.[11]

The hunting grounds provided not only migratory haphazard encampments. Models of Indian life show that in some areas there were specific tribal hunting grounds for family use, to which the small group would return season after season. The patterns of travel for the hunt were deliberate: after leaving the base villages, usually inland, at the start of the hunting season, Indian families created their seasonal hunting encampments near the mouths of streams and rivers. As was previously noted, the archaeological evidence of such camps has been discovered at Forked Creek, Ulmstead Point, Gibson Island, South Ferry Point, Mill Creek, Dividing Creek and in areas near Cockey's Creek.

Fishing wier

The ways of the hunt have sparked the imagination and primal instincts of many Eastern and Western Shore people. The men usually hunted every day in order to get enough meat to last through the winter; the women butchered the anmals and prepared the skins. Historically, the Woodland Indian stalked and hunted deer through cunning techniques. By burning a circle of fire two or three miles in diameter, these Indians would trap a large number of deer. Gradually the hunters would close in on the perimeter of the circle, frightening the deer towards the center. Swiftly, the arrows would fly for the kill. Another method of the hunt was to drive the deer toward the river's edge where alternate members of the hunt team would perch for the final kill. Camouflage was the trick for stalking deer. The Indian hunter would dress in deer skin as cover so that he could attack close to his prey.

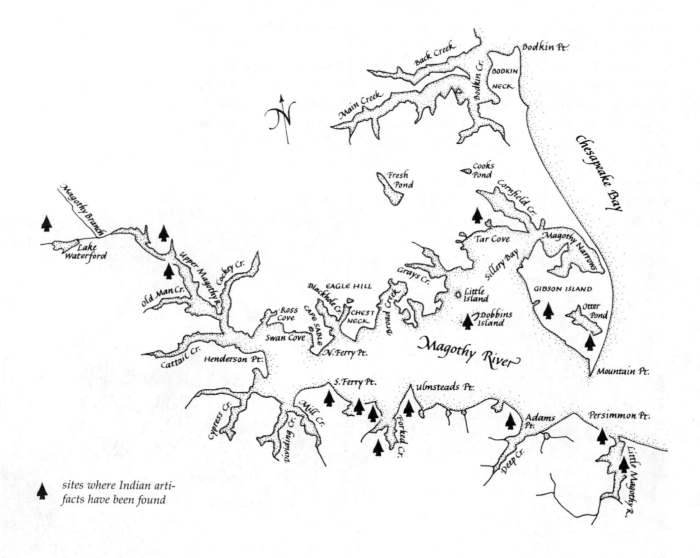

Bodkin Pt.

Back Creek

Bodkin Cr.

BODKIN
NECK

Main Creek

N

Chesapeake Bay

Cooks
Pond

Fresh
Pond

Cornfield Cr.

Magothy Branch

Tar Cove

Magothy Narrows

Lake
Waterford

Upper Magothy R.

Cockey Cr.

Grays Cr.

Sillery Bay

GIBSON ISLAND

Otter
Pond

Old Man Cr.

EAGLE HILL

Blackhole Cr.

Little
Island

Ross
Cove

CAPE SABLE

CHEST
NECK

Broad Creek

Dobbins
Island

Swan Cove

Cattail Cr.

Henderson Pt.

N. Ferry Pt.

Magothy River

Mountain Pt.

S. Ferry Pt.

Mill Cr.

ulmsteads Pt.

Adams
Pt.

Persimmon Pt.

Cypress Cr.

Dividing Cr.

Forked Cr.

Deep Cr.

Little Magothy R.

sites where Indian arti-
facts have been found

30

Fishing activity closely resembled the hunt, the Indians using an admirable art and technique of acquiring their seafood. They found plentiful supplies of crabs, shrimp, eel, fish, clams and oysters. Sometimes they speared the fish; at other times, they would construct weirs or giant fish traps. This was done by driving brush and spears into the bottom of streams and river shallows to create a "v"-shaped barrier. In the center of the weir was a narrow opening through which the fish would swim, much like our modern crab pot. Then the fish would become trapped in small fenced-in sections or large baskets within the weir complex.

For the Magothy Indian and all others in Maryland, community or clan life predominated, even though the small groups moved from place to place in search of food. The archaeological evidence on the Magothy, unearthed by Richard E. Stearns beginning in 1937, is collated in a document entitled, "Some Indian Village Sites of Tidewater Maryland. . ." The assumption in the title includes the notion of "village" life. The pottery implements and tools, as well as oyster shell deposits, were found in various clusters or groupings, indicating that seasonal village life did exist on the river's edge, though temporary.[12]

Setting up a seasonal camp at river's edge.

The notion of privacy was not a part of the Native American vocabulary, even though Native Americans acquired large pieces of territory as tribal personal property. When they made their small "village" encampments on the Magothy for their hunting and fishing activities, they created small huts for protection from the elements. The typical shelter was dome-shaped, about fourteen feet wide, ten feet high and twenty feet long. Branches and saplings, driven into the ground, formed the base, while vines and strips of animal hide were used as bindings. This framework was then covered with sheets of tree bark or woven bulrush mats. These mats could then be lifted to allow air flow during the warmer months. The structure formed one large room, shared by several families, sometimes divided by hanging mats. The floor was made of earth, and fires were built directly in the floor, vented by a hole in the roof. People reclined on sleeping benches set along the sides of the walls, which were made of tree limbs covered with mats. The primary builders and construction workers of those days were the women.

Certainly, social life was engaging, creative, and integral to the work-life of the Magothy Indian. Trading for glass ornaments, beads, and hand-beaten copper was probably just as enticing for the Algonquian as flea market barters are today. One form of social activity which occurred on riverside campsites, was the dance or chant ritual. To prepare for religious events which centered upon dance and song, the Indians would wear their finest specimens of animal bones, teeth, shell necklaces, and feathered constructions. They were worn to celebrate the seasons, various hunt rituals, or mark personal life transitions such as marriages, as well as rites of passage which included birth, puberty, manhood or womanhood. Elaborate tatoos illuminated their bodies to reveal in design their system of belief in the cycles and mysteries of nature.

Specific Archaeological Digs

Magothy pioneers in the actual archaeological digs of the Magothy were Richard Stearns, former curator of the Department of Archaeology; Woodward Burkhart; and T. Milton Oler Jr., member of the Natural History Society of Maryland. In 1937 "Butch" Oler, a summertime resident of the

Magothy who lived on Ulmstead Point, discovered some Indian sherds of pottery and other Indian chipped implements. This discovery led to the first archaeological dig of the Magothy River.

Together this small team unearthed Indian axes, celts, pieces of incised pottery, rhyolite knives for cutting and scraping hides and layers of shell-midden. Several gorgets or stone pendants used for symbolic ornamentation still sit on the shelves of Oler's home in Towson.

Pot sherds were found along the Ulmstead Point and Forked Creek sites. The so-called "Pope's Creek" type was discovered with specimens containing pulverized quartz tempering material. This type of ceramic is considered the earliest type of Algonquian pottery, whose decoration consists only of net and cord impression on the outside of the vessel. (500 B.C. to 250 A.D.) A later type of "Townsendware" (1200 A.D. to 1400 A.D.), tempered with ground oyster shell and usually decorated on and below the rim with notches and geometric designs, was also found. Oler discovered quite a fascinating gorget or decoration of black slate, broken into three or more pieces. Also, a mottled black and white bannerstone of granite was unearthed, a rare find for the Magothy River.

With a considerable amount of erosion having taken place even in 1937, Stearns writes, ". . . probably twenty feet has been washed away, no doubt destroying a large amount of pottery fragments which could otherwise have been restored." He adds that "There is no marked difference in culture on any of these sites; which would indicate that they were inhabited by the same people."[13]

By 1943 many other archaeological discoveries along the Magothy were documented. Although actual areas cannot be published, the general areas of archaeological finds gathered for the first collated study (1943) include Harmony Point, Tar Cove, Gibson Island, Dobbins Island, small areas of the upper Magothy, South Ferry Point, and areas along the Little Magothy River.

Altogether there were some 2,000 sherds, some of which were cord-marked, fabric-marked or fabric-impressed. These terms apply to surface impressions on the found sherds which the Indians applied with a paddle wrapped with cords or covered with a piece of woven fabric or net. Other artifacts included many cooking and pottery vessels marked with a kind of basketry weave, termed "basketry impressed," a type which covers a large classification of sherds with surface designs and markings. Some of these included pots with beach-sand tempering, which consists of sand which has the appearance of having been gathered from the beach. The grains of sand vary in size from minute particles to small pebbles one-eighth of an inch in diameter. Sherds containing this form of tempering material were usually cord-impressed and never decorated. Other artifacts included pieces of what were once large water pots.

Arrowpoints were both stemmed and triangular in shape. The triangular types, which numbered thirty percent of the total, were made of quartz and brown jasper, while the stemmed points were made of quartz, quartzite and rhyolite, and one specimen was made of argillite, all types of hard stone used for multi-purpose tools and weaponry aids. Other stone objects unearthed were fragments of a steatite (soapstone) vessel, a pitted stone, and two abrading stones made of red sandstone with two grooves for smoothing arrowshafts. Many cord-marked sherds with beach-sand tempering continue to be found at various Magothy River sites.

With investigations continuing in the forties, some pitted hammerstones and rubbing stones were found in the shell deposits. The rubbing stones are small quartzite boulders containing one or more faceted surfaces. Mr. Franklin Spriggs, the tenant of a farm near Ulmstead Point, thought they might have been used by white farmers for sharpening scythes; however Stearns claims that they are of Indian origin and have been found on other Indian sites of the Magothy.[15] A number of quartzite boulders were "flaked." This means that force had been applied to hard stone to create a striking platform on it. The Indians flaked stones in the making of weapons or farm tools. Those found on the Magothy were flaked on only one end and were probably used in the hand for chopping. A few pestles were unearthed as well.

Finds at Harmony Point and Tar Cove include many of the same types of artifacts discovered at Ulmstead, Forked Creek and Gibson Island. At least three found vessels bore collared rims resembling the style of ware usually found on the Potomac River above tidewater. Thus, similar artifacts from the Magothy region as well as the Potomac and the Patapsco indicate that the Indians moved with fluidity and freedom around the waters of the Chesapeake.

The Angonquian Indians in a Riverine Setting

Perhaps when one finds a spearhead or fragments of Indian pottery, while walking the Magothy shores, the mind floats into remembrances of past lives lived on Western Shore rivers, lives whose history forms a part of the entire span of river-time in the Chesapeake region. Seeing pictures of what these "fragments" looked like in reassembled models, one admires the craft and art, the lovely designed pottery urns and dishes, the incised and roped designs, or the smooth surface of an early bannerstone. The Algonquian ghosts of these times may still come to watch over modern-day residents of the Chesapeake Bay as they settle into modern crab feasts and barbecues of roasted corn and hot dogs.

Incidentally, the Algonquians knew exactly how they liked their corn and crabs. They were masters of the barbecue and steam pot, for they were our first mentors of riverside feasts and community gatherings. Traditionally, the Indians roasted the corn of the early summer directly on the fire in green husks, while the fish were broiled by placing them on green wooden racks that stood over a fire. Sometimes the Indians would impale the smaller fish on sharpened sticks which were stuck into the flames. Dinnertime was community time where all would gather around the fires to enjoy corn bread called "pone." Native Americans barbecued fish, deer and squirrel; steamed crabs and clams; and roasted duck or goose with a dressing made from deer fat, similar to butter. Succotash was a popular vegetable since the use of corn mixed with beans or squash was practical and delicious.

Community and clan relationships predominated. Mothers and daughters formed strong female bonds by quietly working in small groups on simple functional pottery pieces, cordwrapping the clay or incising the piece with geometric designs. Matriarchal society was strong, with family lines established through the woman's family heritage. Yet, tasks were clearly divided among Indian men and women. A riverine setting formed the very stuff of work and play, for they produced useful yet beautiful, pieces whether they be clothing, pottery, or hunting shafts. Feathers, beads, adornments of deer hide and fur, animal hair and bone, stone, clay, shell, wood, parts of plants—these were the raw materials for transformation into beautiful objects for everyday use. Nature and imagination provided strength and sustenance. Needles for sewing, for example, were made of polished bones. Strips of animal hide formed the thread and cord for the clothing and lacing. Sharpened flint points became awls to pierce holes into the heavy animal hides used for tents as well as for clothing.

Some of the ancient tools pictured were grinders used to make other tools; some were used for pounding grain, such as the hammerstones, rocks of just the

bone
awls

right size and shape to hold in the hand. The planning and designing of such pieces certainly took time, great skill and timing in order to be ready for the hunting and fishing season. For example, pieces of deer antler or flakes were used to shape sharp edges for stone tools and weapons. The Indians pressed the flakes against the edge of a stone, chipping away one tiny piece after another until the edge became thin and sharp. Spearheads, arrowheads, axes, drills, and scrapers for hides were constantly produced. Magothy branches of ash, hickory or locust were fundamental material for the bows and arrows, spears and tomahawks. Bowstrings were made from a strip of deerskin or from deer sinew, from animals of the Magothy who still roam, especially on Gibson Island.

During tales told around modern-day campfires, better known as crab feasts, someone will mention in quiet, reverent tones, "You know, there are Indian buri-

Indian artifacts found on Gibson Island. Clockwise from upper left:
1. pounding stone, well worn on one end
2. rhyolite hoe
3. pounding stone
4. pounding pestle
5. hammerstone with tongue groove
6. pounding stone, ground to fit hand
7. stone quern, worn both sides, used for grinding (Gibson Island Historical Society; photo by Michael A. Dulisse)

als near this point and that place." This kind of talk forms the lore of the Magothy. But to this date, no burial mounds have been documented. However, it is known that religious rituals formed the fiber of life as well as the passage into the "Spirit World." The common practice of burying the bodies in the fetal position signified birth/death and recycling of spirit into the Indian "Great Spirit." For the initial stage of burial, bones were placed in a special structure called a "quiackeson." Indians believed that all the elements of nature—water, lightning, fire, stone, and animals possessed unique spirits of their own.[16]

The Magothy spirits of the past would include the good luck spirit, "Manto," invoked before the hunt or the harvest, and the evil spirit, "Okee," who was respected and kept at a distance through various rituals. The first game or fish of the season were offered as necessary sacrifices to these spirits. When one picks up a piece of an Indian clay pipe, such as those found on Forked Creek and Gibson Island, it is easy to conjure the former circles of friendship as the Indians smoked tobacco, a religious rite of community. This practice, they believed, purified them.

Quite often residents of the Magothy pick up old oyster shells near the river's edge, never realizing that the Indians used parts of this natural shell for trade, especially the small purple section. As the Algonquian Indians of the Western Shore traded more with various tribes, they used a natural form of exchange called "wampum" or "wampumpeaq," the Algonquian term for "white strings." This form of trade money was made with strings of clam and oyster shells cut and shaped into beads. Various parts of the shell were more valuable or less valuable, depending on the specimen of shell.

The wampum, strung onto strips of animal hides and woven into broad belts, held a complexity of meaning. The Indians understood that this wampum was a form of talk. These belts served as mini tape recorders, bearers of messages, secrets and protocol. When wampum was exchanged, a pact or treaty became valid. In fact "no treaty or agreement would be honored unless there had been an exchange of wampum."[17]

wampum

With wampum packed in his kit, the riverine Native American paddled or trekked to other areas of the Chesapeake Bay. Travel was noiseless and swift. Softly, the waterfront Indian moved along one trail at the river's edge to an elaborate system of connecting trails to what is now Baltimore. He then would make trips north to the Patapsco or the area where Frederick is today. Seasonally, he would travel south to the Severn or Potomac using dug out canoes with small swift sails. Through these means, the Indians traded fur pelts from fox, raccoon and small mink, as well as the indigenous crafts and arts so unique to each family tribal unit. Eventually, the Indians traded pelts for guns. These goods would go via the colonial trade ships to England, France, Holland and Spain. Thus, in a way, the Woodland Indian of the Magothy and of all Chesapeake tributaries and estuaries, with a leap of time and energy, became international.

By the late sixteenth and early seventeenth centuries, the life as well as the ecology along the Magothy River, as well as other tidewater rivers, rapidly changed. The pinnacle of sacred tribal life along river banks, so joyously lived, was to end. At this juncture the colonists infiltrated their culture, their ideas and their values upon Native Americans. Skirmishes, territorial battles, degradation, and disease followed.

1. Louise E. Akerson, Baltimore: *Technical Series No. 3*, Baltimore Center for Urban Archaeology, (1989), p. 1. [Ms. Akerson reports that evidence gathered for the study includes ". . . portions of Anne Arundel County . . . Glen Burnie . . . Elkridge . . . northward to Owings Mills . . . east to parts of the Gunpowder River . . . southwest to Curtis Bay. The general area of the Atlantic Coastal Plain . . . the Piedmont Plateau are the wide geographical areas to which this study applies.]

2. L. E. Akerson, *American Indians in the Baltimore Area, Technical Series No. 3*, Baltimore Center for Urban Archaeology, (Dec. rev. 1989), p. 3.

3. Ibid.

4. Ibid.

5. Ibid., p. 7.

6. Ibid.

7. Father Andrew White, S.J., *A Briefe Relation of the Voyage Unto Maryland*, (1634), (Tri-County Council of Southern Maryland, Maryland Hall of Records, Mar., 1984), pp. 21- 22.

8. Thomas Harriot, "A Briefe and True Report of the New Found Land of Virginia" in L. E. Akerson, *American Indians in the Baltimore Area*, p. 5.

9. Father Andrew White, *A Briefe Relation*, p. 21.

10. William Marye, "Former Indian Sites in Maryland as located by early Colonial Records," *American Antiquity*, 1:40, p. 16.

11. Father White, *A Briefe Relation*, p. 22.

12. Richard E. Stearns, "Some Indian Village Sites of Tidewater Maryland," *The Natural History Society of Maryland, Proceeding No. 9*, (Natural History Society of Maryland, Baltimore. July, 1943.)

13. Richard E. Stearns, "Indian Village Sites on the Magothy River, Maryland," *Bulletin of the Natural History Society of Maryland, Vol. VIII, No. 3*, Nov. 1937, pp. 15-19.

14. R. E. Stearns, "Some Indian Village Sites of Tidewater Maryland," pp. 21, 22.

15. R. E. Stearns, "Indian Village Sites on the Magothy River, Maryland," p. 18.

16. Frank W. Porter, III, *The Nanticoke*, (NY. & Philadelphia, Chelsea House Publishers, 1987), pp. 19-39. [All information about the general daily life of the Tidewater Indian is supplied by Dr. Porter].

17. Ibid. p. 33.

CHAPTER 3

Colonial Entrepreneurship and Expansion

Swiftly, the colonials took advantage of the marvelous "Eden" they discovered in the new world; the natural resources of both shores, Eastern and Western, were plentiful, a cause for jubilation and celebration. A tidewater work force of lumbermen, millers, trappers, planters and fishermen plunged into the rigors of life in the wild.

During this time, between the 1600s and the 1800s, the Chesapeake Bay formed a vision of great beauty and abundance for the early pioneer and a natural setting for colonial expansion. In the spring of 1634, Father Andrew White describes the Bay and its tributaries in his personal narrative:

> When you come within the Capes, you enter into a faire Bay, which is navigable for at least 200 miles, and is called Chesopeack Bay, and runneth Northerly: Into this Bay fall many goodly navigable Rivers . . . In the upper parts of the Countrey, there are Bufeloes, Elkes, Lions, Beares, Wolves, and Deare . . . in all places that are not too much frequented, as also Beavers, Foxes, Otters, and many other sorts of Beasts.

> • • •

> Of Birds, there is the Eagle; Goshawke, Falcon, Lanner, Sparrow-hawke, and Merlin, also wild Turkeys in great abounbance, where of many weigh 50 pounds, and upwards and of Partridge plenty. There are likewise sundry Birds which sing,

They traded and travelled on it, fought and frolicked on it, and its inlets and estuaries were so numerous and accommodating that nearly every planter had navigable salt water within a rifle's shot of his front door.

— Thomas J. Scharf, *History of Maryland*, Vol. I

whereof some are red, some blew, others blacke and yellow, some like our Black-birds, others like Thrushes, but not of the same kind, with many more, for which wee know no names. In Winter there is great plenty of Swannes, Cranes, Geese, Herons, Ducke, Teale, Widgeon, Brants, and Pidgeons, with other sorts, whereof there are none in England.

Of the section of the Bay northward Father White claims:

[. . . at the] head of the Bay, there are no more Rivers that are inhabited: There dwell the Sasquehanocks, upon a River that is not navigable for our Boates, by reason of Sholes and Rovkes, but they passe it in canoos; . . . Upon the East side of this Bay lie very many Ilands which are not inhabited, where are store of Deere.[1]

He writes that:

. . . the Sea, the Bayes of Chesopeack, and Delaware, and generally all the Rivers, doe abound with fish of severall sorts, . . . There are Whales, Sturgeons very large and good, and in great aboundance; Grampuses, Porpuses, Mullets, Trouts, Soules, Place, Mackerell, Perch, Crabs, Oysters, Cockles, and Mussles; But above all these, the fish that have no English names, are the best except the Sturgeons. . . also the Tode-fish, which will swell till it be ready to burst, it be taken out of the water.[2]

With this vision of the bay glimmering before them, the colonials set forth to settle into a place where religious freedom could be experienced and where this kind of abundance could offer them quality of life, economically and spiritually. However, this rapid settlement occurred without much deliberation about environmental resources and little thought about the Indian way of life. By the 1700s the colonists saw the value of land that bordered navigable water and settled on the banks of rivers all over the Bay before settling inland. One noted historian relates, "The Bay and its estuaries. . . gave the Tidewater Marylander a facility of communication with one another and with the outside world not possessed by any other colony on the continent."[3]

During the colonial period the differences in Magothy River settlement patterns from those of other Western Shore rivers influenced its general ecology and usage. Initially, in the early l600s, compared with other rivers or creeks of the Bay, such as the Severn or the Patapsco, the Magothy went significantly unnoticed and undisturbed by the early colonists. The focus of attention was in establishing the port towns of Anne Arundell Towne (Annapolis), St. Mary's City and Baltimore. At that time the prevailing attitudes were that "creekes," as the Magothy was called, were considered as "marginal environments, unsuitable for agriculture." A Methodist missionary wrote: "The Indians have their abodes a great way back in the

woods, so that we seldom see or converse with one another." The small tributaries and the backwoods were free territories for those who fled the colonials. Who knows? Perhaps these were the clans who loved the hidden coves of Blackhole Creek or of Dividing Creek or Mill Creek? No doubt, they used obscure necks of land such as the Magothy to sequester themselves from the onslaught of the colonists.

Because of the Magothy's configuration of secret coves and long river branches and its quiet, sequestered woods, its natural wildlife remained pristine, perhaps even harboring remaining family hunting units long after more centralized colonial

centers had been settled by the influx of people from the old world. Frank W. Porter notes:

> Accustomed to dispersing to remote areas and to maintaining lengthy periods of isolation, the family hunting unit would have allowed some Indian families to subsist successfully in their traditional habitat even though much of their land had been usurped by Europeans. Similarly, the

move of the remnant Indian groups to marginal environments would not have proven to be a severe hardship, and would have partially reduced their contact and conflict with white settlers. These Indian families gradually assumed the outward appearance of Euro-Americans through their acquisition of material culture traits. . . . They subsisted on the natural resources and by "selling or bartering the meat and skins of wild game to their neighboring Whites in exchange for goods derived from a foreign technology." [Gradually,] "through time the Indians gained an intimate knowledge of the legal institutions and social customs of the Whites. Their repeated appeals to the county courts about land encroachment, physical abuse, and murder strongly support this point.[4]

Like a shifting kaleidoscope, the land transfer for the colonials formed patterns of movement and a breakdown from large holdings to smaller ones, an evolution begun during colonial times and continuing to the present. Originally the land surrounding the Magothy was deeded from Charles I of England to George Calvert, a prominent Englishman who strongly believed in religious freedom as well as economic opportunity. In 1632 he willed the land to his son, Cecilius Calvert, the second Lord Baltimore, who became proprietor of the Maryland colony. Calvert's primary motive was to set up a secure haven for Catholics.

Impregnated into the *Charter of 1632,* which designated lands to Cecil Calvert, were viruses of a prejudice based upon ignorance of foreign cultures and the rights of a people the English could not comprehend. This charter referred to the Indians as "savages" and potential enemies of the colonists. Unfortunately, the English in their rush to establish colonies and to acquire lands through royal grants, often overlooked, ignored, and usurped the land rights of the Indians, who at this time were still quite vital.

In fact, the twelfth section of the *Charter of 1632* authorized Lord Baltimore to collect troops and to wage war on the barbarians and their enemies who might threaten the settlements. The colonists were to pursue them "beyond the limits of their province" and "if God shall grant it, to vanquish and captivate them; and the captives to put to death, or according to their discretion to save." (Charter of Maryland, Charles I)

Initially the colonial relationships among the Indians were peaceful. Generally, the Maryland colonists developed trade with them and obtained large tracts of land with amicable, though uneven trades. Alcohol and weapons were traded for furs; Indian lands were given away to colonists in return for protection against inter-tribal wars. Since, in the Native American culture, property ownership did not exist, territorial land rights, although respected, could easily be traded for bright trinkets, alcohol, cattle and hogs, or whatever else caught the naivete of the particular tribe. Because of their fluid way of moving with the seasons, at first, the Indians simply moved on to allow the colonists to share land.

Native American traditional hunting and farming activities were disrupted after encounters which began as peaceful gestures between two cultures. The early colonial grantees tried to protect the Indians' privileges of hunting, fishing, and crabbing. But the aggressive settlers usurped land, while the Indian warnings to the colonial settlers went unheard. Thus, the initial peace between the Indians and the early colonials was short-lived. Fur and lumber in such plentiful supply appealed to the new world travellers who took full advantage of the situation through devious methods. The native Algonquians began to use their creative energy to cope with the increasing number of settlers and the preponderance of unfair and illegal practices of traders. Between 1642 and 1698, they attempted to protect themselves and their lands frequently by staging raids or by threatening war. Later, when Indian food and lands became scarce, Native Americans supplemented their diet by stealing and killing the settlers' domestic hogs and cattle. They too, swung into a mode of war for survival. What follows is one story of an Algonquian who was threatened:

> Let us have no quarrels for killing hogs no more than for the cows eating the Indian corn. Your hogs and cattle injure Us you come too near us to live and drive us from place to place. We can fly no farther let us know where to live and how to be secured for the future from the Hogs and Cattle.[5]

Thus, the careful use of land and water by the Indian population gave way to a new way—the colonial way. Harsh measures were taken by the colonists who had little understanding or patience in negotiating with the warring Indian tribes.

Weak treaties were signed, such as the famous treaty between the Susquehannocks and the colonists in July of 1652. Signed under the Liberty tree in Annapolis, this treaty propelled the demise of the Indian on the Chesapeake Bay and its tributaries. Gradually, the Susquehannocks relinquished their claim to jurisdiction over the lands on the west side of the Chesapeake Bay as far as Palmer's Island and from the Choptank to the Elk River on the Eastern Shore. They were afraid of a neighboring tribe of Iroquois and sought military alliance and friendship. But in exchange for this false security, they lost large tracts of land. Gradually, this same type of give-away occurred over all the Indian territories. Wars persisted between the Susquehannocks and the colonials in 1676 and 1677. From 1670 to 1680, wars occurred between the Indians and the new settlers. Tribal wars between the Iroquois and Susquehannocks shattered the peace and tranquility of the land and surrounding waters.[6]

Pillage and burnings of small settlements frequently took place. Tribes began their "Trail of Tears," the migration westward and to the north, searching for places to relocate. For example, the migration of the Nanticoke from Virginia and the Eastern Shore to the Susquehanna River took place in 1744. Fear narrowed the mind of the Indian and propelled that culture into defensive mechanisms, which helped to level and obscure that race. No longer could the legendary Indian feasts be enjoyed between the Algonquians of Persimmon Point (now Cape St. Claire), Deep Creek and Forked Creek and those of Mountain Point (now Gibson Island). They were too busy fighting for their lives.

As the colonials were beginning ventures of open trade of tobacco and furs with Holland, Spain and England, the Indian way of life gradually became extinct due to disease and the loss of lands. In 1642, Captain John Price had been ordered by Thomas Greene, the governor of Maryland, "to destroy their corn, burn their houses, and to kill them or take them prisoner."[7] The colonials, in the Treaty of 1669, relegated the Indians to "certain tracts of land for their exclusive use." This marked the beginning of the idea of Indian reservations, later to be used in the West.

Along with the vanishing Indian pathways of life, the ecology of the Western Shore was never to be the same. Exploitation of the natural resources for profit as well as the lack of awareness of the colonial concerning other cultures, led to the failure to see the rivers and bays as viable connectors between races and color. Over a period of approximately 150 years, the near-complete demise of the Indian took place in Maryland, and by the end of the 1700s, few Indians remained.[8]

In the Tidewater region, population growth and density tripled between 1700 and 1790, and by the late eighteenth century, the Piedmont and western sections of the Chesapeake became more populated. More tidewater farms dotted the waterfront. By 1750 a large influx of a slave labor force and the growing number of white immigrants created many close-knit permanent family farms, replacing the transitory Indian way of life.[9]

With the clearing of vast tracts of trees for the burgeoning lumber trade, and later, the onset of small industries which began to dot the river branches and inlets, the bay became not a waterway for sustaining life, but a metaphor for opportunity and monetary gain. Gradually, a chasm was created.

In the early and mid-1700s, like other Western Shore rivers, the lands surrounding the Magothy were used pragmatically for tobacco plantations and for working lumber and grist mills. Moderate winters, late falls, and early springs, with a gentle effect of waters surrounding the land, created the ideal environment for farming. But the plantations still formed a patchwork of clearings among existing forested lands. While these plantations were being established, the small creeks still provided shelter, due to their forested cover, from various warring factions between colonists and the Indians. Many Algonquians went into these sheltered coves and tributaries to set up small remaining camps; others became hunting and fishing guides for the new white gentry, entering the area, sometimes even dressing like colonists. Other Indian tribes seemed to have lost their spirit for who they really were and became prey to alcoholism and disease. An important missionary noted:

> . . . these detached Indian families living among the white people on the banks of rivers, and on that account called "River-Indians," are generally a loose set of people, like our gypsies they make baskets, bromes, wooden spoons, dishes, etc. and sell them to the white people for victuals and clothe.[10]

Mapmaker Lewis Evans, in 1753, wrote that these Indians who "have no land of their own or fixt habitations: what they get for their Work, they Spend in Rum and their food they beg. . ."[11]

The abode of river-front lands now became sole possession of the colonists: ". . . The earlier colonists took up no land but what bordered on the water; and both shores of the bay (Eastern and Western) and its estuaries were settled. . . before the interior of St. Mary's, Talbot and Kent Counties."[12]

Narratives and Diaries of the Waterfront

A detailed rendering of the superb natural wildlife which once proliferated in the environs of the Chesapeake Bay emerges from early writings and diaries. Hammond in his "Leah and Rachel," an early colonial diary, relates: *"Deer are all over the country, and in places so many that veneson is accounted a tiresome meat; wild turkeys are frequent, and so large that I have seen some weigh near three-score pounds."* He describes the docility of the deer: *"They are as plenty as cuckolds in London. . . and they are so tame that they would almost let you touch them."*[13]

Also mentioned are more dangerous animals: *"Wolves, bears and panthers . . . have abounded in the backwoods."* Less fierce, yet a nuisance, some minute pests were made use of by the colonials: *". . . Squirrels were so abundant and so destructive, that the counties were authorized by the legislature to pay rewards for their scalps."* At this point in time bison and bears were seldom seen and rarely hunted, but quail, pheasants, ortolans, snipe, woodcock, raccoon, opossums, wild pigeons, and hares *"were everywhere to be shot, and, as every man and boy carried a gun habitually, [to] supply game upon all tables."*[14]

The earth itself was described as having all the necessary natural resources to make it a great place to colonize. Early seventeenth century diaries and chronicles relate:

> *The greatest variety of soil overlies this diverse geological structure, varying from the peaty or sandy loams of the bay sections with their deposits of oyster shell and marl, to the ferruginous clays of the secondary region, the rich and crumbly loams which rest over the beds of granite and limestone. . . .Valuable bog iron ore may be*

found in the swamps of Dorchester; and nearly all the various oxides of this metal are deposited either in clays or among the rocks in the several parts of the State. Copper and marbles are found adjacent to the clays and irons; and the five hundred square miles of coal fields are a treasure, the value of which is scarcely yet fully developed. Other minerals, equally rare and useful, having commercial value and being found under peculiarly favorable circumstances, are characteristic of the State's resources. Zinc, red and brown ochre, steatite, manganese, building slate, mica, baryta, tripolis, granite, asbestos, kaolin, breccia limestone, fire-brick clay, corundum, are amongst those productions which have already been developed.[15]

Another historian notes that the "iron deposits [in Maryland] were so rich that they littered the surface of the ground."[16]

So, too, the Magothy River contained rich geological sources of iron and coal deposits and layers of fine sand called "hour-glass sand," and clay deposits for firing brick.[17] In fact, in 1731 the Magothy River became a key area for the establishment of the first alum plant in the United States, called the Baltimore Iron Works, started by Dr. Charles Carroll. Here, the deposits of iron-ore contributed to the manufacture of alum, a composite used in the making of gun-powder. "The ore was mined along North Ferry Point and Cape Sable, then barged to Baltimore where the manufacturing took place."[18]

In another part of his early Chronicle of Maryland, Hammond speaks of the forests and orchards:

The soil of Maryland impartially encourages the growth of both the hardwoods and the soft; and the hickory flourishes beside the maple, the white pine beside the white oak, the persimmon with the beech and the wild elm with the sassafras and the dogwood, as if each found here its favorite habitat—wild fruits, are to be found growing naturally in the fields and forests; and all spontaneously in the deep soils of the glades. All early travellers in, and writers about Maryland, have noted the fact that, even before the first generation of settlers had passed, the country was thickly planted with orchards of apple and peach trees, which seemed to grow in the most flourishing way.[19]

Of course, the forests of the Western Shore rivers were meccas for lumbering activity, forming a firm basis for trade. The lure of the riverside edges also provided the colonial with land conducive for planting orchards. Riverside grapes grew wild and the nuts fell from the trees. Hammond continues:

The country is full of gallant orchards, and the fruit generally more luscious and delightful than here [England], witness the peach and quince, the latter may be eaten raw savorily, the former differs and as much exceeds our as the best relished apple we have doth the crabb, and of both most excellent and comfortable drinks are made; grapes in infinite manner grow wild, so do walnuts, chestnuts, and an abundance of excellent fruits, plums and berries, not growing or known in England; bread and bear [beer], and pease besides English, of ten several sorts, all exceeding our in England; the gallant root of potatoes [sweet] are common, and so are all sorts of roots, herbs and garden stuff.[20]

In 1679, two early Dutch traders wrote in their diaries of the plethora of ducks on the Eastern Shore, a memoir which creates awe in the hearts of contemporary Bay people and one which connects with the oral history of the Magothy and Western Shore rivers:

I have nowhere seen so many ducks together as were in the creek in front of this house. The water was so black with them that it seemed when you looked from the land below upon the water, as if it were a mass of filth or turf, and when they flew up; there was a rushing and vibration of the air like a great storm coming through the trees, and even like the rumbling of distant thunder, while the sky over the whole creek was filled with them like a cloud, or like the starlings fly at harvest time in Fatherland. There was a boy about twelve years old who took aim at them from the shore, not being able to get within good shooting distance of them, but nevertheless shot loosely before they got away, and hit only three or four, complained of his shot, as they are accustomed to shoot from six to twelve, and even eighteen and more at one shot. . . . They rose not in flocks of ten, or twelve, or twenty, or thirty, but continuously, wherever we pushed our way; and, as they made room for us, there was such an incessant clattering made with their wings upon the water when they rose, and such a noise of those flying higher up, that it was all the time as if we were surrounded by a whirlwind or a storm.[21]

During the colonial period, subtle shifts of ecological values occurred. Hunting was not only necessary for sustenance, as it had been for the Native American, but was now to be used for profit and gain:

The colony armed every man; in fact, it compelled every man to carry a gun and learn how to use it, and it compelled all ships at first to pay their port dues in gunpowder and lead, so that every man might become a sportsman. A good shot with the rifle or fusee, who might kill fifty squirrels a day, could earn 100 lbs. of tobacco, that is to say, 12s. [shillings] 6s. [pence] for their scalps, less the cost of the ammunition. If he shot a wild turkey, it was 2s to him. . . If he knew how to call them, he might easily bag three or four a day. . . A deer "in grease" was worth five or six shillings; so that there was profit in wood-craft to the skillful pot-hunter, and every servant had his Saturday afternoon in which to learn how to shoot.[22]

These "Saturday afternoon" shooting groups historically form the beginning of the long tradition of hunting for pleasure and for social bonding which still continues today. The natural abundance of wildlife beckoned. With more population, however, some resources began to dwindle. During the colonial period, on the Magothy as well as all over the Bay, wildlife as it had been for thousands of years was beginning to disappear entirely. The last Atlantic grey whale disappeared in 1695; the last bison in Maryland was hunted and killed in 1775; the last heath hen in 1800; the last gray wolf disappeared in 1850; the last elk in 1874; the last passenger pigeon in 1903 and the last panther in 1930.[23]

Pioneer Settlers of the Magothy

Many of the Magothy's wealthy land owners during the colonial era of the 1700s first resided in either Annapolis or Baltimore, renting out "plantations" to tenant farmers. These renters were either plantation tenant-farmers, yeomen, or indentured servants. Slaves accompanied them as part of the labor force. People who ventured into the "hinterlands" or "backwoods" such as the Magothy usually were of the most adventurous kind. The predominant characteristic of Magothy pioneers was that of independence, high individuality, ruggedness and practicality. Early river-life became land and farm-centered;

Charles Carroll of Carrollton, 1737-1832 (James Barton Longacre, 1794-1869, after a painting by Field, courtesy of the National Portrait Gallery, Smithsonian Institution)

whereas the more sophisticated river-front areas of Annapolis or Baltimore became town-centered, with vast colonial plantations stretching outwards.

The land was deeded to Magothy inheritors, who were primarily prominent wealthy families from England. These early land-holders (many of whom lived in Annapolis or in Baltimore) played a role not only in the early governing structures of Maryland, but in some of the organic developments of the land surrounding the Bay.

One stellar land-holder, Charles Carroll of Carrollton, owned hundreds of acres of the land on the north side of the Magothy which was financed through The Farmer's Bank of Maryland, one of the settlement's earliest banks. Descended from the Charles Carroll family of England, Charles was born in Annapolis in 1737, and was educated in France at the College of English Jesuits at St. Omer. After he was sent to the Jesuit College at Rheims, he studied law at Bourges and then went to Paris. When he returned to America at twenty-seven years old, he became one of the richest men in America. He was made a member of the First Committee of Observation established in Annapolis in 1775, and was elected a delegate to the Provincial Convention during that year. Instrumental in withdrawing the instructions from England to "disavow in the most solemn manner all design in the colonies of independence," he was one of the delegates to sign the Declaration of Independence on August 2, 1776. Also in 1776 he helped to draft the Constitution for Maryland. He became a Senator in 1788 and in 1797 and, in July of 1828 in his 90th year, surrounded by the notables of the country, laid the corner-stone for the Baltimore and Ohio Railroad. Charles Carroll was one of its principal trustees.

As trustee of The Farmer's Bank and owner of vast tracts of property, Charles Carroll held the responsibility of deciding what was to be done with the land, how it was to be developed and how it was to serve the needs of its people who were to live there. In this exceptional case, the concerns of land use and ecology became closely knit with the entrepreneurship of bankers and financiers. Charles Carroll persuaded farmers of both Anne Arundel and Howard Counties to discontinue or reduce their tobacco acreage. Ahead of his time, he noted that soil was robbed of nutrients "by that greedy though aromatic, weed, tobacco." He advocated the use of fertilizer (lime) together with crop rotation such as wheat or corn, followed by nitrogen-fixing clover, thus "providing food for mankind while restoring food to the soil." Later, methods of fertilization would become distorted and over-used, contributing greatly to the degradation of the Chesapeake Bay.

Colonial settlement spread northward into the area of Anne Arundel County during the mid-seventeenth century. Around 1651, the five "hundreds," or formal areas of settlement, had been established.[24] Broadneck and Towne Neck Hundred were located between the Severn, the Magothy and the Bodkin. The lands on the north side of the Magothy became known as "Towne-Necke Hundred;" the lands on the south side were designated as "Broadneck Hundred."

With colonization and the clearing of lands for orchards and farms, the densely forested riverside areas slowly began to thin. The colonial lumbermen of the riverine properties discovered the value of the great white and red oak found on the Western Shore of the Chesapeake and the rich sources of chestnut, for lumbering and barging to the coastal New England towns. Gradually, almost imperceptibly, people began to replace trees. At the end of the seventeenth century, Anne Arundel was the most heavily populated county in Maryland; it was considered the most wealthy county in the colony since its tidewater regions were so well-suited for growing tobacco and, later, for wheat growing. The Magothy on both its north and south sides was no exception. Early land grants of both Broadneck Hundred on the south side and Towne-Necke Hundred on the north

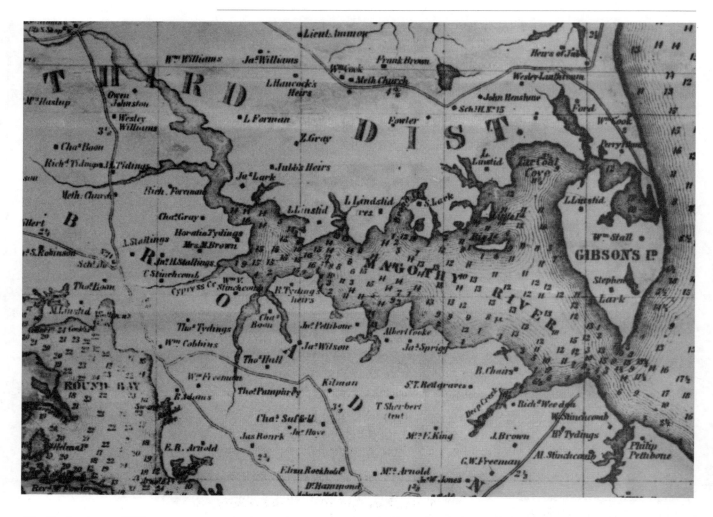

The Martenet map, 1795 (Maryland State Archives, Maryland Hall of Records Map Collection MSA SC 1427-187)

side show that farms, or "plantations" were being deeded and divided. Land along the Magothy indeed was becoming a part of large holdings by early colonial entrepreneurs such as Charles Carroll of Carrollton.

Other pioneer grantees of land on the Broadneck and Towne-Necke peninsulas included owners of vast tracts which bordered the Severn as well as the Magothy: On June 15, 1650, a grant of land was made to:

Robert Burle, 450 acres, on ye no. side of Chesapeake Bay; Abraham Holman also had a grant this year; in 1651 to John Covell, Ralph and Wm. Hawkins; in 1652 to Richard Ewen, 600 acres near Fishing Creek, on ye Bay side, with title above ye no. point of Severn River; also, to Richard Young and James Homewood; in 1659, to John Hawkins, Philip Harwood, James Rigby, William Fuller, Elizabeth Strong and Matt. Clark; in 1658 to Nathaniel Utie; in 1661, to William Cronch; in 1662 to Henry Woolchurch, William Hopkins, William Pyther, Richard Deaner, Thomas Underwood, Alice Durand, Robert Taylor, Absalom Dawson, William Stayd, Thomas Turner, Robert Lusby; in 1663 to Matt. Howard, Edward Skidmore, Robert Tyler, Abraham Dawson, Sarah Marsh, John Aiken, John Green, John Homewood and Emmanuel Drew.[25]

During the early period of colonization and farming on the Magothy, slaves and indentured servants comprised most of the work force needed for the labor-intensive cultivation of tobacco. Consequently, by the end of the eighteenth century, black slaves accounted for nearly half of the county's population (Wesler, 1981:96).[26]

A picture emerges of the Magothy and its people of the Colonial age. The farms here were held by wealthy landowners who used indentured servants from London and Bristol and slaves to work them. Later, they rented them to tenant farmers, such as the Quakers who immigrated here and formed farming communities. But slaves performed a major part of the early work of tilling the soil; thus the African-American became intimate with the environment and with the early methods of farming, drying, and rolling the tobacco to river landings for trade and transport.

Pioneer Magothy Workers

A closer scrutiny of some of the early Magothy workers allows the creation of a more specific picture of colonial waterfront people. The indentured servants who worked the lands, for the most part, did not have a great reputation. In fact, public opinion of these people was unfavorable. William Bullock described them as "idle, lazie, simple people. . . such as have professed idlenesse, and will rather beg than work."[27]

Various sketches of early prototypes of Magothy farmers come from original journal entries of the day: From Bristol came "... servants to his majesty's plantations... some are husbands that have forsaken their wives, others wives who have abandoned their husbands; some are children and apprentices run away from their parents and have been tempted on board by menstealers, and many that have been pursued by hue-and-cry for robberies, burglaries, or breaking prison, do thereby escape the prosecution of the law and justice."[28] Another 17th century diary entry describes early settlers as "convicts, paupers and dissolute persons of every type."[29] These unfavorable, more idiosyncratic people certainly came over on the ships to the new country, but recent historians concur that the early colonial servants came predominantly from "the middling classes: farmers and skilled workers, the productive groups in England's working population."[31] These were people from predominantly agricultural backgrounds, the yeomen and the laborers, also those engaged in clothing and textile trades, clerks, accountants, and grooms. From London and Bristol came the pioneer settlers, a people who escaped the rigid class society of the Old World to begin anew on the estuaries and inlets of the Chesapeake. They would rise out of what England called "The Commons" and gain wealth, self-esteem, and independence while at the same time exploiting both the Indian and the natural resources surrounding them.

Although the first batch of colonists drove out the Native American population, successive flocks of people from England and Holland, escaping the Old World for freedom and prosperity, quickly forgot this darker side of colonization. From their point of view, life had to be survived in a rugged place. Thus, through persistence and diligence in working for large plantation owners who were of the English gentry, the indentured servants earned enough money to buy their own land and establish close communities of their own kin,[30] usually extended families who to this day still own and live together on large acreages of land on the Magothy. Pioneer family names, from early English gentry as well as from merchant class and farm stock, remain today. Family names as the Brices, the Worthingtons, the Stinchcombs, the Heaths, the Hydes, the Ogles and many more still persist on both the north and south shores of the Magothy.

Historical Magothy Farms

Out of the stillness of the Magothy's pristine shoreline could be heard the sounds of trees being felled for lumber. During the mid 1700s, along the Western Shore rivers, small spaces began to be cleared for homesteading and farming. The Magothy farmer was adventurous, keen-spirited, and immensely practical. He wanted to make not only a living but a profit. Families of both free men and slaves worked hard clearing the deep woods. These plantations, even though they might be on vast hundreds of acres of land, were only small clearings in the forest. Recently, as a few of these early plantations have been excavated, a picture emerges of buildings which were impermanent, built on or in the ground without foundations. These structures, termed "earthfast," apparently did not last; however, this type of construction suited the planter of Anne Arundel County, because it was cheap and fast; and materials could be used from the natural woods surrounding the waters.[31] In fact, the forest around the Magothy supplied one of its old residents with wood for housing and fencing: In 1754 John Gray of the Magothy River on "Eagles Hill" (north side), patented his land which contained the following improvements:

> . . . one dwelling house 21 foot long, 15 foot wide post in the ground, wood chimney, covered with pine clapboard built 12 years, 1 logg hut 15 by 12 built 6 years, one old 40 foot tobacco house very sorry condition, 46 apple trees in orchard, 254 panels very old fence, about 10 acres of cultivated land.[31]

Romantic notions of snug, neat farms, tucked along the waters edge are erased. Historically, the environs of the river farms and others were rather shoddy. Donna Ware, historian, speaks of Anne Arundel County in the 1700s:

> . . . the buildings, fields, and landscape were not aesthetically pleasing. Houses were generally small, often with dirt floors and no chimneys. If there was a chimney, it was frequently made of wood and stick, rather than brick. Tobacco houses or barns were unpainted and appeared dilapidated. The majority of fields were untidy and looked abandoned. On a family farm of 50 acres . . . only 10 to 20 acres were cultivated with corn and tobacco. The rest was wooded or recuperating "old fields" where cattle wandered freely.[32]

Practicality and some ecological concerns did exist during early settlement of the area; however, colonial farmers were willing to "sacrifice aesthetics for economic thrift. In a mobile agricultural system, unkempt old fields restored soil fertility and structures related to tobacco cultivation were semi-permanent. Durable painted barns, and . . . dwellings, were considered a waste of capital."[33]

Differences in housing structures occurred between various Western Shore rivers: while the wealthy gentlemen of Baltimore and Arundell-Towne (Annapolis) used brick imported from England to create their mansions, the working tenant farmer and slave of the Magothy primarily used wood from the chestnut tree or logs made out of pine. The beginning of what was to become extensive land clearing and tree-cutting contributed to the vast tree loss of the Western Shore. As was previously noted, around 1600 almost 100 percent of the state was forested with trees twenty percent taller than those of today. By 1900, only twenty percent of the trees remained.

Farm life was arduous. Fences, houses, tools, sheds, curing barns, even clothing had to be hand-made. During the eighteenth century, survival instincts of the sixteenth and seventeenth centuries relinquished to a way of life measured by success. The settlers became a tenacious lot; they were staunch, vigorous, capitalistic and ready for new opportunities.

While Annapolis and the Severn River were becoming the center for government and the hub of social life for the wealthier classes, the Magothy became a key river for the great work of settlement and survival, its environs a source for plenteous supplies of corn, wheat, tobacco, furs and lumber along with abundant amounts of seafood and fowl. Thus, the architecture of grand houses surrounding Annapolis differed from the more humble, pragmatic cabins and farmhouses of the Magothy hinterland.

On the Magothy, families moved into small log houses to farm large tracts, mills sprang up, barges were built to carry produce and lumber to ports all over the new country—from Baltimore to Annapolis and Virginia. Tobacco and furs were transported as far away as Holland, Spain, and of course, England. More trade brought more people.

New technologies and entrepreneurship thrived. But environmental change seemed to accelerate with each colonial innovation. For example, instead of using the Native American method of punching divots into the ground to plant seed, not displacing much soil with their crude hoes, the colonial farmer by the 1800s began using iron plows which cut up to a foot into the soil. Plant life was disrupted, such as the wild orchids which used to proliferate. Silt and sedimentation had quadrupled over the past 350 years, and by the turn of the 19th century, almost every acre of the forest in Maryland had been clear-cut.[34]

Mills of the Magothy

Mills of the Magothy were a life-force for the colonial planters and lumberjacks, providing work and productivity for the progressive builders of a new country. The millers prepared the lumber for building or for trade, and the corn and wheat for the making of flour, establishing a link in the chain of a work ethic which formed the impetus for riverfront development.

Bare traces of these early mills remain. In 1994, the old mill located at Lake Waterford, the headwaters of the Magothy, was demolished for a county project to widen the spillway. Orange-yellow speckled foundation stones of the old mill house there remained, before the bull-dozers roared in for demolition. These mill stones were the remnants of an early Magothy mill dating to the mid-1700s. This mill was Wallace's Mill which can be found on a 1795 Martenet Map. Early land plats reveal that in 1727 it was owned by Adam Dash and was then called the Adam Dash Mill. Later it became known as the Wallace-Dash Mill. Its last recorded owner was a Mr. Boyd. Its history can be traced back into a larger system of a grist and saw mills owned by Charles Waters, one of the wealthiest mill owners in the new colonies. This particular mill ground corn and wheat, farmed on a large adjacent piece of property owned by the Pumphrey family, an original colonial family in Anne Arundel County. To this day, the old grist mill stone lies on the ground near the tennis courts, testimony of historic Magothy mills.

Traces of another mill, not far from the Adam Dash Mill, can be found on the east side of the Magothy Bridge near a narrow part of the river. An old "mill race" remains, reminding Magothites of the industriousness of early river people. Perhaps this was a part of a system of mills near the Lake Waterford Mill. No historic reference can be found in connection with this mill race. Farm land adjacent to these important headwaters of the Magothy River was used for growing tobacco, corn and wheat and later was sold to the Bower family who created a homestead there and a summer camp. This area evolved into what is now called "Lake Waterford," a public park in Anne Arundel County. But some of the old barns remain among the suburban houses, even now.

A Magothy mill which predated the American Revolution, built in 1721, was called *Maggety Mill*. It was located at the mouth of Muddy Run, and owned by John Summerland of Anne Arundel County. It became known as "Summerland's Mill" and was used as a lumber mill. In 1727 it was sold to John Worthington, merchant, which also included a large tract of land called "Margaret's Choice" on the north side of the Magothy. In 1753 the land and mill were sold to a Mr. Stevens. The land then shifted from Stevens to one Thomas Sparks in 1755 and in 1769 was sold to George Conoway, an Anne Arundel County planter, and his wife, Rachel.[35]

The author and her husband, Robert, by the millstone near Lake Waterford.

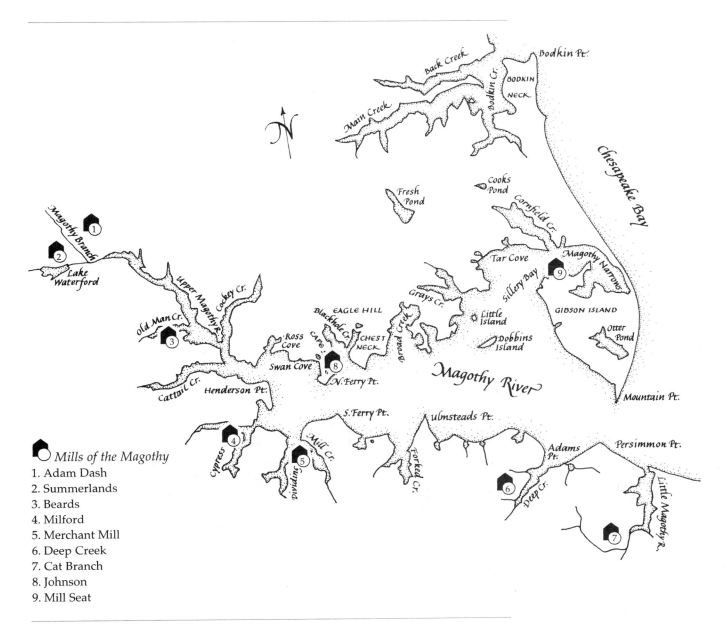

Back Creek

Bodkin Pt.

Main Creek

BODKIN
NECK

Bodkin Cr.

Chesapeake Bay

Cooks
Pond

Fresh
Pond

Cornfield Cr.

Magothy Branch

Tar Cove

Magothy Narrows

(9)

(1)

Sillery Bay

(2)

Lake
Waterford

Upper Magothy R.

Cockey Cr.

GIBSON ISLAND

Grays Cr.

Little
Island

Otter
Pond

Old Man Cr.

EAGLE HILL

Blackhole Cr.

(3)

Ross
Cove

CAPE

CHEST
NECK

Dobbins
Island

Broad Creek

Magothy River

Swan Cove

(8)

Cattail Cr.

Henderson Pt.

N. Ferry Pt.

Mountain Pt.

S. Ferry Pt.

Ulmsteads Pt.

Persimmon Pt.

Mill Cr.

Adams
Pt.

(4)

Cypress

(5)

Forked Cr.

(6)

Deep Cr.

Little Magothy R.

Dividing

(7)

⬟◯ *Mills of the Magothy*
1. Adam Dash
2. Summerlands
3. Beards
4. Milford
5. Merchant Mill
6. Deep Creek
7. Cat Branch
8. Johnson
9. Mill Seat

A Magothy mill named *Milford* was established near Cypress Creek at Magothy Branch. In 1683 this land, called "Milford" and "Taylor's Lott," was deeded to Thomas Sparks of Baltimore County and to Elizabeth, his wife, in 1756. The original land plats for Anne Arundel County show that Thomas was a planter who sold some of his tracts of land to James Norman of Anne Arundel County.[36] Norman was a "sayer" or "sawyer" meaning a person who operates a saw mill. The property surrounding the mills "a short distance above Cromwell's

old mill site," was called "Cave" stones. Cromwell was the last owner of the mill before it was sold to Charles Waters in June, 1834. Waters represents the pragmatic, industrious type of river-front entrepreneur, now the wealthy miller of the new colonies. Like many other Magothy pioneers who succeeded through vast acquisition of lands near the waterfront, the ownership of his chain of Magothy River mills proved to be a source of great wealth.

Millstones from Beard's Mill, now located at The Old Stone House (photos by Joan B. Machinchick)

Beard's Mill, on Old Man's Creek, dating back to 1698, was located conveniently near the thick forests and was accessible to the creek and eventually the river. The original land patent (1687) included 1161 acres and was called Huckleberry Forrest (now the community of Berrywood). This farm extended to Cattail Creek. Richard Beard, the miller, was a man of extensive interests. He owned the first lot laid at Londontown on the South River; he also built several other grist mills, one of them near his stone house, "Beard's Habitation," It has the distinction of being built in 1749 or earlier, one of the earliest houses built on the Magothy River. Near the house were found several of the original millstones. Later, he sold 438 acres of his land to Thomas R. Robinson. The "old stone house," invariably connected with the life of the miller, still stands south of the mill site on Route 648. Inhabited through the years by John Tydings beginning in 1837, it was later owned by Laura Tydings Garcelon.[37] At present, it is owned by the Dr. Stephen Hittle family, who continue to improve it and to retain its historical significance. [For a full description of this home, refer to pages 117-119.]

Lumbering became a way of life for the early Magothy settlers, extending into the early twentieth century. One lumber mill is located on Blackhole Creek, established by the Johnson family, of Johnson Lumber Mills. In 1902 Wilmer Johnson purchased a huge tract of chestnut timber and erected his first sawmill, on the north side of the Magothy, renowned for its rich sources of chestnut timber. He appointed his nineteen year old son, Joshua Fred Johnson, "to take charge of it." Under his son's guidance the new mill prospered. Joshua married Mabel Virginia Jubb, of a family who owned extensive property on Cape Sable on Blackhole Creek on the north side of the Magothy. Later, another larger mill was constructed by the Johnsons at Marley Creek.[38]

One mill reference in the early land plats on the north side of the Magothy, refers to a mill called *Mill Seat* located at Holland Point near Gibson Island.[39] This could have been a grist mill since historic references have been made to the "rich cornfields" of "Cornfield Plain," nearby. On the south side of the Magothy was stationed a mill at Deep Creek, quite an excellent spot for such an operation because it was convenient for the barges to load and unload at the landing so near the wide mouth of the Magothy. One historical reference notes that: "the old mill at Deep Creek washed away."[40] This event probably occurred in the great rain of 1749, sweeping away many mill dams of this area. Another mill was developed afterwards with water collected from the Cat Branch stream, which flowed from the north slope of the hills into Little Magothy Creek. The procedure for milling was to raise water levels which could collect in ponds or lakes through constructing a dam. Then the water could be controlled by opening a contrivance on a mill-race which would send concentrated amounts of water rushing to operate the wheels of the mill. During Governor Horatio Sharpe's ownership of Broadneck lands (1763), the waters from this particular Cat Branch Dam were lifted from a "pond" connected with the Little Magothy River. Through a primitive hydraulic system, the water could be carried via canal to his property near Whitehall. (Governor Sharpe owned extensive lands on both sides of what is now US Route 50 which, at that time, was only an oyster shell path. Thus, waterways of both the Severn and the Magothy connected indirectly.)

Knowing that various creeks of the bay were named either after early settlers or as descriptions of their function, one can assume from its name that there also was a mill at Mill Creek on the south side of the Magothy. However, no historical documentation exists as proof. But in the Maryland Gazette of Feb. 2, 1795 there was a *Merchant Mill* advertised for sale on the *"So side of Maggety,"* perhaps the same as the unnamed one on Mill Creek.

The mills on the Magothy are testament to the life of the Magothy worker, and formed some of the first industries on the waterfront. The network of planters, lumberjacks, millers, indentured servants, and slaves contributed to the foundations of what the Magothy stood for in its staunch work ethic of the eighteenth and nineteenth centuries.

1. Father Andrew White, *A Relation of Maryland Together With a Map of the Country, The Conditions of Plantation, His Majesties Charter to the Lord Baltimore: A Readex Microprint, 1655* Sections 18, 19.

2. Ibid.

3. J. Thomas Scharf, *History of Maryland from the Earliest Period to the Present Day,* Vol. 1, (Baltimore: J. B. Piet, 1879) p. 2.

4. Frank W. Porter, III, "Behind the Frontier: Indian Survivals in Maryland," *Maryland Historical Magazine,* The Maryland Historical Society, Vol. 75, No. 1 (March 1980), p. 50.

5. T. J. Scharf, *History of Maryland,* p. 2.

6. Barry Kent, *Susquehanna's Indians, Anthropological Series #6,* Pennsylvania Historical Museum Commission: Harrisburg, PA, (1984).

7. Frank W. Porter, III, *Maryland Indians: Yesterday and Today,* Baltimore: Museum and Library of Maryland Historical Society, 1983, pp. 40-56 [All subsequent references to the demise of the Indian of the Northeast Corridor are from this source].

8. Frank W. Porter, III, *The Nanticoke,* (NY & Philadelphia, Chelsea House Publishers, 1987), p. 52.

9. Daniel Blaker Smith, "Narratives of Early Maryland, 1633, 1634" *Inside the Great House: Planter Family Life in 18c. Chesapeake Society,* ed, ed. Clayton C. Hull (NY: Barnes, 1946) p. 177.

10. F. W. Porter, p. 42

11. F. W. Porter, p. 50.

12. J. T. Scharf, p. 2.

13. Hammond, "Leah and Rachel" and Alsop in History of Maryland, p. 2.

14. W. T. Scharf, pp. 2-5.

15. Hammond, "Leah and Rachel," in *History of Maryland,* T. J. Scharf, p. 6.

16. John W. McGrain, *From Pig Iron to Cotton Duck:* (Baltimore County Heritage Publication, 1985), p. 11.

17. Robert J. Brugger,*Maryland, a Middle Temperament: 1634-1980* (Johns Hopkins University Press, in assoc. with the Maryland Historical Society, 1988), p. 66.

18. Robert F. Gould, "Eminent Chemists of Maryland," *Maryland HIstorical Magazine,*Vo. 80, No. 1 (Spring, 1985), p. 19.

19. Hammond in T. J. Scharf, *HIstory of Maryland*, p. 13.

20. Ibid. p. 6.

21. Jasper Dankers and Peter Sluyter, "Journal of a Voyage to New York and a Tour in Several of the American Colonies," in T. J. Scharf, *History of Maryland*, p. 4, 5.

22. T. J. Scharf, p. 71.

23. *The Baltimore Sun*, June 16, 1993, p. 9B.

24. James C. Bradford, ed., *Anne Arundel County Maryland: A Bicentennial History 1649-1977*, (Anne Arundel County and Annapolis Bicentennial Committee, 1977) pp. 92-93.

25. Elihu S. Riley, *A History of Anne Arundel County in Maryland*, (Annapolis: Charles G. Feldmeyer, 1905) pp. 29-30. [This reference was also used for information about Charles Carroll].

26. R. Christopher Goodwin & Associates, Inc., "Phase I Archaeological Investigation of the Robert Thieme Minor," p. 19.

27. William Bullock, "Virginia Impartially Examined. . . (London, 1649) in *The Chesapeake in the Seventeenth Century, Essays on Anglo-American Society* (Chapel Hill, 1979), p. 56.

28. Ibid.

29. Ibid. p. 47.

30. Smith, ed. *Seventeenth Century America*, article by Mildred Campbell, pp. 63-89.

31. Donna M. Ware, *Anne Arundel's Legacy: The Historic Properties of Anne Arundel County*, (Anne Arundel County, 1990) p. 7.

32. D. M. Ware, *Anne Arundel's Legacy: Historic Properties* . . . p. 8. [This information originated from an original land plat of Eagles Hill, Maryland State Archives: patented Certificate of Survey #440, 1754].

33. D. M. Ware, "The Evolution of a Tidewater Settlement System: All Hallows Parish, Maryland, 1650-1783," *Anne Arundel's Legacy*, p. 10.

34. *The Baltimore Sun*, June 16, 1993, p. 9B.

35. Gladys P. Nelker, *Town Neck Hundred of Anne Arundel County, The Land, 1649-1930*, p. 80. [I am indebted to Mrs. Nelker's painstaking research of early Colonial land grants.]

36. Ibid. [All subsequent references to early land grants and transfers can be found herein.]

37. Nelson J. Molter, *An Illustrated History of Severna Park, A.A.C. Maryland* (Linthicum: Anne Arundel County Historical Society, 1969), pp. 66-67.

38. Harold E. Slanker, Jr., *Anne Arundel County History Notes,* (July, 1993) p. 2.

39. John McGrain, "Molinography of Anne Arundel County, 1971." [This study, taken from early land plats of Anne Arundel County with references to mills and their placement, is approximate. *My River Speaks* uses this information with verification from other sources. Thus, except for the mill at Lake Waterford, actual locations are estimated.]

40. Broadneck Jaycees, *Broadneck, Maryland's Historic Peninsula,* (Annapolis: Fishergate Publishing Co., Inc.), p. 11.

PART II

Historical Points
of the Magothy

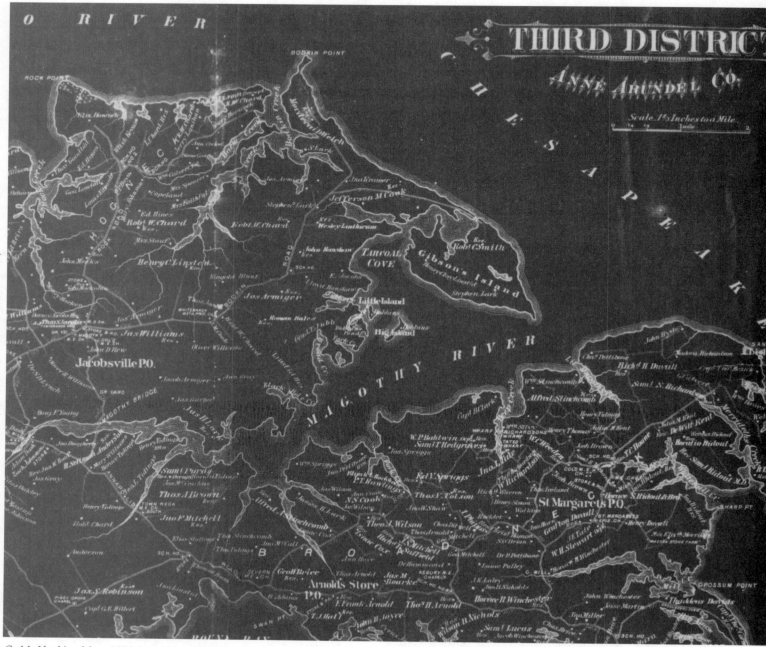

G. M. Hopkins Map, 1878 (courtesy of the Maryland State Archives, Maryland Hall of Records Map Collection MSA SC 1427-193)

North Side of the Magothy

Gibson Island

When Captain John Smith sailed the Bay in 1608 during his exploration of the upper Western Shore, he noted in his journals the land of "Seven Mountains." By contrast with the Eastern Shore, the Western Shore land mass surrounding the tributaries on that side seemed mountainous. In fact, all of the early maps of the period depict actual mountains in the vicinity of Gibson Island, Bodkin Point, as well as "inland" on the Towne-Necke Peninsula. Captain Smith never explored the Magothy. He noted that the lands of the Western Shore were "... *well watered, the mountains very barren, the vallies very fertill, but the woods, extream thick, full of Wolves, Beares, Deare, and other wild beasts.*"[1] He was on to larger harbors such as the Patapsco which eventually became a part of the harbor of Baltimore as the land developed.

Exactly what happened between 1609 and 1850 when this island on the insignificant little "creeke" became known as "The Newport of the Magothy?" Its transformation occurred slowly, beginning as farmland and working land, as did all other Magothy River land acquisitions. In 1651, all the lands of the Magothy were named "Lord Baltimore's Plantation" and were granted to Cecil Calvert from Charles II of England (*Virginia Farrer Mapp of Virginia discovered to ye Hills*

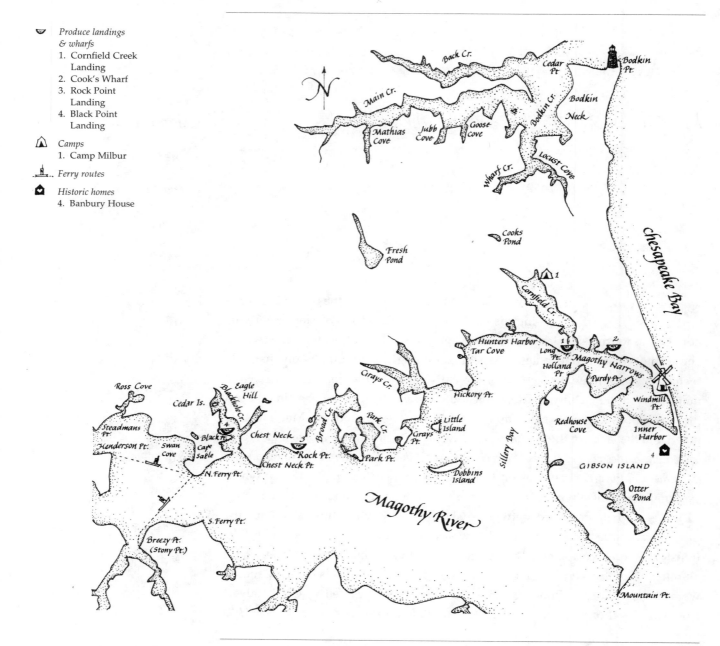

Produce landings
& wharfs
1. Cornfield Creek
   Landing
2. Cook's Wharf
3. Rock Point
   Landing
4. Black Point
   Landing

Camps
1. Camp Milbur

Ferry routes

Historic homes
4. Banbury House

Back Cr.

Cedar
Pt.

Bodkin
Pt.

N

Main Cr.

Bodkin Cr.

Bodkin
Neck

Mathias
Cove

Jubb
Cove

Goose
Cove

Locust Cove

Wharf Cr.

Chesapeake Bay

Fresh
Pond

Cooks
Pond

Cornfield Cr.

1

Hunters Harbor
Tar Cove

1

2

Long
Pt.
Holland
Pt.

Magothy Narrows

Purdy Pt.

Windmill
Pt.

Ross Cove

Eagle
Hill

Grays Cr.

Hickory Pt.

Redhouse
Cove

Inner
Harbor

4

Cedar Is.

Blackhole Cr.

Little
Island

Park Cr.

Broad Cr.

GIBSON ISLAND

Steadmans
Pt.

Black Pt.

Cape
Sable

Chest Neck

Grays
Pt.

Sillery Bay

Henderson Pt.

Swan
Cove

Rock Pt.

Park Pt.

Otter
Pond

N. Ferry Pt.

Chest Neck Pt.

Dobbins
Island

Magothy River

S. Ferry Pt.

Breezy Pt.
(Stony Pt.)

Mountain Pt.

1651 [1670], (Md.HR. G 1213 - 269). Successively large parcels were deeded to various prominent gentlemen: Between 1668 and 1687 Cecil Calvert, the Lord Baltimore, granted the northern part of the island to Paul Dorrell (376 acres). Between 1663 and 1672 the southern part was granted to Thomas Homewood (140 acres); James Orrouck received 190 acres and Richard Moss acquired 100.

In 1726, 711 acres were patented to William Worthington, who also owned multiple land holdings around Cornfield Creek and west of the peninsula, extending as far down the north side of the Magothy as "Pointe Lookout," or Cape Sable, and encompassing North Ferry Point, Steedman's Point, Swann Cove and Pea-Patch Point. (Later, Thomas Hyde acquired Mr. Worthington's acreage on Gibson Island in 1789 and 1790.) In 1771 the southern part of the island was resurveyed into what was called the "Seven Mountains." (*Griffith Map of the State of Maryland, 1794 [1795] (Md. HRG 1213-356)*. An early map records the name of "Stoney Pointe," on the southern tip of Gibson island, marking the entrance to the Magothy River. (*Griffith Map of the State of Maryland, 1794 [1795] (Md. HRG 1213 356)*. Later this became known as "Mountain Point" (From the "Tentative Preliminary Plan for Development of Gibson Island, Maryland, Olmsted Brothers, Brookline, Mass. October 1921).

It was not until 1793-1794 that the name of John Gibson, Jr., appeared on the patent charts. Gibson, a wealthy businessman who owned The Gibson Corporation, a land holding company, had responded to an advertisement in the *Maryland Journal and Baltimore Advertiser*, dated August 24, 1792, which announced a Trustees Sale of 2240 acres of land lying *"on the bay between the Patapsco and Magothy Rivers."* Aptly it is described: *"This land is remarkably valuable for the Fertility of its soil, and Conveniency of its situation to Baltimore, Annapolis, and other markets; it abounds with Plenty of Timber and Wood, has the Advantage of productive Fisheries, and Variety of wild fowl—It is adapted to every species of Country-Produce."*

By 1793-94 John Gibson Jr. had acquired all of the lands of this most eastern part of the peninsula and the land became known as "Gibson's Island" (*G.M. Hopkins Map, 1878*). At that time, other families recorded there were Robert C.

The soft waves of the Chesapeake speak

a language of strange romance

and yonder Gibson Isle slopes green

to wooded shores of dreams serene . . .

—from a poem by
Folger McKinsey

Smith, Henry Clay Linstid and Stephen Lark. These men also owned large properties off the island, extending down the peninsula, west and southwest into Cornfield Creek, Broad Creek, and beyond to Cape Sable and were held in conjunction with the Farmers Bank of Maryland. Some were jointly owned by the statesman, Charles Carroll of Carrollton.

In the late 1800s the lands of Gibson Island were divided into three farms: Lendy Linsted (Linstid), then Henry Clay Linsted – 500 acres; H. L. Thomas, then Michael T. Horner – 250 acres; and James, then Thomas and Carroll Bond – 250 acres. Stuart Symington then bought the three farms in the early 1920s. Notable heirs of Gibson's lands were John and Anne Ogle, Martha and Horatio Gibson; also John Robinson, Ruth and John Davis, and Richard I. Jones. Still residing on the island are descendants of the early settlers, Katharine Worthington and Brydon B. Hyde.

The farming activities of the island in the eighteenth century duplicated those of the entire Magothy. Initial tobacco planting gave way to planting a wider variety of vegetables and fruits such as peaches, tomatoes, and watermelons. In the 1700s, entire waterfront plantations consisted of enclaves of farm families, including slaves and indentured servants who timbered the land, barged the lumber, traded and transported crops to various ports of call including Baltimore and Annapolis, as well as those of New England. As was noted earlier, oystering, fishing, and hunting for fowl and game formed a means of subsistence as well as profitable sources for trade. The farms continued to exist into the mid-1900s.

In a charming historical journal, *Hearsay*, written by Louisa B. Reynolds, early letters and diary entries relate the personal history of what drew early twentieth century people to the north side of the Magothy peninsula. A diary entry of Sept. 28, 1918, written by Carroll Taney Bond, Chief Judge of the Court of Appeals of Maryland who lived with his mother in an old farmhouse on the island, reveals a wild, untamed farmland:

> *Several mornings I rowed over to Cook's wharf facing back to the flowing East across the Bay. Almost stealthily the day waxed and expanded. . . . The opening of the day has the suggestion of agelessness which the sea gives, and like the sea denies the importance to little man and his woes. . . .*

This particular diary continues on Saturday, March 20, 1920:

> This afternoon took the Annapolis Short Line train down to Elvaton, and from
> there rode with John Ellison in his car down to the farm to take a look and pay off.
> . . . The country road [Mountain Road] was as usual abominable; at times my head
> struck hard on the top in bouncing. The farm in good order, but the care of it is like
> a heavy weight upon me. It sets much like an undigested dinner. . . . Even today
> the brown winter grasses, and the lively green of the pines, the broad sweep of the
> fields and water were good for the soul of me."[2]

A turning point in the history of the island occurred in 1923 when an ex-confederate captain made a quick deal. Just how did this valuable piece of property known as Gibson's Island sell for $165,000? The story goes that while drinking some cool mint juleps, some amazing "land deals" were made on the north side of the Magothy. The land, originally owned by Captain Jefferson Cook, along with what is now Bodkin Pointe, as well as lands stretching along the Patapsco towards Baltimore, was sold to Dr. Hugh Young who then sold it to W. Stuart Symington Jr. Dr. Young, a noted urologist, relates in a piece entitled, *A Surgeon's Autobiography,* an amazing insider's view of this transaction:

> Since 1910 the Chesapeake Bay has been the scene of a great part of my outdoor
> life. In that year Mr. Carroll T. Bond, now chief Judge of the Maryland Court of
> Appeals, asked me if I would like to help an old ex-confederate, Captain Jefferson
> Cook, who owned large properties on the Bay and the Magothy River about 20
> miles from Baltimore.
>
> Captain Cook had outfitted blockade runners to the confederacy during the
> Civil War. He had a small mortgage on his farm and begged Carroll Bond to find
> someone to take enough of the land to lift the mortgage. I was not particularly
> interested in water-front properties, but agreed to see him. 'How much land will
> you give me if I lift the mortgage?' 'As much as you want,' said the Captain. So
> I drew a line across the peninsula, the deal was closed, and we measured the acreage
> later. Here I built a bungalow [This is the first house off the island on the bay side.]
> To one of the numerous parties that we gave there came Mr. W. Stuart Symington,
> Jr. He expressed amazement at the beauty of the spot and asked who owned Gibson
> Island adjacent. After his fourth mint julep he said that he was going to buy it and

make it a haven for yachtsmen and golfers. And so he did, in a grand and glorious way, without regard to expense, so much so that he went broke and dragged along with him his sympathetic brothers. But in the meantime he had organized the Gibson Island Club with splendid golf links. He did not live to see the organization of the Yacht Squadron that has played such an important role in maritime activities and afforded Baltimoreans (and many others) a chance to enjoy the incomparable Chesapeake Bay.[3]

Dr. Young draws an early sketch of some of the history of yachting on this river:

While Commodore of the Gibson Island Yacht Squadron I was instrumental in inaugurating the ocean race from New London to Gibson Island, and I was brought into intimate contact with many important figures in yachting.[4]

At this point in the early 1920s, the character and the essential nature of waterfront living gradually changed from farm enclaves and plantations to places for family recreation and rest from the burgeoning cities of Baltimore and Washington. Ghosts of the plantation days peer out at residents who had moved into old houses to find reminders of farm life in the late 1700s and 1800s. People have unearthed a slave dungeon, several ice-houses, blacksmith quarters, farm artifacts and even stone secret passageways said to have been used during the Underground Railroad.

On Tuesday, September 13, 1921, a diary entry by Judge Bond expresses deep regret at having to move away from Banbury House, the lovely family farmhouse situated on a knoll that commanded a panoramic view of the Bay and the old ships in and out of Baltimore: *"Today we moved from the farm all our goods and chattels. . . . My boat and canoe are still on the shore, and raft is in the water."* This house is still called "Banbury House" today and is referred to as Judge Symington's "cottage" with its smokehouse, toolhouse and lovely surroundings.

As one drives from the causeway onto Gibson Island a historical monument in honor of Judge W. Stuart Symington, Jr. stands at the entrance to the island. The monument, designed by D. K. Este Fisher, Jr., honors this man as founder and first president of the Gibson Island Club, a man who had the vision to create a natural environment with land preservation for wetlands and woods and natural forests. More importantly, here was a Shangri-La for family togetherness and for real relaxation. Mrs. Stuart Symington named all of the roads after English or Scottish names because of her affection for those countries. She was also responsible for creating the famous Gibson Island chairs built for the club lawn, later to be used by many river-front families all over the Magothy because of their charming look and comfortable design.

In an address given at the Golden Jubilee Party by Richard Porter Thomsen, the history of the island and its inhabitants is revealed:

Monument to Judge W. Stuart Symington, Jr. (photo by Joan B. Machinchick)

> *My father, Sam Thomsen, assumed his duties as superintendent of development in the summer of 1922, . . . I was nine at the time, and my father drove me down in an ancient Model-T Ford panel truck. . . The trip from Baltimore took two and a half hours; the Mountain Road was fifty percent oyster shell, thirty percent clay (or mud), and twenty percent potholes. The grand finale was the ceremony of being dragged across the soft sand of the causeway by a team of two black horses.*
>
> *Once arrived at this Shangri-La, there was a single dirt road that circumnavigated the island. . . . There were three farmhouses: The Bond House, which overlooks the second hole of the golf course, was the first clubhouse, and was later the abode of Judge Stuart Symington; the Horner House, which is on the bluff overlooking the Magothy River, and where the Thomsens resided; and the Brown House, which was in the northwest part . . . So there we were in 1922: with dirt roads, well water pumped by hand; kerosene lamps; wood stoves for heating and cooking; and party-line telephone service which was shared by that whole end of Anne Arundel County.[6]*

In this diary entry a specific note refers to the use of African-American employees of the Magothy:

Most of the early road and golf course construction was done via manual labor, including digging up tons of muck for greens, and there were literally hundreds of black employees who lived in a special camp, working five and a half or six days a week

Historically, Gibson Island and its people represented a unique environment, especially in the twenties and thirties, a time when life seemed simpler, softer, more gentile. Taking a peek through a kaleidoscope of time remembered, the Gibson Island journal, *Hearsay*, recalls details of the beginnings of the trend towards using the early farmlands for recreation and relaxation:

The clubhouse had its formal opening May 30th, 1924 . . . had imposing pillars on the majestic porch, no screening, and very colorful awnings. The front lawn was resplendent with umbrella tables, Gibson Island chairs, bells for service, and some shaded deck chairs. The rotunda had no roof, no screening—just a dance floor with a tree growing right through the middle of it. While some people danced romantically under the stars, others sat on the front lawn and observed. One of the young people of that day said, "If you could sneak up the beach with your beau without being seen, you had it made."

• • •

Mrs. Bidwell, loved by many, was hostess. She kept the youngsters and the oldsters in line. Nobody minded driving from Baltimore as the ride, though rugged, was beautiful. In the Spring blossoming peach orchards lined the road. Thursdays and Saturdays were special party days; the lobster buffet each Thursday was the highlight of the week. There was spirited dancing doing the Polka, the Big Apple, and the Conga. Children were permitted to come to the dances until 10:30. Mrs. Elder, hostess a little later on, followed the old traditions. There was always an attendant in the ladies' room, the men wore black ties to dances, and the ladies brought their fans.

1924 architectural rendering of the Gibson Island Club House (from Hearsay)

When the clubhouse fire occurred in 1937 the entire community turned out to help. Water was pumped out of the Bay by the island fire engine, which to this day is well-preserved and used in Fourth of July parades. Shortly after, the clubhouse was repaired and continues as the hub of the island to the present.

Hearsay continues to relate the history of a specific drink popular on Gibson Island and referred to by many other elderly Magothy River descendants all over its shores—both north and south:

Gibson Island chairs on the lawn of the Club House over-looking Chesapeake Bay (photo by Joan B. Machinchick)

> *The most popular drink was the mint julep. These delectable concoctions made by the hundred were served with much flair. Someone said his pleasantest memory of the Club was a seat in a Gibson Island chair on the Club lawn at sunset with a frosted perfectly-made mint julep.*

The clubhouse featured marvelous parties and dances and became the center for "warm, friendly, cozy . . . meeting place[s]." The Grill or bar was the only part of the Club opened in winter, but in summer it turned into "an inviolable male sanctuary" until a few of the mail pilots [admitted some girls] . . . and somehow Louise Bailliere and Sally Symington, and some of the other "girls," were admitted. According to the journal, *Hearsay*, the "barriers were down."

The island with all its traditions of yachting, golf, family gatherings and parties, tennis, paddle ball, swimming, Fourth of July parades, and big band dances, still holds to strong family values and staunch environmental concerns. Much of the land has been carefully zoned and preserved for natural forest, wetlands and coves where moratoriums for building are in effect. As a result Gibson Island remains a haven for wildlife. Deer abound. Waterfowl of all species use the quiet

Above: St. Christopher By-the-Sea as it appeared in the 1930s with its thatched roof (Hearsay); right: a 1997 view (photo by Joan B. Machinchick)

habitat of Red House Cove. Wetlands remain in their natural state as havens for the Great Blue Herons and other lovely species of birds. However, some species of animals no longer remain. No more goats wander about the island as they did in the twenties, thirties and forties, clustering around what was once called "Goat Point," now Purdy Point. The horses and stables are gone, as well as the mules and the donkeys. Currently, nature trails have been carved out by the Gibson Island Garden Club whose focus is to preserve and beautify the natural resources of the island. Carefully designed recreational areas nest among lovely historic houses, once the farms of old.

St. Christopher-by-the-Sea, an historic, waterfront Episcopal Church, was founded and designed by Mrs. Stuart Symington along with D. K. Fisher and R. E. Taylor and consecrated in 1931 by the Right Reverend Edward T. Helfenstein,

Bishop Coadjutor of Maryland. The church bore a distinctive feature in the thirties—a charming thatched roof. The bell, still rung to this day before each service, was found on a sunken Danish freighter.

Several historical houses remain refurbished on the Island. One of these, called "Islecrest," once had a jail, a dungeon, an icehouse, and a hidden room where it has been reported that the slaves congregated for the "Underground Railroad" so heavily used prior to the Civil War. The house contained an early schoolroom (1880), still remembered vividly by some of the students, a chapel, and an old graveyard.

To fulfill the needs of the incoming early families making Gibson their permanent homes, a school was established in the Gibson Island Clubhouse in 1944 by Miller and Carol Sherwood. In l956 the *Gibson Island Country School* was built outside the gate adjacent to the Island. Sally Symington Henderson was its founding headmistress. Many of its rooms are dedicated to various Gibson Island contributors such as Captain Nathaniel Kenney, founder of the Gibson Island Junior Fleet.

The transition from farmlands on the island to land used for family vacations and recreation, then for permanent living, occurred steadily in the mid-thirties and forties. Gradually, Gibson Island became a respite for people of Baltimore, Washington D.C., Wilmington and Philadelphia, who used the island for their summer "cottages." Eventually, the lure of waterfront life drew them permanently to the shores of the Magothy, and the "summer places" were renovated into year round residences. Many of the houses dating from the twenties still proudly stand, bearing distinctive features. Some homes sport little stages, built for musical performances and plays; some have Gothic mantels and fireplaces with bread ovens. Gibson Island is a place where many of the residences mirror the world travel of their owners, with Italian, Spanish and Oriental influences in their architecture. Reflecting the English and Scottish style, many houses had

"Islecrest," one of the early farmhouses of Gibson Island. (courtesy of the Gibson Island Historical Society, photo copy by Michael Dulisse)

towers built for water front viewing. Some of the homes still have "walk-through" chimneys with arched fireplaces. When the grading was done for new housing, the oyster-midden from early Indian oyster feasts was found to be three feet thick, a poignant reminder of the Native American presence which layers the early history of the Magothy.

Cornfield Creek Plain

Originally a part of Charles Carroll of Carrollton's extensive land holdings on the north side of the Magothy, the Cornfield Creek Plain, named as such on the *Martenet Map, 1795*, was developed and divided in the same manner as was Gibson Island. Large tracts were farmed in tobacco in the early and mid-1700s; later they were farmed for peaches, melons, and wheat for grist mills in the 1800s, usually by a tenant plantation farmer or "planter" as they were called. Gradually, these parcels were divided into smaller farms because the typical tenant farmer bought additional smaller size parcels which he could afford. Also, family plots of land were divided into equal portions for family heirs and heiresses, creating the inevitable breakdown of magnificent stretches of Magothy farms. Areas around Tar Cove (named "Tarcoal Cove" on *the G. M. Hopkins Map, l878*) were called Jubb's Delight and the entire area stretching from the west side of Gibson Island and off-island into Cornfield Creek was known as "Cornfield Creek Plain." Worthington's "Courtesy" and Homewood's "Addition" were all working farms by the mid-1700s. Staunch, early Anne Arundel County planters of the area were Zachariah Gray in the mid-1600s, John Peasley (1685) and John Nicholson (1688).

During the 1800s, other property owners around Cornfield Creek were: Wesley Linthicum, John Hanshaw, E. Jacobs, Lloyd Hanshaw and Thomas Pumphrey—family names which remain as a living testament of the long history of waterfront family enclaves of the Chesapeake.

Visualize a man such as Jacob Allwell who bought land around Cornfield Creek in 1753 and dubbed it "Allwell's Choice." A prototype of the industrious colonial planter, he was savvy, industrious and pragmatic. He knew the value of riverside crops which grew prolifically with the warming effects of Magothy spring, summer and fall weather. The enclave of workers on his property included slaves and hired hands to accomplish his pragmatic goals of survival, as well as profit from the land. The value of riverside farms was enormous; once the crop was harvested it could easily be barged to various markets in Baltimore and Annapolis.

Magothy Narrows: Holland Point on Gibson Island. (photo by Michael Dulisse)

The tobacco was rolled or pulled by donkeys or horses onto landings or "wharves" such as "Cook's Wharf" or "Cornfield Creek Landing" on Long Point. The various landings, both on the north and south sides, formed a nucleus for trade. From these landings the melons and peaches, the hauls of fish, even the lumber, would be barged or ferried to the Baltimore or Annapolis markets by bugeye, skipjack and ram, ships that reigned before the advent of truck farming. Oysters and fish usually were hauled in flat bottomed boats to larger craft called buy-boats, which remained in deeper waters.

Hogsheads of tobacco being loaded on boats for shipment.

During the eighteenth and nineteenth centuries people from established towns such as Annapolis and Baltimore used riverfront lands as their sources of great wealth. For example, the prominent Thomas Homewood of Baltimore, whose historic home, Homewood, still stands on the Johns Hopkins University Campus, and William Worthington, "gentleman" of Annapolis, held extensive lands in 1676 and 1730, adjacent to Cornfield Creek, named "The Compliment." These lands were rented to the tenant farmers who raised tobacco there in the early eighteenth century.

Dotting the landscape of the Cornfield Creek Plain was a working windmill, referred to specifically on an early land plat which specifies *"a windmill . . . at one of the points in the Cornfield Plain . . ."* This windmill was one of the major working machines efficiently using the energy of the wind whipping off the Bay to drive mill stones for grinding wheat and corn. Most likely, "Windmill Point," near Gibson Island, was the site for it, since many points of land were named after pragmatic functions or topographical features.

Lloyd Hanshaw as well as Jefferson M. Cook were farmers prominent in this area of Cornfield Creek during the 1800s and at the turn of the century. Later, in 1916, William Cook farmed the land extensively in corn, tomatoes, cantaloupe, squash and strawberries. Henry Alfred Cook also farmed large parcels of land bordering the Bodkin and the Chesapeake Bay. People of the Magothy could always depend on "the great fresh-from-the-field Cook produce at the end of the peninsula," reports Franklin Fick, elder resident of the area.

Many stories told by Magothy River residents refer to the Cook family, their farms, their vegetable-tobacco landing and the venerable "Cook House." The Fick family came to the area in 1917 and were primary witnesses to life around Cornfield Creek and Longpoint. Franklin Fick's memories of old wharves, historic houses, and farmlands, now filled with myriad developments, recall the fiber of life at the turn of the century. He remembers that the produce taken from his great-grandfather's farm would be hauled to Cook's Wharf by mule. With a far away look, he tells the old stories his grandfather told, about the overflow of peaches rolling off the wagon and the farm workers' children who would trail the farmers for convenient free drop-offs. When the produce was deposited at the "Cook's Wharf," the rest of the day would be spent socializing, perhaps ending with an impromptu picnic or crab feast with the Cook family.

Mr. Fick relates a memoir about a camp near his house on Cornfield Creek:

I used to go to the summer camp here when I was a boy. It was called 'Camp Milbur' and it was a Boy's Brigade. We had drills every day and learned the discipline of rifle drill. We had a drum corps and regular bugle calls. I remember when the old porch of the camp served as a kitchen. We even had special quarters for sleeping on an old side-winder tugboat donated to the camp from somewhere in Baltimore.

In Burgess' *This Was Chesapeake Bay*, the donor of this boat, the *"S.W. Smith,"* is verified as the Bethlehem Steel Corporation.

Another former Camp Milburite, John Talbot Gass, resident of Severna Park, enlarges a picture of what Camp Milbur used to be. Mr. Gass had joined the Boys Brigade, Company D, in 1919 when he was twelve years old. He recalls:

*Camp Milbur, formerly known
as Camp Broening, in 1921.
(photos courtesy of John Gass)*

"Camp Milbur was a wonderful part of my life." He informs that The Boys Brigade was an organization which concentrated on building character through male mentoring and disciplined routines. It was church affiliated with the Brantley Baptist Church of Baltimore, and had its meetings at headquarters in an old fire house on Mulberry Street in Baltimore. The original name of Camp Milbur in the early twenties was Camp Broening, named after the Mayor of Baltimore. Mr. Gass reminisces:

> *As soon as school was out we'd take the train from Baltimore to Jones Station and be ferried on the* Desdemona *or the* Maid of the Mist *from a landing on Cypress Creek over to the camp on Cornfield Creek. Many of us stayed for over a month, meeting our families and girlfriends on weekends.*
>
> *The regular program at the Brigade included all kinds of water sports—canoeing, swimming for miles, high diving, calisthentics, baseball games, military drills and marching. We learned bugle calls and various formations. Our barracks was an old side-winder ferry from Baltimore [the S.W. Smith]. At the camp, long swims from two to eight miles long, were the norm. We used to take swim tests by swimming with our hands behind our backs for long distances. From the camp on Cornfield Creek we'd sometimes swim to Cypress Creek!*
>
> • • •
>
> *We had a cook, but the fellows and girls (weekend visitors) were responsible for setting and waiting on tables, and for cleanup. Social life of the camp was intense.*

Camp Milbur in the 1920s.
(photo courtesy of John Gass)

Mr. Gass recalls that when the girlfriends visited with their parents as chaperones, those mostly associated with the Brantly Baptist Church,

> We were one big family . . . We had a lovely time sailing . . . The fellows would toss
> the girls into the water from the boats. Then we'd trail a line, and if they'd miss they
> would have to swim near Long Point, entering Cornfield Creek, for one half mile!

It was at Camp Milbur that Mr. Gass met his wife, Evelyn Kansler Gass.

Mr. Fick, still residing at the grassy, wild edges of Cornfield Creek with his wife Anna, gazes across to view Long Point on the other side. He adds, "We used to fish near here, my father and I, and would get loads of crabs with a dip-net. We'd get two dollars per sugar barrel at the Baltimore Fish Market back then in the 1920s." Franklin shares his love of the Creek with all his "critter friends" including a muskrat who burrows into the marshes still preserved there.

He also resurrects his great grandfather's stories of the old lighthouse at Bodkin Point. Even though the Bodkin Creek runs out into the Chesapeake, invariably it was linked to the "Town-neck Hundred" and the Magothy River through its lighthouse, throwing beams of light, shining out in the night waters of the peninsula.

John Gass in his Boys Brigade uniform. (photo courtesy of John Gass)

Bodkin Point

Many of the same plantation owners on the Magothy farmed lands bordering Bodkin Creek, extending to the Bodkin Point. The earliest recorded name for Bodkin Point dates back to 1794. The first land grant was deeded in 1673 to Richard Mascall; the land was known originally as "Mascall's Adventure." Only ten miles to Baltimore, this land surrounding the Bodkin was central in the early history of the peninsula, since many of the same people owned land on the Magothy as well. The interchanges between peoples and goods linked the Bodkin with the Magothy much as the south side and the north side were linked by its system of ferries and the socialization of early pioneers. For example, John Gibson, wealthy landowner of Gibson Island and lands west of it on the Cornfield Creek Plain, also owned most of what is now the Bodkin Peninsula.

One of the early opportunists who bought extensive Magothy lands between 1737 and 1832 was the famous Charles Carroll of Carrollton. By the early 1800s Carroll had amassed estates totalling over 70,000 acres, some of which were in Pennsylvania and New York. Much of it, however, was the entire north shore of the Magothy. In 1810, Carroll purchased from John Gibson, owner of Gibson's Inclosure, two lots known as the "canal," containing 365 acres with the same boundaries as the future Pinehurst Development. Among his properties was Bodkin Neck, later called Bodkin Farm. At that time the property sold for $13.68 per acre. For the entire sum of $5000, land of this scope was transferred. Pinehurst-on-the-Bay was developed there in the 1920s by the Robinson family.

The inevitable breakdown and parceling of the Bodkin's lands occurred very early in the 1800s. The specifics of wheeling and dealing for the land on the north side of the Magothy, including some of what is now Gibson Island and Bodkin Point, tells a woeful story of land transfer among the early colonial land owners. For example, Gibson's Inclosure, including parts of what is now called Gibson Island, went to Charles Carroll because of a defaulted mortgage. The land, including Bodkin Point, was previously owned by Annapolitan William Worthington, who defaulted to the Farmers Bank of Maryland, then partially owned by Charles Carroll of Carrollton. Richard Caton, Charles' son-in-law, was appointed as agent for his real estate holdings. Eventually, Richard Caton became Carroll's estate manager. His purpose was to sell parcels as needed, but to keep enough land to enjoy the hunting, fishing, and other sports which the Chesapeake offered.

In 1820 Caton sold five acres of Bodkin Island to the United States of America for the construction of a lighthouse at the mouth of the Patapsco River for Bay traffic to the city of Baltimore and for a vantage point of observation to the south.

Seniors of the Magothy report that their "grandfathers used that light as a marker as they would enter the Magothy River peninsula in the late of the evening." This lighthouse was built on Bodkin Point and served until 1858. It was 35 feet tall, cylindrical in shape, and made from stone, with a 34' x 20' lightkeeper's house adjacent to it. The lighthouse was then replaced by another light at Seven Foot Knoll. The hurricane of October, 1914, toppled the original structure and for over 40 years the tower and house were submerged under water. The remains of another beacon light, which at one time could be seen from both the bay side and the Magothy side, sits at a short distance outside the Gibson Island Gate on the Bay side. In October of 1882, Henry C. Dunbar, a magistrate of Anne Arundel County, purchased the whole of Bodkin Neck, 461 acres, for $25 per acre.[6]

All of these transactions, and most of the financial purchases on the north side of the Magothy, were titled through the Farmers Bank of Maryland; thus Charles Carroll of Carrollton can be called the grandfather of the Magothy as orchestrator and overseer of much of the Town-Necke Hundred (north side of the Magothy) and adjacent environs on the Bodkin.

In 1884 the lands of the Bodkin Farm, as it was then called, were sold to Cyrus N. Robinson and Charles A. Robinson. The Robinson brothers shipped the produce from Bodkin Farm to Baltimore by barge. By the 1900s the principal crop of the Bodkin area was fruit, the peach orchards consisting of over 6,500 peach trees. There were several hundred pear trees and 30,000 Wilson early blackberry bushes, as well as an assortment of apple, apricot, plum, grape and quince trees. Cantelope and watermelon were also grown for the Baltimore market. On February 1, 1922, after Cyrus Robinson died, the lands were sold from the Robinson family (including Myrtle E. and Mary M. Robinson) to the Pinehurst Company for the purpose of land development. At that time, the community of Pinehurst developed a "public" beach which was to attract many residents of Baltimore, who would take side-winder ferries to swim, picnic, go boating, do some fishing and, of course, engage in "Saturday night dance[ing.]"[7]

As the land on both the north side and the south side of the Magothy and the farms in the Bodkin area began to be sold, a gradual transformation took place. The vast acreage of land held by the absentee landowners such as Worthington, Carroll and Caton, began to be populated with resident farm families. This marked the beginning of the family enclave or clan, some of which still persist today, with the original family descendants still holding the roots of their ancestry. In fact, in speaking with members of these original families such as Hyde, Worthington, Caton, Brice, Stinchcomb, Cooke, Fick, Heath, Steedman, Robinson, and many more, one senses the pride of place, coming from family roots, and experiences the endurance of long histories.

Long Point

Characterized by many variable and complex "neckes" of land jutting and carving slices of beauty into the waters, the Magothy River speaks of one particular point, Long Point, which protrudes into Cornfield Creek. The history of this community of colonial land is stated in very early grants from Cecil Calvert, Lord Baltimore. In 1665 *"Cecilius, late Lord Baltimore, . . . granted to Elizabeth Balding (formerly Dorrell). . . 60 acres of land on N side of Magety River."* In 1684 John Nicholson purchased 50 acres of this land. In May of 1746, Nathan Nicholson, *"planter of AA County"* sold the property to Jacob Alwell. The land bounds on *"Back Creek, Peasley's Lot, Murphy's Choice, and Pawson's Plain."* These early land designations, named after the family clans, are the lands now forming the communities of Long Point, Hickory Point, Milburn, and Sillery Bay. Other early owners of lands surrounding Long Point were Edith and William H. Chairs. In 1922 they purchased the land from Hezeakiah Linthicum, who had owned it since 1838. In 1923 this whole section of land formerly called "Long Neck," was deeded to the Long Point Corporation by Jacob M. [H] Kahn.

Early maps of the area name the waters near this point "Tar Coal Cove," preceding the name, Sillery Bay. It is a cove off Sillery Bay and is presently called Tar Cove. The mystery of this historic nomenclature was solved when a current resident repeated the oral history of great grandparents: in the 1800s, boats would enter this cove from the bay in order to have tar coated on their hulls to protect their surfaces. A boat yard of the cove specializing in this operation became well known throughout the Western Shore; albeit, the cove acquired its name, Tar Coal Cove. A fresh pond of the area is alluded to on Tarr Cove, named "James's Pond." A small portion of this once pristine point of land is now preserved as a community picnic area. Historical records display another fascinating name, which hints at the abundance of wildlife that once thrived: a northeastern cove of what is now Long Point was called "Otter Slide."

Dobbin's Island

The delightful island-jewel, a magnet for picnickers and boaters as they enter the mouth of the Magothy, serves as a beacon for water-craft and a protective shelter from Bay storms. Now a little island eroding away, it has become a focal point for rendezvous on the Magothy. The *G.M. Hopkins Map of 1878* lists this island as "Big Island" and the one behind it as "Little Island."

Originally in November of 1769 the twelve acres were surveyed and patented to William Gambrell. This property was recorded in the original land grants as, "*12 a. lying in Magotty R . . . opposite the dwelling plantation of Zachariah Gray, next to Rasburry Island* "(now called "Little Island"). On July 26, 1803, it was deeded to "John Gibson of Annapolis," the same gentleman who owned much of Gibson Island during this period. Gladys Nelker, historian of Magothy land grants, in the journal, *Town Neck Hundred,* reveals that there was a large working plantation on Dobbin's Island which produced tobacco. She notes that in 1807 John Gibson sold the island to Horatio Gibson who in turn sold it to Richard Caton in 1811. Between 1812 and 1829, the lands of both Big and Little Islands were

A 1963 picnic on Dobbins Island. (photo by Joan B. Machinchick)

owned by Basil Hanshaw, Brice Worthington and Charles and Anne Hanshaw. Gradually, Big Island and Little Island assumed the name of Dobbin's Island, after it was sold to the Dobbin family in the late 1800s. Judge Penneman bought the property in 1930, and it is now a Penneman family holding.

Legends and stories about these two islands persist today. The question is posed, "Why is it called 'Dutch Ship Island?'" When Paul Hundley, an underwater archeologist with the Department of Natural Resources, telephoned with this pertinent question, the great "dig" into oral history and recorded history was initiated to try to find clues to this mystery. Elderly residents relate that Dutch coins were found washed along near-by shores and collected as curious artifacts of the Magothy. Recently some old ship's planks which date to the mid-1700s were discovered in this area by a team of underwater archeologists. Research is now under way to identify these planks. Nelker relates an incident in *Town Neck Hundred* which might connect with these archeological findings. She repeats oral history of the area: "a Dutch ship sank near the mouth of the Magothy and washed behind these little islands."[8]

A lively exchange of foreign trade between Maryland, England, Holland and Spain is verified historically by Richard Walsh and William L. Fox, noted Maryland historians. Thus, Big Island could have been a great refuge from storms or a place for traders to moor and replenish their reserves. All that we know is, to residents of the Magothy, this island is called "Dutch Ship Island." The mystery beckons still to this day, but the Dutch coins still sit on shelves of Magothy residents, their dull glints lighting memories and whispering of the mysteries still unsolved.

Other legends and stories hover over Dobbin's Island like transparent kites. Nelker reports that John Mellin, in a story for the *Maryland Gazette*, relates that during the Civil War, soldiers would get gunpowder out of a source near the Magothy, carry it to Dobbin's Island and hide. When the tide went out they would traverse the sand bars over to "Rasburry Island" (Little Island) and cross to the mainland on Gray's Creek. Perhaps boats which surrepticiously entered the

Magothy, during the Revolutionary War, probably harbored behind Dutch Ship Island. Thus far no documentation supports this theory, but a crop of lore about covert activities during the Revolutionary War has been handed down by senior residents. [For stories refer to Chapter 9]

Gray's Creek, Broad Creek, Park Creek, Chestneck Point

On the north side of Dobbin's Island rest the quiet coves and natural marshlands of Gray's Creek, Broad Creek, Park Creek, and Chestneck Point—lovely borders for protected areas. These house the herons, terns, waterfowl, turtles, crabs and fish which remain in splendor. Historically, the proximity between Gray's Creek and Dobbin's Island was a fascinating one. At low tide invited guests of the Penneman family, the owners of Dobbin's Island in the thirties, would be hauled over from Gray's Creek to Dobbin's Island in a "horse-drawn fancy carriage which would be sparkling clean, washed down by a servant of the family both before and after the ride."

Blackhole Creek

The process of amassing land on the north side of the Magothy continued in the 1800s. During the colonial period, property was purchased through the Farmers Bank of Maryland, managed largely through prominent Annapolis gentlemen such as John Brice, William Worthington and Dr. Charles Carroll. The lands were now perceived as great potential for acquiring more wealth. The unique area of Blackhole Creek had been heavily wooded in valuable yellow pine and chestnut; thus it became a mecca for business through supplying lumber for the burgeoning Baltimore as well as for the New England coastal towns which valued this kind of wood. From the point jutting out from Blackhole Creek, the lumber barges would carry the wood to Baltimore and up the coast of New England to build the new America.

Nellie Watson canoeing with friends on Blackhole Creek: top: with Ruth in 1919; bottom: with Miss Kellum in 1922. (photos courtesy of Nellie Watson)

A circular ring of trees surrounding the creek forms a verdant enclave of great beauty. Its marshes and woods lean into the waters forming long, deep shadows. In 1739, 100 acres of this land was sold to Richard Bayley; the creek, now known as Blackhole Creek, was then named after him and was called "Bayley's Creek." In 1752 John Brice of Annapolis, and Mordecai Hammond, of the prominent Brice and Hammond-Harwood houses, respectively, held lands there for investment purposes.

The highest point of land encompassing these acres on the Magothy, as well all of Anne Arundel County, is called "Eagle Hill," named after the numerous eagles which had swooped around this point. Originally cited as the "Mount of Wales," and later "Great Hill," this peak dominates the land which frames Rock Point, Chestneck Point, and Blackhole Creek. Encompassing lands, reaching as far to the north as Broad Creek and Park Creek, date to the 1680s and were called "Hall's Parcel." In 1727 this land around Park Point and Broad Creek was named "The Barrens" because much of the land jutting into the river was termed "barren." [The early connotation of the word meant "without evidence of habitation . . . lands which were connected with wide expanses and large empty spaces."] In 1690 Major Edward Dorsey owned 850 acres of it, followed by subsequent owners such as James Homewood (1772) and William Worthington (1773), gentlemen of Anne Arundel County who also owned large tracts on Gibson Island. Worthington sold his land to a planter, Oneal Cromwell in 1776, as well as parts of "the Mount" to Samuel Crane in 1777, who took advantage of the price which included "a free cart" or "waggon" road "leading to the water." This was highly desirable for transporting farm products to landings, where they would be ferried for shipping to Annapolis, Virginia or Baltimore. This particular landing was used later by the Johnson family to haul lumber to Baltimore markets via barges from the landing at Chestneck Point. Parcels of "The Mount of Wales" as it was known then, went to William Maccubin in 1778, *"excepting 1 a.[cre] on Great [Eagle] Hill . . . laid out for Oneal Cromwell."*[9]

This was prime land of the Magothy, a high "mountain" peak, commanding stunning vistas of the Magothy waters of variable moods, lights and shadows. In 1784 James Meek, a planter of the county, was deeded 128 acres, a part of the entire piece called the *Mount of Wales*. Other familiar families acquired parts of the "Mount," some of which stretched to Chestneck Point. These were Samuel Crane [Crain], John Gibson, Zachariah Ashley, and Benjamin and Sarah Hancock. Some of this land bordered *Bayley's Creek,* the original name of Blackhole Creek. Later, Blackhole Creek assumed its new name from a primary landholder, a Mr. Thomas Black, as well as from its appearance as a "hole," circled by trees; formerly it was *Black's Hole Creek.* Others bordered lands of *Homewood's Creek,* a small branch of water northeast of Blackhole Creek, which is now subsumed into the entire Blackhole Creek area. Eagle Hill, the land high above the Magothy, still stands richly wooded and pristine, owned in part by the Looper family. On this particular site an original land grant deeds the land to Thomas Homewood. About 100 years ago a house was built high upon the hill on Blackhole Creek, historically called "Mulberry House." Now it sits upon a spacious preserved tract of land. With its ancient white mulberry trees, its wildflowers dotting the hillsides, its venerable southern magnolias, and lush Martha Washington hawthorns, wild azaleas and mountain laurel, Mulberry House stands as a symbol for the Magothy's rich, nostalgic past. Nelker reminds river people of how the "back entrance is larger than the front entrance, because country people usually use the rear door. Of course, the water can be seen from every room."[10] The entire area of Eagle Hill remains well preserved, its lands slanting into the gracious Broad Creek, Park Creek and Blackhole Creek.

In the early 1920s, the lower lands bordering Blackhole Creek were sold for fifty cents to two dollars per acre, according to William G. Rothamel, long-time resident of the Magothy. As a son of William H. Rothamel, who in 1904 was general caretaker for a local family, Bill recalls that in 1910, J. Fred Johnson "milled Chestnut trees across from Hammerbacher's. . . . There was a mill on Blackhole Creek . . . later it became one of the Johnson Family Lumber Mills."[11] This lumber mill was later verified by Mr. Wilmer M. Johnson of the Johnson Lumber Company. Mr. Wilmer M. Johnson relates that they would use a landing at Blackhole to barge their rich loads of chestnut which were cut from Cape Sable on the west side of Blackhole Creek. An early land grant describes a *cart road leading to Black's Point, where landing formerly was and where road ran in the lifetime of Thomas Black.*" (The landing apparently was no longer in use by 1826 at the time of this deed).[12] Mrs. R. Kent Schwab of Eagle Hill affirms the presence of this landing: "You can go to the 'Point' [Chest Neck Point] and see strange steps leading to rubbles of a stone platform which edges into the water. There are some buried vats . . . They look like storage containers . . . near the side of the hill."[13]

Mr. Rothamel adds, "At Black's Point [Chestneck Point] there was a landing for boats and produce and lumber pick-up." He wistfully continues, "In those days the river was a busy place, but it sure was clear and green. . . . There were so many crabs and fish that you only had to swoop them up with a net to make a good catch."

Marie Angel Durner, former Judge of the Orphan's court, recalls a humorous story about Black Hole Creek, adding to the lore of information about this pristine area. She recalls when her dad, Jack Fick, bought a tiny island, a "dream come true," for him. It was called Marshall's Hunting Ground after a previous owner, but became known as "Angel's Island." He used the island for hunting. Gradually the island disappeared due to erosion and "that was the end of his dream; you could call it his folly." However, a small island within the sheltered cove of Blackhole Creek, named Cedar Island, still exists, now protected for osprey nests there.

North Ferry Point

Rivaling Gibson Island and Eagle Hill for its high vantage points of river views, perches North Ferry Point, originally called "Pointe Lookout" on the *G. M. Hopkins Map, 1878.* Early land grants at the Maryland Hall of Records show that in 1649 a wealthy English merchant, Thomas Welbourne, was granted 1200 acres on Cape Sable; it was broken into parcels in the mid-1700s. Rich in Indian artifacts and colonial sherds, Indian experts relate that the Algonquian Indians in this area loved the high ridges for good sun and wind to dry hides and meats.

In 1813, Charles Carroll of Carrollton purchased a large portion of Cape Sable from John Gibson. Shortly thereafter, a small group of people including Richard Caton, Alexander Mitchel and William Mechin formed the Cape Sable Company to search for coal deposits; ore for making alum, used as a base to form gunpowder; and sand for making glass. An obscure article found in the Baltimore Museum of Industry states:

North Ferry Point, viewed from the Magothy River. (photo by author)

> *The chemical industry had its start in Maryland in 1812 when Gerard Troost, an enterprising Dutchman, assisted in the formation of a factory on the banks of the Magothy River, near Baltimore, to manufacture copperas (iron sulfate). The president of the company was Richard Caton. He, along with Gerard Troost, a professor of mineralogy at the Philadelphia Museum, and professor of geology and chemistry at the University of Nashville, . . . directed the establishment at Cape Sable, Maryland, of the first plant in the United States for producing alum. This plant soon freed the country from the need to import alum.[14]*

Between 1821 and 1822 Dr. Charles Carroll, who had acquired a fortune as a merchant, planter, shipbuilder and investor, then acquired Cape Sable, and hundreds of acres to be deeded as part of the original Cape Sable Company. Later the company was subsumed into the Baltimore Iron Works and moved its plant to Baltimore. In a conversation with Bill Rothamel, this history is verified. "As a lit-

tle boy helping my Dad, I remember that on the edge of the Magothy River bank, where the Gilbert family lived, we dug out old alum factory foundations, which were taken from an old pavilion on North Ferry Point. I remember that horses used to haul the alum refuse and place it on the hill near Swann Cove."

Other geological features of North Ferry Point include findings of amber and coal. The precious amber and "hour glass sand" would pour out from very thin layers of coal along the high cliff-side of Ferry Point, even to the 1970s. Several residents remarked that it was an "expedition" to paddle over to Ferry Point to look for valuable amber: "We would find good specimens, have a great swim, and paddle back."

A long line of notables have owned the properties of Cape Sable from the 1800s onward: These include John Gibson, John Brice and Mordecai Hammond. Other property owners of the 1920s included Joshua Linthicum, Thomas Bittisen, H. Melvin Bull, William Gilbert, Edward Ward, Frederich L. Hammerbacher, G. H. Hammerbacher and Paul Watson.

Recalling the gentler days of North Ferry Point, Bill Rothamel recalls: "There was a picnic pavilion jutting out into the Magothy where a steam excursion boat owned by Linthicum would drop off people from Baltimore to have waterside picnics. . . . The foundations of the pavilion were made from Chestnut and had Chestnut poles which my Dad and I dug up. . . .They dated way back! . . . Boy, were they heavy!" This pavilion could have been used as early as the 1780s. This history is affirmed in a reference to a "County Ferry" via a land grant patented to John Gray in November of 1769 refering to: the *land adjacent to Baker's Folly, former landing place for the County Ferry.*"[15] [See Hopkins map of 1878, p. 70]

In the mid to late 1800s, the transformation of river lands used for subsistence in early settlement, occurred; gradually little riverside amusement parks, church camp parks for relaxation and fun, and small "hotels" sprang up on the Magothy and on all Western Shore rivers in the same manner.

Many residents recall the stories of the various ferries or launches on the Magothy River transporting people from the south side where they would get off the W. B. and A. Railroad or the Annapolis Shortline train at Elvaton, Jones Station or Arnold Station, ride a mule or donkey cart to the river's edge, and be ferried across to the north side. The darkened bricks from the ferry landing still wash up on the beach at North Ferry Point. Other recreational ferry landings were at White's farm in Whitehurst, Mill Creek and Dividing Creek, Deep Creek, and Pea-Patch Point as well as on Windmill Point in Cornfield Creek [See maps, pp. 72, 104 and 126].

On North Ferry Point a large plantation existed in colonial days. Like all river-front plantations of this sort from Gibson Island, Cornfield Plains, Cape Sable, "the Heath," and into Cypress Creek, especially around Cape St. Claire on the south side, remnants remain of an old colonial root cellar; a typical farmhouse or tenant house where the tenant farmer lived with his family; a colonial well; old burial mounds where the alum refuse was accumulated; and a foundation for the icehouse. Each large parcel formed self-contained working farms, much like medieval compounds. On this particular piece of high ground, in the mid-1900s, Nellie Watson, decendant of an original family, reports, "We used to come to Ferry Point to get our milk . . . oh my, was it fine! I remember how the cows would wander to the water and go wading."

To this day, smaller family compounds still exist there, with all members of the extended family settling comfortably on remaining parcels. On Cape Sable such clans remain: Hammerbacher, Watson/Banner, Price, Councill, and the Macleoud/Van Metre, Joseph and Natalie Leach family homesteads. When the Robert A. Taylors bought North Ferry Point acreage in 1974, only five families had owned it since the mid-1800s. Now people of the Magothy name this preserved point, "Taylor's Point;" in this way riverfront lands still continue to acquire their names and albeit, their personalities.

Mrs. Nellie Watson of North Ferry Point pinpoints some details of settlement in the early 1900s. When the Watsons came to "the Point," they settled on the bor-

Molly, a favorite cow, at North Ferry Point. (photo courtesy of Nellie Watson)

Cow at North Ferry Point. (photo courtesy of Nellie Watson)

Dr. Paul Watson's observatory. (photo courtesy of Nellie Watson)

ders of Blackhole Creek in what is called the Big House, a sprawling, comfortable cedar-shingled dwelling so typical of waterfront family homes of the twenties. Furniture from Baltimore was hauled to their house on a large "barge," since "there were poor roads and little direct land access." Mrs. Watson muses: her husband, Dr. Paul Watson, "built an observatory for viewing the stars and such . . . now it is someone's swim-house!" People would come to this observatory for evening classes in astronomy. Mr. Bill McDonough, long-time resident, now living away from the Magothy, relates that the observatory contained a celestial clock drive in the 12-inch reflector telescope whose motor turned with equatorial drive. It was built for Paul S. Watson, curator of astronomy at the Maryland Academy of Sciences. According to Mr. McDonough, it was the first privately owned telescope in the U.S. to view "Sputnik," on October 4, 1957. [This was the first satellite, launched by the U.S.S.R., to orbit the earth.]

The Hammerbacher family, who have resided on the Magothy at Cape Sable for approximately 100 years, relate that the land was either largely forested or in huge farms when they purchased it. Before that, large tracts of 1,000 acres or more were owned and farmed by the Heath family, now residing on Cape Sable. This property, known as "The Heath," was one of the large farmland stretches on the north side of the Magothy, inland. Along with Linsted's land and John Gibson's extensive holdings, they were parcelled into smaller sections in the 1800s.

On Cape Sable, remains are visible of another small historic place connected with the old ferry system on the Magothy. Reported by William Rothamel, an old artesian well, or what he called "a spring," was cleaned out by him and his father. It measured six by eight feet and had old leather and wooden buckets and three wooden pump stocks. This well was "used during the Civil War. . . and also when the British blockaded the Bay during the War of 1812," reports Natalie Leach, a centenarian who has lived on the Magothy since the early 1920s. "The water was hauled down to the ferry at North Ferry Point, . . . and ferried over to the other side for troops there because the Bay was blockaded." This particular artesian spring can still be located, but it is boarded up for safety purposes. These artesian springs were valuable in an age when dug wells were scarce. Other natural springs existed on various Magothy sites, such as near Cornfield Creek; another was reported on Gibson Island. Around one such spring, a tranquil, secret place on Cornfield Creek, an Indian adze and arrowpoints were found by Franklin Fick. The Indian ancestors of the Magothy knew a valuable source when they found one! Dug wells were not a practical endeavor for Native Americans who did not have the proper tools for such work; they simply used natural springs for water sources. Most of these springs surfaced from a large source under the Magothy River area called the Magothy Aquifer. Later, the colonials began to dig wells; however natural sources of spring water were strongly preferred.

Sturton's Cove and Swann Cove

Sturton's Cove and Swann Cove on Cape Sable bear the same history of adjacent lands. These quiet coves were named either after owners who bordered the waters or by the natural wild life known to gather there. Traditionally the whistling swans have enjoyed the splendor of marshes and quiet waters of this particular cove, which, with its old covered boat house, still remains as it was in the 1920s.

Today, stretching into the Magothy from Cape Sable are Ross Cove, Steedman's Point, The Grachur Club and Camp Whippoorwill, the Girl Scout camp. This later became Laurel Acres. The large span of land which comprised Magothy Villas (1800s) was deeded to the Grachur Club in August, 1911 by Dr. Guy Hunner and his wife. Each of these waterfront points shares a common heritage. Owned by various early colonists since the 1600s, the Steedman's Point, Sturton's Cove parcels

Boathouse at Swann Cove.
(photo by Michael Dulisse)

were originally known as "Hallet's Lot." The great-granddaughter of Myrtle Steedman, Berry Griebel, relates that the original owners were three Scotchmen, the Steedman brothers, who loved the views and used the lands for peach orchards. She adds: "I felt secure being able to come to the river to spend the entire summer just swimming, crabbing, and feeling the cool breezes and knowing the water's ripple in my dreams." Her description of Steedman's Point was that it became so much a part of her, "something like a spiritual friend."

1. Frances d'A. Collings, *The Discovery of the Chesapeake Bay, An Account of the Explorations of Captain John Smith in the Year 1608*. Chesapeake Bay Maritime Museum, (1988), p. 14, 15.

2. Dr. Hugh Young, "A Surgeon's Autobiography," Harcourt Brace Javanovich, Inc. 1940, in Louisa B. Reynolds, *Gibson Island Hearsay*, Gibson Island Historical Society, Baltimore, Reese Press, Inc., (1978), p. 7. [All subsequent quotes are from this journal]

3. L. B. Reynolds, *Hearsay*, pp. 1-5.

4. Dr. Hugh Young in L. B. Reynolds, *Gibson Island Hearsay*, pp. 1-5.

5. "Diaries and Letters," an unpublished collection collated by The Gibson Island Historical Society.

6. Mark N. Schatz, Fred M. Petrow, Marie Angel Durner, eds., *Anne Arundel County History Notes:* "A History of Pinehurst", John M. Robinson, (Jan. 1990), pp. 3-5.

7. John M. Robinson, "History of Pinehurst, Part I," [For a continuing history of this topic consult "History of Pinehurst," Part II.]

8. Gladys P. Nelker, *The Town Neck Hundred of Anne Arundel County, The Land 1649-1930*. (Westminster: Family Line Publications, 1990), pp. 53, 54.

9. Ibid., p. 93.

10. Ibid.

11. This information was verified by oral history by Wilmer M. Johnson of the Johnson Lumber Company, Oct. 1995.

12. Gladys Nelker, Ibid.

13. Oral History related by Mrs. R. Kent Schwab to author, Oct. 21, 1997.

14. *Maryland Historical Magazine,* Vol. 80, No. 1 (Spring, 1985), p. 19.

15. G. P. Nelker, *Town Neck Hundred*, a study of original land grants of the Magothy River, p. 107.

CHAPTER 5

The Upper Magothy River

Cockey's Creek

Cypress Creek

Cattail Creek

Old Man Creek

Cockey's Creek and the Camp Experience

Located on a point of land jutting into the Magothy and abutting Cockey's Creek, other points of noted historical significance were known as Cuckhold's Point, Peasley's Inheritance, Brice's Security, Mill Seat, Steven's Connection and What's Left.

Remaining on Cockey's Creek today, complex inlets and coves provide wildlife protection and marshy areas of habitat for nesting waterfowl. Originally this creek was named after an early colonial inheritor, William Cockey, who was granted 100 acres of surrounding land in 1681. Previously the creek was called Cuckhold Creek, and, along with Cuckhold Point, was named after an annual indigenous North American weed still found there. But with time, it became known as Cockey's Creek, just as many other creeks and coves acquired their names from owners of lands surrounding them. This area includes what is now Chelsea Beach, Cockey's Addition and Brice's Security, and was the site of a grist mill, marked on the *Martenet Map of 1795* [Refer to section on Mills of the Magothy]. This was also a prime hunting area in the early 1900s,

A summer home at Magothy Beach, built in 1927. (photo courtesy of Mrs. H. W. Schindler)

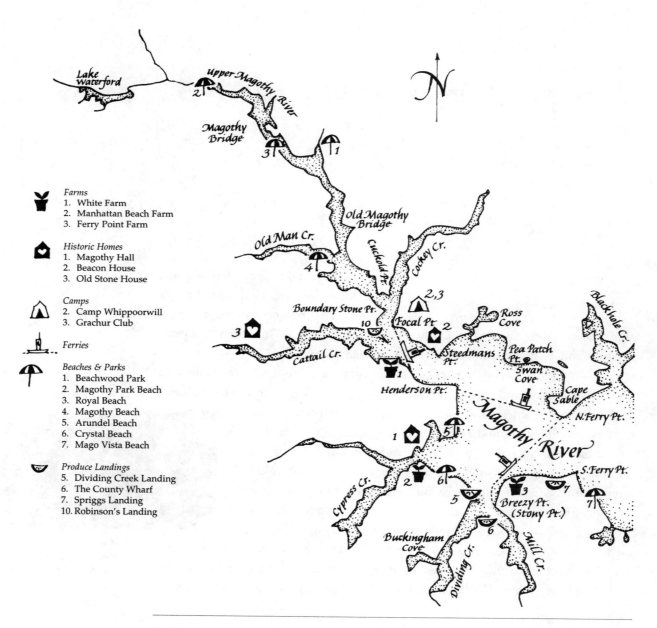

Farms
1. White Farm
2. Manhattan Beach Farm
3. Ferry Point Farm

Historic Homes
1. Magothy Hall
2. Beacon House
3. Old Stone House

Camps
2. Camp Whippoorwill
3. Grachur Club

Ferries

Beaches & Parks
1. Beachwood Park
2. Magothy Park Beach
3. Royal Beach
4. Magothy Beach
5. Arundel Beach
6. Crystal Beach
7. Mago Vista Beach

Produce Landings
5. Dividing Creek Landing
6. The County Wharf
7. Spriggs Landing
10. Robinson's Landing

Lake Waterford

Upper Magothy River

Magothy Bridge

Old Magothy Bridge

Old Man Cr.

Cuckold Pt.

Cockey Cr.

Boundary Stone Pt.

Focal Pt.

Ross Cove

Blackhole Cr.

Pea Patch Pt.

Swan Cove

Cape Sable

N. Ferry Pt.

Cattail Cr.

Steedmans Pt.

Henderson Pt.

Magothy River

Cypress Cr.

Breezy Pt. (Stony Pt.)

S. Ferry Pt.

Buckingham Cove

Dividing Cr.

Mill Cr.

where some of the early hunting shacks were built. They were among the first houses built on the Magothy. The locals call the environs surrounding this creek "Indian Village" because of the large number of artifacts and layers of oyster-midden found, dating to the Indian seasonal camps which undoubtedly were clustered there.

At the convergence of Cockey's Creek and the Magothy, deep into the dense woods, sits the Grachur Club, a unique waterfront camp. It is one of the sites along the Magothy frequented by church groups from Baltimore in the early 1900s, who flocked to the riverbank for recreation, rest and prayer. Continuing this tradition, the Grachur Club is located at a point of the Magothy which has broad vistas towards the mouth of the river, as well as views of sequestered coves towards Cockey's Creek.

An original hunting lodge, built on Cockey's Creek in the 1920s. (photo courtesy of Howard W. Schindler)

The camp experience on the Magothy was a particular indulgence of Baltimoreans and Washingtonians from the twenties through the seventies. Founded in 1912 by Claude Bingham Whitby, a member of the Grace Methodist Church of Baltimore, the Grachur Club was to concentrate upon the character-building, integrity, and development of moral judgment for the male youth of the church. [The name, Grachur, evolved as a derivative of Grace-Church Club.] Whitby noted that the community needed something to "hold its teenage boys." Taking a small group of these boys and stressing strong moral values, good character, camaraderie through recreational pursuits, and engaging in social action among those less fortunate, Whitby's vision caught hold and proved successful. The Magothy River provided the backdrop for fun, friendship, and the resulting development of strong Christian values. Boys learned from their peers and from the older men of the club and developed what is called among club members, the "Spirit of Grachur." To Whitby this elusive spirit encompassed the "spirit of truth."[1]

At first the club met at C. E. Henderson's property on the south shore of the Magothy, so convenient to the W. B. and A. Shortline Railroad. Escaping fragmented city life, people would step off the train and then walk to Henderson's, on the south side of the Magothy, where a small shack was used as headquarters for picnic supplies and gear. Memories of swimming and cavorting off "Henderson's sand bar" at the Point were shared by members. In 1914 because of the growth of membership, the club bought property at the head of Cockey's Creek. In 1915 the Grachur Club was legally chartered with its purpose drawn and affirmed as an "educational, social, athletic and social service-oriented" club. Christian values formed the core of belief, and the club grew through hands-on hard work, initiative, and holding a clear vision of its real purpose—the bonding of youth to older members, family and church. The members had to paddle from the south side to the north side of the river by a flotilla of canoes which they kept at the Henderson property. In the thirties a motor launch (*The Little Emma*) carried them between South Ferry Point and North Ferry Point.

In 1920 adjacent property was purchased through the Grachur Club to be developed later in the thirties as a boys camp for the underprivileged of Baltimore called "Whippoorwill Hills." (This site was located where the Girl Scout "Camp Whippoorwill" now stands.) This new land segment extended Claude Whitby's outreach of implanting strong moral values and stressing strength of character for the youth of the underprivileged. Church services at both camps were required each Sunday, the "talk sessions" extending long into the night around the camp-fire, river sounds of water quietly lapping along the shores.

Claude Whitby Memorial Chapel, the Grachur Club Stone Chapel. (photo by Michael A. Dulisse)

A quaint water-side open air chapel, complete with stone pulpit and pews of river-slate and granite, was built and dedicated in 1928 as the Claude Whitby Memorial Chapel. Currently it remains, offering quiet moments of reflection during contemporary Sunday services with its special celebrations for Grachur campers, including award-granting, anniversaries and services centering around small turns of events in campers' lives. Fond memories of campers include "closed weekend religious services at the clubhouse" with Coley at the piano, his morning cigar spreading a filmy haze throughout the room. Many weddings were conducted there, and, even now, these happy events are celebrated at water's edge.

Noteworthy is the quintessential camp experience for the Grachur Club of the early twenties to the forties and fifties. The Magothy River camp ritual began upon arrival with a thorough cleaning of the cabins. Then the cabin was bug-sprayed and shut tight for awhile, while the campers carried gear from the parking area by wheelbarrow. The first thing the younger members did was to change into shorts or a bathing suit. "Their clothing was placed carefully on a clothes hanger and hoisted to the ceiling where it remained awaiting the trip home. By three o'clock the beds were made up and it was time for the first swim of the day." The "cool-off swim" was so enticing, men and boys together plunged into the Magothy's shimmering waters.

Camp activities, which had been popular during the Depression, continued as tradition during the post-war years, forming the early spirit of carefree times on the Magothy. Team competition was a large part of the Labor Day events: sailing, canoe races, canoe tilting, swimming, diving, horse-shoes, softball and ping pong tournaments—all were means of accumulating points for the Labor Day Trophy. Volleyball play went on for hours, and there seemed to be at least four teams in competition during a busy weekend. The shout, "Ice cream point!" signaled a life and death struggle, but with simply playing the game there were no losers. One unique type of Magothy River game was initiated by the Grachur Club. Young members would play football on the beach or on the sand bar. One of the members notes that their "football" consisted of a sock filed with rags, easy to catch and hold and soft enough that it did not cause injury. The only ill effect was "sore feet from running on the sand until the bottoms of the feet were raw."

Many courtships occurred with the Magothy as benevolent and secret back-drop. After the war the "juniors" of the depression years courted their "wives to be" at the Grachur Club. The boys of Grachur jaunted to riverside docks to find girlfriends and perhaps end up with a free meal. Usually the ritual included the "Camp Secretary" who was the person to stay the summer to answer phone calls, take reservations and to coordinate supplies. He would usually have two other juniors staying with him, who would have the time to explore other shores of the river:

> A deal would be worked out whereby each (helper) would share one of the free meals provided for the Camp Secretary. Since only one person had to remain at camp to answer the telephone, the other two could use a canoe to investigate the renters or owners of shore property that had bored or lonely daughters just waiting for a visit from nice boys of Grachur. There always seemed to be girls and they were as anxious to see the boys as the boys were to see them. The most popular girls were the late risers since they would have brunch around eleven o'clock. This was ideal because the girl's mother always invited the boys to come to the Club for swimming and thus the third member of the team got some relief. . . . The parents of the 'river girls' were pleased that their daughters had company.[2]

In fact, a Mrs. Connor owned five rental properties across the river from the Totem Pole. To entice prospective renters she would assure people that there were "always fine, upstanding young men" just across the river. She promised the girls that if they would lounge on the pier, a Grachur canoe would be there within the hour.

Spare, vigorous routines characterized Magothy camp life from the 1920s to the 1940s, including the constant fetching of water. In the early twenties, the perishable food was cooled by being lowered into a well. Hank Dorsey, a member of the club, recalls one occasion when the rope broke and the entire weekend supply of food dropped to the bottom of the well. A very tiny member of the club was lowered into the well and retrieved the food with a shovel. Also a natural spring on the property provided cool water. Pots and pans were placed in a wheelbarrow, carried to the spring, filled, and brought to camp. Later, an artesian well was located which flows up "like a fountain" even to this day. These cool springs could be found right in the water, and all the campers loved the springs, swarming to the "cool spots" on sweltering summer days.

The club featured "River-Shows" in the 1930s and 1940s. "People all over the river used to paddle in their canoes to watch the plays. These were elaborately costumed vaudeville acts and little plays, sometimes with a full chorus of the Grachur Glee Club, bellowing their music across the river."[3] Other riverside rituals included events such as "Dog-house Weekend," a male-time away from home, primarily for either "work weekends or for volleyball, non-stop," depending on the season and the need. Many Grachurites mention what are known as the "bull sessions." These casual talks among members would range through all subjects of life. In 1919 and 1920, Grachur veterans of World War I would converge, engage in some memory sharing, then sing their collections of poetry and songs learned from their army camps and naval stations. Spicy sea-chants led by Abe Cole and famous army classics like a "Day at the Zoo," led by Fred Maag, were sung in chorus by all. The famous Grachur greeting, "Wahoo!" was derived from the chorus of this song.[4]

To this day, traditions of this kind are carried throughout the Magothy's community clubs, yacht clubs, and camps, extending long lines of rooted history into the present. The Grachur Club still stands today as a symbol of what draws all people to the river's edge—the chance to recreate away from the complex life of the neighborhoods or the city, to pare down to the simple, to enjoy the freshness of the waters and clear air. Surrounded by friends and family, they form bonds between generations, the links of real life.

The gradual development of the modern day Camp Whippoorwill, from a previous large farmland owned by Captain Robinson, typifies the demise of working farmlands. Before the 1920s, Captain Robinson owned a huge farmhouse which was used later as the first Girl Scout quarters. The Captain's house stood on a hill surrounded by trees and fields and served as a landmark for the country folk for miles around. It is said that Captain Robinson kept a light burning in the third-floor window to guide the large produce boats and ships that sailed up and down the river.[5] The point of land which extends at the confluence of the Magothy and Cockey's Creek is the site of the present day Girl Scouts' *Camp Whippoorwill*. In 1923 Claude Whitby sold a large tract of nineteen acres to the

Senior Girl Scout Mariners board the ferry, Diana *for transportation to Camp Whippoorwill in 1950. (photo courtesy of Jacques Kelly)*

Seabee Co.,Inc. Subsequently, the Girl Scouts of Baltimore City acquired the land originally known as "Ellsworth's Apartments." The Girl Scouts in those days would eagerly gather at the train station in Baltimore to travel to the stop at Jones Station to be carted to South Ferry Point, where they would then board the ferry, *Diana.* Happily they glided into the Magothy world of secret coves, deep woods extending to sparkling vistas of open water at the Magothy camp. This was the world of canoeing, swimming, and hiking through the waterfront pine woods.

Many now-grown Magothy children recall the camp songs sung around a flickering fire, the french toast cooked on their own "buddy-burners," the ooze and chocolate of a good "s'more," and the classes in pottery in which clay from the banks of the Magothy was used for hand-made projects. Now this point of land at the Girl Scout camp and the Grachur Club lands is marked by a replica of the original hand-carved totem pole, standing as a symbol of Magothy River camp life; it staunchly protects the property from the intrusion of extreme modern day development.

A historic beach exists in the area of the Upper Magothy River near Cockey's Creek called *Beachwood Park*. Known as Boone's Purchase in 1790, granted to Richard Boone, it became a part of the lands owned by one of the wealthiest men in Maryland, Charles Waters, who owned grist and lumber mills. Named Beachwood Park in the 1930s, it originated as a place for African-Americans of the area to congregate for recreation and prayer, similar to the development of the Grachur Club and the Mago Vista Beach Club. At that serene park, many baptisms of the church were performed in the clear waters of the Magothy. Bus loads of the community from Baltimore would come on weekends to celebrate church holidays and to relax together. Gradually, it became a small amusement park with ferris wheels and various joy-rides for children. People picnicked, paddled, swam and basked in the sun, the lush pine smell drifting over the water. Of course the fishing was unparalleled.

The covenants which governed property purchases in this area were restrictive to the African-American community and resulted in a Supreme Court Decision in 1950, which allowed equality in all neighborhoods with restrictive covenants. This affected all waterfront communities and other communities of Maryland and the United States. Sadly, earlier restrictive covenants had allowed the African-American community to live on waterfronts only as "servants." Franklin A. Owens, who owns a waterfront home on a knoll at Cockey Creek in Beachwood was the first African-American to own property on the waterfront there. He notes, with dismay and a far-away look, that the Riverdale Inn would not sell groceries or goods to the Black community. He remembers the old days

The totem pole marking the lands of the Grachur Club near Camp Whippoorwill at river's edge. (photo by Michael A. Dulisse)

at Beachwood Park when "fun was so simple as a little merry-go-round which the kids would pedal by foot," and when "the crabs and the fish-fries would be eaten in the dark of the evening. . . . and when stories would be flung out like flies and laughter . . . all over the place." Later, he notes that "rowdy characters began to litter the place and it became rather run-down." Beachwood Park closed in 1954 due to tax foreclosures.

As the Magothy edges into the shaded glades of woods and narrows into the upper end, closer to its headwaters, small "cottages" once used as summer houses still cling to its banks. Reportedly, here was excellent territory for the bootleggers to make their brew and to frequent a "speak-easy" for some evening forays. One such cottage, renovated by Sue Sherrill, literally "opened doors" to its history. Discovered in the house was a trap door for hiding from the law, reported Irene Duncan, former owner. Mrs. Duncan states that the house was originally deeded to Lucy Duncan in 1930 and "was a 'speak-easy'. . . with upstairs rooms for 'accommodations.'"

Family life on a Sunday afternoon at one of the small cottages near Beachwood Park on the upper Magothy River, early twentieth century. (photos courtesy of Mrs. Irene Duncan)

On a part of the Upper Magothy River stretches *Magothy Beach,* now a planned residential park for picnics and beach activities. Residents whisper and conjecture about the "mystery ramps" jutting out from Magothy Beach into the river: They seem to go nowhere, just jutting into the water from a submerged "Iron Pier," marked by a steel pole protruding from the river. One possible explanation could be that they are the antiquated rail tracks once used in the twenties and thirties for loading lumber and heavy cartons of produce onto permanent carts which would be stationed there. According to Bud Schindler of Cockey's Creek, "Magothy Beach was a well-known docking and landing area.

The lumber rams would carry the white pine (the material used on the first Schindler house on the Magothy, 1927) and unload its cargo onto the dock and into the cart which traveled on two rails. They curved upward at the ends like a sleigh so that the cart would not fall into the water ar the end of the loading ramp. The double rail permitted the cargo in the cart to be more easily pulled by mule or oxen to be hauled to its destination." When truck farming became the mode of transportation, the lumber would then be rail-carted to the trucks from the docks. But to this day, residents shroud the "Iron Pier" with mystery.

In this area of the upper Magothy sits another house named "The Lord's Manor," built in 1929. Its gracious appointments include a ballroom on the third floor. Residents of the area relate that it was built by a German Count and the cove where it now stands is called "The Count's Cove." Good times on the Magothy extended even to royalty!

Of the lands surrounding Riverdale, local history was traced to 1681 when Thomas Sutton owned all of Huckleberry Forest, which stretched between the Severn and the Magothy River. The land holdings shifted and were broken into smaller parcels. Grace Van Meter Schofstal, niece of the last large landholder, Captain Raphael S. List, relates the local history of Royal Beach, Sunset Knoll and Riverdale on the Magothy. Each of these communities was a separate farm when Captain List, a Chesapeake Bay boat pilot, bought one of them in 1912. Miss Grace describes the old farmhouse: "It was long and rambling. It had white pillars on the side facing the road, a screened porch across the river side and lots of rooms. But . . . notice I did not mention bathrooms! Bowl and pitcher were in each bedroom and one of those 'two-seat Chic Sales Specials' was in the backyard." She remembers the farm as "a bit of paradise with neatly whitewashed out-buildings, grape arbor, grass-covered wharf and orchards." She recalls the night the captain named his farm. "One evening Captain List took a walk through the orchard all the way to the point that he loved best. He told the family that as he sat on an old peach basket, looking down the river, he suddenly turned and saw the beauty of the sunset going down over the knoll that rose behind the orchard. When he came home he announced that the farm was to be called 'Sunset Knoll.' In 1925 he realized his dream when he built a year-round home on the water complete with all conveniences!" (This is now the Fink house.)[6]

On the Upper Magothy, the river diverts into complex systems of narrow creeks and long-stemmed river branches. These include Old Man Creek, originally called Beard's Creek, and Cattail Creek. The river meanders west, cutting into banks which housed small vacation "cottages," which later became year-round residences during the forties.

Magothy Bridge

A narrow part of the Magothy, before it slips into a small stream which flows from one of its sources, Lake Waterford, is covered by Magothy Bridge. Originally it was known as "Dougherty's Bridge," named after John F. Dougherty, whose land bordered this area. He was a waterman who owned the bugeye, Florence, and who used to sail and carry produce to Baltimore from various Magothy River landings such as Richardson's Wharf and Tate's Landing. Prior to his ownership, some of this expanse of land on both the east and west side of the bridge was owned by Zaccary Bentz in the 1800s.

In the early twenties, Anne Meyers, another local land-owner, and John Dougherty feuded over the name of the bridge. Some residents, including Ms. Meyers, preferred to call the bridge the "Anne Meyers Bridge." When the old wooden bridge collapsed in the twenties, it was rebuilt, moved, and dubbed "Dougherty's Bridge." Later it was mapped as Magothy Bridge. It was rebuilt again in 1980.

Fascinating oral history about this area is reported by William Rothamel, Jr.: "During the Revolutionary War period, there used to be an island near the bridge . . . . It has since washed away, but the British fleet hid there ready to take Fort McHenry."[7] Later, the island was dubbed "Hale's Island," named after waterfront landowners. He informs that many artifacts from the period, such as Revolutionary War buttons and muskets, were found and are preserved at the Smithsonian Institution. (However, no exact historical reference was concurred, nor found regarding this information.)

The ruins of a mill race, used for overflow, on the west side of the bridge can still be found there. This mill site, probably connected with the larger grist mill originally of John Water's, on Lake Waterford's edge, was owned also by a Mr. Wallace, succeeded by Adam Dash (named the Wallace-Dash Mill).[8]

Herbert Dougherty, John's son who still resides on the east side of the bridge, would sell soft-shell crabs from the Magothy for twenty-five to thirty cents a dozen to "Bushman's Towne Hall," a local gathering place to eat a "shore" dinner, buy groceries, candy and ice-cream. Now called Riverdale Restaurant, the tradition continues as boaters and waterfront people still frequent the place for some excellent crab cakes and bay seafood. The nearby Waterbury Inn developed in the same way, beginning as a small general store for boaters, later becoming a gathering place for the local community. The twenties and the thirties, muses Herbert, was the time when everybody knew everybody else. "People gathered to celebrate birthdays, traditional holidays, and for just everyday small talk."

In the early 1900s at Magothy Bridge, a stretch of its gentle, rolling beach-front was used for swimming and picnics. Herbert Dougherty relates that this was the only free beach on the Magothy, since all others, like Crystal Beach and Mago-Vista Beach, had restrictions and charged people money to enter. He notes that people like Wilmer Johnson from Johnson Lumber Company would come and visit with his father and enjoy the cool springs which were plentiful in these waters. John H. Dougherty would offer small boats for hire there so people could paddle and picnic on private spots up the river. "The fishing was also excellent," continues Herbert. "We caught perch, white and yellow, and bass, and catfish. The crabbing was so great. The softies would be scooped up with a long-handled net in large fat groups. Grandfather would cart them by horse and wagon to the fish markets in Baltimore." Wistfully, he adds, "I stopped crabbing when the waters got too cloudy in the fifties."

Old Man Creek

The Magothy branches from this point to Old Man Creek. In the early 1920s sat a little boat-yard called "Beall's Boat-Yard." Here you could buy "a beautiful hand-made boat—so spe-

Top: Upper Magothy River, facing Cockey Creek, 1998; right: Old Man Creek from Stewarts Landing, 1998; bottom: Cattail Creek from the Berrywood community pier, 1997. (photos by Joan B. Machinchick)

cial . . . or you could rent one," muses Mr. Dougherty. Residents report that John E. Beall of Old Man Creek was the "artisan of the creek;" each boat was made of "lovely molded wood."

At a narrow point near the headwaters of Old Man Creek was a very early grist mill, marked on the *Martenet Map of 1795.* It was named "Beard's Mill" after its owner, Richard Beard, son of A. Matthew Beard who owned 454 acres, a portion of a large tract of 1161 acres known as Huckleberry Forrest (Berrywood Community forms a part of this tract). Beard's Mill operated on Beard's Creek (now Old Man Creek) from 1698 to 1726. Later, it was owned and operated by Richard Robinson and the name of the mill changed to "Robinson's Mill."

The Old Stone House

A venerable fieldstone house fondly referred to as "The Old Stone House," built in approximately 1749, weaves its many layers of the past into Magothy River history. Viewing the house now, one would not even suspect that it ties into river life, with its fieldstone back-side facing the bustling Baltimore-Annapolis Boulevard. Here three millstones form a part of the pathways leading to the main and side entrances to the house, remaining as persistent reminders of the historical pragmatic uses of the Magothy River. In the 1700s and 1800s, the farmlands surrounding the house edged onto Cattail Creek and Old Man's Creek and were also bounded by a small branch of water called Wolf Pitt Branch.

One of its former owners, Colonel Elijah Robinson, in the late 1700s owned a bugeye schooner, *The*

The Old Stone House today.
(photo by Joan B. Machinchick)

Above: some clay pipes found in the Old Stone House. Below: the stone well on the property. (photos by Joan B. Machinchick)

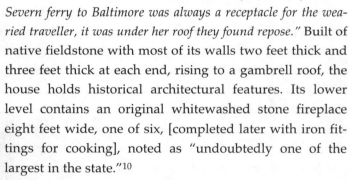

Nancy, which harbored in Cattail Creek.[9] The schooner hauled farm produce from a landing at the *"end of a lane running from the Old Stone house to Cattail Creek,"* to the markets in Baltimore and Annapolis. On this property lived thirty-one slaves, whose names are listed on an original tax record. These African-Americans formed a part of the task force of the Magothy. They were the tillers and farmhands who built the houses and provided its owners and surrounding markets with bountiful supplies of watermelon, tobacco and corn.

The most recent owners, Dr. and Mrs. Stephen Hittle, conjecture that perhaps this house was used as an inn; undoubtedly it formed a hub of hospitality and rest for the "wearied traveller." An obituary in the *Maryland Gazette,* April 27, 1815, notes that *"Mrs. Mary Roboson died Sunday morning last (April 23) relict of Colonel Elijah Roboson. . . . Her venerable mansion, situated on the public line from the Severn ferry to Baltimore was always a receptacle for the wearied traveller, it was under her roof they found repose."* Built of native fieldstone with most of its walls two feet thick and three feet thick at each end, rising to a gambrell roof, the house holds historical architectural features. Its lower level contains an original whitewashed stone fireplace eight feet wide, one of six, [completed later with iron fittings for cooking], noted as "undoubtedly one of the largest in the state."[10]

An aura of warmth and hospitality hovers in this room. One can feel the presence of its former owners, the Robinson and Tydings families who, through concerted efforts of its slaves and tenant farmers, worked the lands and milled the grain; they would gather around this huge fireplace to rest and enjoy the great warmth from its fires. The late Hammond S. ("Skip") Carr of Round Bay lived here as a child. Other notable occupants were Mrs. Laura Tydings Garcelon of Round Bay, the last of two families who owned it for a stretch of 245 years. What post-revolutionary tales and plans were made here, when Colonel Elijah "Robosson" [the name was misspelled in an early document] met with his men? One important military meeting connected with the Severn Battalion of militia on June 19, 1777 is recorded in a journal found at the house:[11]

> *. . . It is hereby ordered, that the military company of the 22nd Regiment, meet on Saturday the 24th instant, at 11 o'clock, at Colonel Robosson's old Fieldst[one]. It is expected that the commanding officers of companies will be industrious in warning their men to attend on the above day, and we're prepared with pen, ink, and paper, to take a list of the absentees.*

　—*John Gassaway, Lt. Colonel, Oct. 14, 1795*

Dr. Stephen Hittle, present owner of The Old Stone House, stands beside the enormous fireplace in the lower level of his home. Below: some of the artifacts found at the house. (photos by author)

And of the Civil War, what stories were told by Richard Tydings, former resident of the Old Stone House and member of the Confederacy? The Magothy still holds some secrets, which may connect with a plethora of muskets and cannonballs dating back to the Civil War, found at the end of the creek by a resident, Mr. McNamara.

A stone well stands among large lilac and mulberry bushes, and an ancient cemetery holds graves of its succession of owners. Now overgrown with vines and brambles, its secret tales lie hidden with its occupants. Here rests Colonel Robosson, with his wife, Mary Warfield Robinson, John Tydings and many of the John Tydings family. The house has been renovated by its succession of owners who have kept in mind the original appointments in style and spirit.

Connected with this large parcel of land bordering Cattail Creek and Old Man's Creek, sits a pre-civil war manor house named "My Lord's Gift." It undoubtedly stood gracing the farmlands and mill sites which formed their network among these branches of the upper Magothy River. William Gibbs owned 200 acres of the land surrounding the house in 1684, a part of the original Huckleberry Forrest, known as "Gibb's Folly." When the land was sold to the Robinsons in 1709, a part of the tract went to Thomas Robinson who married Rachel Bear, Matthew's sister. Their son, Oneal Robinson inherited 311 acres in 1735 from his parents which became known as "My Lord's Gift." Oneal's son was Colonel Elijah Robinson, the inheritor of the Old Stone House. A portion of the land which surrounds My Lord's Gift was sold to the Williams family in 1796 after the Colonel died. The house was built in approximately 1812-1817, but the kitchen was added in 1888. Prior to that time, cooking was done in the slave quarters and food carried into the house. (This custom, used extensively in Maryland, provided some protection from fires.) In 1919, David Ross, developer, builder and owner of Riverdale, leased it to Mrs. Frederick Johnston who used it for a summer tea room named the "Breeze Inn." The house exudes its river charm, with its width being one room wide in the manner of most of the period farmhouses, allowing river breezes to flow through. The scent of its boxwood bushes and the patina of old brick paths linger in memories of its visitors. A series of owners since then have renovated the old farmhouse. Its most recent owners are Mr. and Mrs. James Crawford, who acquired it in 1982 from Mr. and Mrs. Leslie Smith.[12]

Cypress Creek

The Cypress Creek area, beautifully wooded and pristine, formed a clandestine cove of the Magothy where it was known to have sheltered runaway indentured servants or convicts during the colonial days. It remained pristine and unsettled until the twenties when the W. B. & A. Shortline electric railroad connected rural Anne Arundel County with Baltimore. At that time, around 1914, a gentleman named Folger McKinsey fell in love with a farm "gently washed along the southeastern shoreline by Cypress Creek." He purchased 600 acres, some of which bordered the Magothy River. At that time he observed the "wild white waterlilies toss[ing] gently in the shallow headwaters of the creek." He noted a "failed peach orchard

The wild white waterlilies tossed gently in the headwaters of the Creek

—Folger McKinsey

covering the sandy acres." Apparently, the former owner, Horatio Tydings, was "brought to disaster" because of failed crop.[13]

Folger McKinsey, a poet and writer, known as the "Bentztown Bard," was the poetic voice of Maryland for more than forty years, publishing his witty insights in the *Baltimore Sun*. Born in Elkton, Maryland in 1866, McKinsey spent most of his life on his quiet estate near Severna Park on Cypress Creek. In his prolific writing, he dubbed himself the Bentztown Bard after "that part of Frederick where my wife and I in our romantic youth went to live." A protege of Walt Whitman, McKinsey used the nature and simplicity of the Magothy River as prominent themes for his poems. He loved the Maryland country scenes, waterways and the people he would meet in what he called "routine life situations."

Magothy Hall
(photo by Peter Geis)

He resided at Cypress Creek in a two story brick farmhouse previously owned by Horatio Tydings known as "Magothy Hall." He describes his house: "This house faced a sandy beach with a long view downriver to Gibson Island." The McKinseys were an integral part of the fabric of close social life on the Magothy during the twenties when everybody knew everybody else. The young couple enjoyed canoeing, often camping out on Dutch Ship Island. They were honored guests everywhere and were at all the parties of the Tydings, Stinchcombs, Worthingtons, Stuart Symingtons, Linsteads, Brices and Arnolds. A one-track lane ran through the farm, then through the neighboring Arnolds' farm to the village depot at Robinson Station. In 1908, the advent of the Annapolis Short Line Railroad through the area of Anne Arundel County formed the impetus for development of the south side of the Magothy because of immediate accessibility from Baltimore. Residents reached Robinson Station by wagon and team, then would be picked up upon arrival from Baltimore, heavily laden with market goods from the Lexington Market. Prior to the automobile, residents note that the old mule carts could take them over from the railway.

Once settled in after the long railroad ride, Folger McKinsey would love "to walk out on the farm, savoring the broad hayfields, the plantings of peach trees that still bore fruit for the steam packet to load at the landing for Baltimore, the lush meadow with teams of horses and the great barn with its fieldstone wall." Dense pine woods had engulfed the abandoned sections of peach orchard; fields and woods sheltered a great population of "wildings–bluebirds and bobwhites, fox and coon and possum."

Days of quiet reverie and forays into waterfront adventure marked McKinsey's summers. People gathered for parties and for the the celebration of important events. On the banks of the Magothy during the twenties and thirties, Orlando Ridout IV recalls the social life in this relaxed, informal setting of the Magothy:

> The creative verve of Baltimore after the turn of the century was lively and excit-
> ing. Among other activities, the Saturday Night Club was an informal get-togeth-

er of writers, musicians, and artists: Hans Schuler, the sculptor; Leo Trotsky, the violinist, leader of the Naval Academy Band, . . . H. L. Mencken regularly attended together with the Benztown Bard [Folger McKinsey]. A customary summer outing brought these fun-loving men to the McKinsey's place on the Magothy. In the morning the boys would hitch up the teams, fork hay on the wagon beds, and drive up the land to meet the electric car at the depot. Replete with band instruments and bursting with the latest fun stories, the club members loaded onto the farm wagons and headed for the shore. Grandfather would present himself as "Joey, the Jail Poet," in an outrageous costume of broad white and black jail stripes. . . . Such wondrous foolishness! The grown men after a few beers and cold water-melon, formed up their noisy band and drummed and tooted across the lawn and back a great number of times. Singing and skylarking like a gang of fun-loving schoolboys were the sages of Baltimore on a country outing.

Mr. Ridout remembers that his grandmother and her girls did "lovely kitchen work" in preparation for these gatherings: ""the fried chicken, inevitable fresh lima beans, fresh potato rolls, delicious peach pies and all lush bounty of the land was spread for the revelers." When the picnics and parties were over, the guests would prepare to return to the city filled with river memories:

When the last beers were drafted from the ice-filled washtubs, and the final watermelon brought from under the cool artesian well. . . they doffed their party hats, packed their noisy instruments, and boarded the wagons for the railway depot.[15]

Folger McKinsey (1866-1950). (photo courtesy of Orlando Ridout, IV)

1. Carl Behm, "The Grachur Story: 1912-1992." All succeeding material quoted will be taken from this booklet.

2. *The Grachur Club 70th Anniversary Booklet,* 1972 (a collection of anniversary key-note talks by Grachur Club members) p.10.

3. Information supplied by Phil Beigel, a member of the Grachur Club, Jan. 18, 1997.

4. *The Grachur Club 70th Anniversary Booklet,* pp. 10-15.

5. Gail R. Blaisdell, *Maryland Living Magazine* , July 7, 1968.

6. Elaine Leigh, in "A Bit of History," an account of the history of Sunset Knoll, researched by Alex Fowler with oral history by Grace Van Meter Schofstal. 1970, p. 1.

7. Oral history related to the author by William Rothamel, Jr., April 1989.

8. Refer to chapter 3, mill section, for further details.

9. "Inventory of the Good and Chattals of Colonel Elijah Roboson late of Anne Arundel County, deceased . . . (Appraisal of goods) . . ." Jan. 13, 1787. [Researched by Dr. Stephen Hittle. From Roboson journals, 1799. Copies of journals and tax lists (1799) from The Old Stone House donated by Dr. Hittle to author.]

10. Lise Becker, "The Old Stone House, Huckleberry Forest" in *Anne Arundel County History Notes* ed. Marie Angel Durner. Vol XIII, no. IV, (July 1982), p. 1.

11. John Gassaway, Lt. Colonel, Oct. 14, 1795 [Research notes provided by Dr. Stephen Hittle, current owner of The Old Stone House], p. 2.

12. Orlando Ridout, IV, "The Old Stone House" in *The County Chronicle*, Glen Burnie, Maryland, Friday, Oct. 1947.

13. Ibid. P. 2.

14. Orlando Ridout, IV, "My Grandfather, The Bentztown Bard," in *Anne Arundel History Notes,*(July, 1991), p. 3.

15. Ibid. p. 4.

CHAPTER 6

Journals from the South Side

Dividing Creek

Mill Creek

Mago Vista Beach

Ulmstead Point

Forked Creek

Deep Creek

Cape Saint Claire

(Persimmon Point)

Little Magothy River

On the south side of the Magothy, colonization and gradual land development took place more rapidly than on the north side, since its proximity to the bustling social and political life of Annapolis provided a boost for early colonial settlement. In the 1920s the W. B. & A. Railroad stopped more along routes near the southern edges of the Magothy, including Jones Station and Robinson's Station, which were easier to reach than those of the northern side.

In the mid-1700s and the early 1800s the land remained within colonial family holdings. It was used extensively as working farms complete with a mini-feudal system of master, tenant farmer, itinerant worker and in some cases, slave. Like the north side of the Magothy, tenant farmers and slaves worked large areas of waterfront farms, from 500 to 1500 acres, owned by prominent Annapolitans or Baltimoreans. In the early twenties, the gradual splitting of the large parcels took place, as the focus for property ownership shifted to smaller family farms. During the late 1920s, thirties and forties, the land gradually shifted to residential and recreational use for summer houses.

One such farm area, known as White's Farm, was split into smaller lots for waterfront living. This area, adjacent to Cypress Creek, now called Whitehurst,

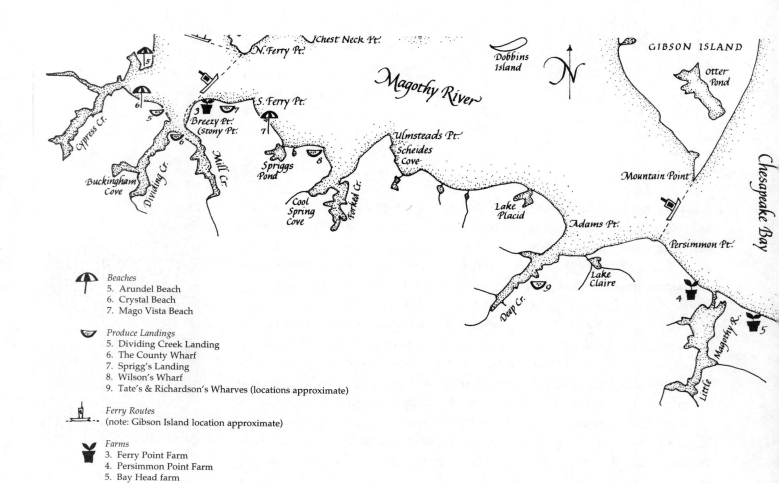

Chest Neck Pt.

N. Ferry Pt.

5

Magothy River

Dobbins Island

N

GIBSON ISLAND

Otter Pond

6

5

S. Ferry Pt.

3 7

Breezy Pt.
(Stony Pt.)

7

Cypress Cr.

6

Dividing Cr.

Buckingham Cove

Mill Cr.

8

Spriggs Pond

Cool Spring Cove

Forked Cr.

Ulmsteads Pt.

Scheides Cove

Lake Placid

Mountain Point

Chesapeake Bay

Adams Pt.

Persimmon Pt.

9

Lake Claire

Deep Cr.

4

5

Little Magothy R.

Beaches
5. Arundel Beach
6. Crystal Beach
7. Mago Vista Beach

Produce Landings
5. Dividing Creek Landing
6. The County Wharf
7. Sprigg's Landing
8. Wilson's Wharf
9. Tate's & Richardson's Wharves (locations approximate)

Ferry Routes
(note: Gibson Island location approximate)

Farms
3. Ferry Point Farm
4. Persimmon Point Farm
5. Bay Head farm

was once a huge produce and dairy farm owned by Dr. White in 1910. Along with the Whitehurst Community Clubhouse and docks, small community marinas have developed along this point and at Cape Arthur, Mago Vista, Forked Creek, Deep Creek and near the Little Magothy River.

Dividing Creek and Mill Creek

Two meandering creeks, *Dividing and Mill Creek*, provided safe harbors and gracious wind-protected lands for crops. From these areas along the south side, still residing on the Broadneck Peninsula are the Worthington, Tyding, Welch and Ogle colonial family descendants. In the late 1800s and early 1900s, the farms, now between 200 to 500 acres, were held by large waterfront families including those of Alfred Stinchcomb, Edward V., Williams and Franklin O. and Harry L. Spriggs, Thomas Welsh Adams, Jack Wilson, M. P. Baldwin, Captain B. Clark, Charles Pettibone, W. P. Baldwin, and Sam Redgrave. Other significant families who lived on Broadneck include those of P. T. Rawlings, James Lark, Thomas and William Richardson and William Tate. In fact, several families owned some of the vegetable and produce landings on the south side such as Richardson's Wharf, Tate's Wharf, Wilson's Wharf and Sprigg's Landing. (See Map, p.126. Also see the G.M. Hopkin's Map of 1878 for more inclusive listings of early families of the Magothy.)

A diary entitled "*Some Stinchcomb History, As I Understand it,*" by Victor E. Stinchcomb, Jr. (1925-1989) weaves threads of a tapestry which forms a viable history of the south side of the Magothy. Many of these same families had owned other properties checkerboarded all over the Magothy. In the 1880s between Dividing and Cypress Creeks, Alfred A. Stinchcomb owned 226 acres of what now includes Manhattan Beach, stretching from Spriggs Pond. At that time these land holdings comprised what is now the old Crystal Beach and South Ferry Point. Victor Stinchcomb writes that in 1874, there was a "farmhouse near the point of the Magothy River and Dividing Creek" where his father, Alfred A. Stinchcomb lived. In 1921 this property was sold to J. Brooks Melchor for development into what is now Manhattan Beach. An anecdote relates that while sur-

The yacht, Hobgoblin *on a mooring in Mill Creek. Birchwood community pier is in the background. (photo by Joan B. Machinchick)*

veying his new property, Mr. Melchor, finding an old Indian axe and other artifacts, called the community after the Indian name—"Manhattan."[1]

Another of the Stinchcomb family holdings, "Ferry Point Farm," was significant since it formed the connection for the county ferry running from South Ferry Point, a known site for the produce and lumber barges to trade and pick up goods, to North Ferry Point. Victor Stinchcomb relates that "the Stinchcombs let the County have a parcel of ground directly south of the boatyard for use as a county wharf, in the old days when farmers took produce to Baltimore by boat." Today this is the site for the Ferry Point Yacht Basin, which operated during the twenties to the present. The Stinchcomb Ferry Point Farm holdings had included a part of what is now *Mago Vista Beach*. Later the Walter Stinchcombs moved to Cox's Place, which is now Anne Arundel Community College property.

Misty morning on Dividing Creek, 1997. (photo by Michael Dulisse)

On many waterfront farms the main house had been built on what are perceived as inland pieces of property; however, the farms themselves edged the waters of the Magothy and were deemed more important than the houses. Farther east along the Broadneck Peninsula, another of the Stinchcomb holdings was titled Persimmon Point Farm, at Cape St. Claire. Three hundred years old, it is distinguished as the oldest of the family estates fronting the west side of the *Little Magothy River* and is a clear example of how the pioneer families "hopscotched" their land-holdings all along the Broadneck Peninsula.

Also on Mill and Dividing Creeks, early land grants reveal that James H. Lark and Joseph Wilson held waterfront farming properties there. Lark's farm was called Bushy Neck Farm, its principle crop being tobacco in the 1880s. Other inheritors of this primary property fronting the Magothy's broad expanse were Emma Gardner, Robert L. Werntz, and Mrs. Maurice Ogle.

Pioneer riverfront families such as James S. Wilson and Samuel T. Wilson farmed along these shores from 1887 to as late as 1945. A part of this area was owned by Emma Gardner and became the property of Robert L. Werntz in the early 1900s. A manor house was built there in the mid-1800s which was formerly occupied in 1939 by Mrs. Maurice Ogle of the Governor Ogle family. This house still stands, bearing warm memories of Magothy's clear, blue-green waters with the perch leaping in shining moments. The serene porches and verandas of the house overlook Mill Creek and was formerly owned by Naval Academy Professor Michael Saarlas and his wife Nancy. The house whispers its memories of ren-

dezvous and small parties when, in the late 1800s and early 1900s, according to oral history, it used to be a small "hotel" where the ferry side-winder steamers dropped off the city-folk from Baltimore for a brief getaway.

George Stinchcomb, who had originally owned and farmed the *Crystal Beach* area, sold to real estate developers as early as 1921 where a recreational beach for swimming, picnics and simple row-boats provided public access and space for ferry boats to drop off passengers in search of a brief outing away from the burgeoning

A typical recreational beach of the Magothy where people gathered to enjoy the riverside.

city. Gradually, as with all these little beach areas, merry-go-rounds and ferris-wheels, waterslides and pony rings sprung up along Magothy shores.

Crystal Beach, well known by many Baltimoreans and Annapolitans, was loved by all. According to Herbert Drucker, historian of Manhattan Beach and its environs, the area of Crystal Beach had become a public amusement area by 1929. Mr. Drucker continues: "Crystal Beach on the Magothy is anticipating the largest season since 1929. All kinds of amusements can be found at this resort . . . dancing in the newly decorated ballroom, bowling, billiards and swimming keep the crowds happy. A large dining room has been built on the boardwalk to take care of the thousands who relish Maryland shore dinners."[2]

In this same general area, but nearer the Mill Creek shore, Robert A. Stinchcomb and his wife Eve had a "boat yard" now called *Ferry Point Yacht Basin.* Here, in the 1800s, the bugeyes, skipjacks and lumber-jacks would load and unload tobacco, produce and lumber for Baltimore and Annapolis markets. The "County Wharf" at the point where Mill and Dividing Creek meet was the logical home of the large ferry boat, *Diana,* which carried passengers from South Ferry Point to North Ferry Point and other landings on the north side. Boat yards gradually evolved into what we now call marinas, but in those days, the yards were used primarily for building and repairing boats as well as leasing smaller rowing craft for pleasure; they also provided small food items for sale such as candy, milk, gum, and a few other necessities. At the present, the Ferry Point Yacht Basin still continues its heritage of providing docking, as well as steamed clams, shrimp and excellent crabs at its charming little "Tiki" Bar.

According to the account of Christian Zeichner who still resides on Dividing Creek, in the 1920s the waters there were clear and cool, with flowing green sea-weed growing tall out of the water. He reports that huge turtles used to get caught in the propellers of the small motor boats and would be set free by concerned boaters. He remembers the variegated water-lilies growing wild in *Buckingham Cove* as well as the waterside laurel, shining with color every spring. The multitude of hooded mergansers would cavort in the dense silent woods along Mill and Dividing Creek. Mr. Zeichner reports that the candy store called "The Spit" was popular where the creeks meet.

A quiet, preserved point of land on the south side of the Magothy which today casts pine-green shadows upon the waters, is known as "Henderson's Point." Named after the Richard Henderson family, this point of land still bears all the naturalness of how it must have appeared in the twenties and thirties. Proudly preserved by the Gordon Riley family, who purchased eight acres of this point, its serene revered house perches comfortably among protective shade trees, shining in the afternoon slants of light. The late Gordon Riley became one of the pioneer conservationists on the Magothy, fighting against its development in the fifties and sixties. Staunchly working with the Magothy River Association, Riley initiated many citizen programs of monitoring the waters for pollution and fighting overdevelopment. Marguerite Riley shares the real river lover's memories as she relates how she came to know the Magothy. In 1933 "we came to summertime on the river—three teenagers out of school all decided to rent a summer cottage, an aunt or a grandmother taking turns to be with us. . . . We (Gordon Riley and I) got to know each other on the river. . . our courtship in his canoe." When they were married in 1933, they bought the "hill on the Magothy with nothing but trees."

In the late 1800s and into the early 1900s, on the south side of the Magothy, large family tracts such as those owned by the James Wilson, Walter Stinchcomb, William Spriggs and R. Tydings clans, were divided into 50 to 100 acre tracts. On the west side of Mago Vista Road, rests a spacious mid-nineteenth century house, once the center of a large orchard and truck farm owned by James Wilson of Baltimore. Originally it was known as the Wilson House or Strawberry Plain; later it was called Cloverlea, built around 1848. Like most farmhouses of that era, it was built to be two rooms deep, so that the waterfront breezes could flow through. Two small out-buildings included a brick milk house, brick meat house and a frame kitchen with a massive brick chimney. This kitchen has been altered and enlarged into a small house.[3] Wilson used the main house only in summer and permanently after his retirement from the businesses he owned in Baltimore (a shipping line and a cannery). A landing at the edge of Forked Creek named Wilson's Wharf formed a hub for his new business of hauling seafood and farm produce to Baltimore. (See Map, p. 126)

Mill Creek, 1986.
(photo by Joan B. Machinchick)

Mago Vista Beach.
*The new dance pavillion built
in 1934. (photo courtesy of
Christian Zeichner)*

Mago Vista

Mago Vista Beach evokes warm, centered memories with-in the hearts of many Magothites. This beach was trans-formed into a recreational area, originating from the early farm lands of Ferry Point Farms owned by Walter M. Stinchcomb in 1897. Harold H. Benson recalls that his father, Robert Crisp Benson, contracted to build houses on the land sur-rounding Mago Vista in the 1900s and developed the actual recreational area of MagoVista Beach in l928. At that time Mago Vista opened to the public sporting two bathhouses and a beautiful dance pavilion, enclosed from the elements, jut-ting into the Magothy.

A postcard in the collection of Jack Kelbaugh identifies what looked like a rus-tic beach-front building as "Mago Vista Cotillion." Signs were attached to the rafters announcing pertinent details such as, "Orchestra every Wednesday and

Saturday, or "Positively no tagging." Rows of wooden picnic tables lined the perimeter of the building. This original site was destroyed August 23, 1933 by an electrical fire caused by the high water from the "Hurricane of '33." In 1934, Mago Vista was rebuilt by the Robert Bensons who included a new enclosed dance pavilion that was "mostly over the river," named the "Marine Pier," with sprightly decor in nautical motif.[4]

A description of the new hall in the *Anne Arundel County History Notes* describes Mago Vista in the thirties:

A ship's rail, life preservers, and a ship's wheel adorned a soda fountain next to the dance floor and adjacent areas furnished with table and chairs. The bandstand was surrounded by a drawing of a whale's mouth: later, the "whale" was replaced by a replica of a lifeboat in which the band sat. The ballroom ceiling was given the atmospheric treatment by a number of electric lights representing stars and by "clouds" projected by light boxes on either side of the room.[5]

Riverfront life flourished; Saturdays were the big dance nights for Anne Arundel citizens who swayed to the music of "The Townsmen" and Russ Cullen's band from Baltimore. Jitterbug contests were the rage with the awarding of trophy cups to the breathless winners. The open air picnic structure, built by the Bensons, housed wooden tables and chairs which were rented for the day. Prices varied for preferred seating. It would cost 75 cents for four-seat tables in the center area, to $1.23 for six-seat tables along the water-front edges. An inland building named the "Rustic House" held picnic tables, benches, and grills which could be used in inclement weather. People usually brought their own food, but could purchase sandwiches and light refreshments. No picnics were allowed on the beach itself, and alcoholic beverages were prohibited throughout the thirty-eight years the Benson family operated Mago Vista Beach.

Old timers of the river will remember the long-distance swimming and the lively picnics enjoyed on Magothy's unpolluted shores. Amusements for the young and the "young at heart" included canoeing, high-diving, roller-coastering, or taking a ride on the "Toonerville Trolley," a miniature train ride which delighted children of all ages.

A new structure built by Robert Benson known as "the Clubhouse" became the focal point for church picnics, family outings and a cool, beachy place to relax. This area extended from the clubhouse into two perpendicular pavilions, swimming piers, a high slide into the water plus a high diving board and merry-go-rounds. In fact, Captain Mac McLeoud recalls that "that diving board did me in. . . . My eye, which was once injured during the dive, was never the same. I became blind in one eye from then on. . . . But coming to Mago Vista when I was eight, living in Baltimore, . . . my, that was a real treat! All week long, during weekdays . . . Sunday school picnics were held there. In fact that was a good reason for going to Sunday School," he adds with a chuckle.

As with Crystal Beach, Magothy Beach, and Royal Beach, rental boats were available for "paddling." Personal accounts such as those of Eileen Schaeffer, a long time resident of Mago Vista, became a part of Magothy and western shore oral history. Mrs. Schaeffer recalls the days when "you spent all day swimming, got 'black' from too much sun, . . . got yourself in trouble making noise." Wistfully she remembers the long summer days there, shooting marbles, watching and hollering at "those fellows doing the watermelon jump" off the high dive. She recalls that "Doctor Wilmer from the Wilmer Institute at Johns Hopkins would come down on his boat to rendezvous at Mago Vista: ". . . when you were canoeing, if you would grab the end of a rope you could get a free tow. . . . We would lie on floats around the piers as if we owned the place," she muses softly.

She also remembers the little caretaker's house for the old Benson farm. Houses such as these were gradually built around Mago Vista as rental cottages. Mrs. Schaeffer recalls that "Mr. Owens and Mr. McKinsey had eight four-room cottages that they rented in the summer to people from Baltimore or Glen Burnie." She adds more pertinent details of the clubhouse:

The Mago Vista Clubhouse had a large ballroom with a sparkling glass movable dome. There were long picnic tables and chairs. Tables at the sea-side cost $1, whereas the inside tables cost only 75 cents. In front of the club house was a board-walk lined with the old "Gibson Island Chairs," a lovely chair designed for Gibson

Islanders with enough arm room to hold a mint julep. There was also a sign which
restricted this club which said, "For Gentiles Only . . . no colored allowed. . . ."

Like many beach owners, the Mago Vista Club admitted only white persons of
non-Jewish descent—definitely not a proud part of Maryland history. According
to Mrs. Schaeffer, another class distinction along the Magothy was that the "poor
whites" in the twenties lived along the creeks; whereas the older, established family clans lived near open river. However, at the turn of the century, living directly on the riverfront was not considered a priority; most of the early farmhouses
were set way back to take advantage of warmer shelter from the wind. Mrs.

Mago Vista Beach.
Left: 1939. Top right: the new
pier , built in 1934, showing
swimming area; with sea nettle
net. Bottom right: eating pavil-
lion. (photos courtesy of Eileen
Schaeffer)

Schaeffer asserts strongly, "The creeks are far quieter places, more serene, . . . away from all the noise and ruckus we have now."

Other stories and legends of Mago Vista persist. One anecdote repeated by many Magothites is the story of how several ladies playing cards there in the large ballroom, fell through the rotted floor planks into the antiquated, smelly septic tank below. After they had been rescued, that was the end of the card game for the day.

By 1960 the entire beach had been designated as a private club called the Mago Vista Beach Club, owned and managed by Harold Benson. Benson sold the beach club in 1966 to be operated by new owners, and in the early 1980s the old structures of the Mago Vista Beach Club were demolished to make way for the development of a new town-house waterfront community called "The Moorings." The era of the old beach clubs on the Magothy had ended. Souvenirs of Mago Vista Beach, including paper napkins, spare tire covers for the rear of an automobile, and a plate for the front bracket of an automobile, are sought after by river history buffs.

Forked Creek and Ulmstead Point

The Bugeye, Edith M. Todd, leaving Spriggs's farm on Ulmstead Point with a load of watermelons in the 1930s. (photo by Milton Oler)

Historically, the area now called Ulmstead Point, bordering Forked Creek, was a significant center of farmland, so necessary for a burgeoning economy; pride and hard work of waterfront farmers became evident. Early landowners of this pristine stretch were Albert Cooke and James Spriggs [see Martenet Map of 1795, p. 54]; reportedly, the 400 acre point was owned primarily by James Spriggs in the 1800s. In 1890, 101 acres of the land in the Bayberry area were given to James' daughter, Ruth when she married. In 1910, it was sold to Henry Stainback and his wife Nora. Ruth Stainback, Henry's daughter, then married Franklin Spriggs in 1929, and they farmed the land on the south side in the thirties and forties. The Spriggs family operated the farm, producing prolific amounts of watermelons, tomatoes, and peaches, transporting the produce from what was called *Sprigg's Landing* in bug-eyes to Baltimore from the borders of Forked Creek.

In a letter written in 1967 by Franklin B. Spriggs, postmaster of Arnold, Maryland, details of the truck-farming of the early twenties, connected with Forked Creek, come to life. A picture emerges of the high energy and persistent work of Magothy farmers. He writes:

My father and uncle, (Frank O. Spriggs and Harry L. Spriggs) began farming this in 1909 and raised peaches, tomatoes and watermelons as their main crop, dispatching these crops by hauling down to Forked Creek by farm wagons and ferrying by boat out to a two-masted Bug-eye which in turn sailed to Baltimore to be sold by commission merchants on a percentage basis at the dock....They would ship daily, at the height of each crop, an average of 1,000 baskets of tomatoes, 1,000 baskets of peaches and 3,000 watermelons. Some of these watermelons grew so large one year that the captain of the Bug-eye refused to handle them as they weighed 70 to 90 pounds apiece.

Franklin continues with some bleak economic news of farming during the twenties:

This truck farming was composed of hard work, blood, sweat and tears as on one occasion my father shipped 10,000 baskets of tomatoes to the cannery and when the receipts of the sale came back he owed the commission merchant $8 besides the expense of baskets and picking on the farm. I assure you this was one where the tears were prominent.

What emerges from this picture are a staunch, rooted Magothy people, still using the land in the twenties for livelihood, though it could sometimes be quite a meager one. Noticeable is a historical continuity stretching back into those times on Forked Creek when the Indian tribes once moved in seasonal camps to "farm" the oysters and clams and to hunt the waterfowl and fish the waters. Native American traces, the inevitable layers of oyster-midden, provided rich sources of "fertilizer" for the farmers like Franklin and Harry Spriggs. So too, lay-

Ulmstead Point farmland in the 1930s.
(photo by Milton Oler)

ers of history fold into our memories just as the stories of the Magothy rest like silk sails upon a gentle breeze.

Other historic land owners of spacious farm lands of this area bordering the south side of the Magothy were Charles B. "Buck" and Lillian Lynch in 1943. Also, Professor Robert L. Werntz, who had a private prep school for Naval Academy applicants, purchased what is now "Ulmstead Estates" in the early 1900s. In the area of Forked Creek, Mrs. Maurice Ogle, of the Governor Ogle family, inherited the land in the 1930s from Professor Werntz. When Charles Barnard Lynch bought it in 1946 a "new experiment" on the Magothy emerged. "Mr. Lynch turned the huge tract, which includes Ulmstead Estates and Bayberry, into a model farm, using innovative techniques to improve the sandy soil. . . . An active and progressive citizen, he introduced Belgian draft horses, Aberdeen Angus cattle, and Chester white pigs to the vicinity."[6] The old "horsebarn" used for the prize Belgian draft horses still exists and completes a Magothy waterfront farm tableau.

Reminders of the past Magothy River social and farm life persist in the communities of Bayberry and Ulmstead. The *Spriggs-Lamb House*, listed on the

Maryland Register of Historic Properties,[7] is a typical mid-nineteenth century farm-house, a three-section frame whose main section is two-and-a-half stories high and five bays wide under a gable roof. The extensive property, which had originally surrounded the house, dates to 1760. A summer kitchen with a loft above is connected to the main house by a small wing. Although the house now contains modern amenities, its gentle charm remains as it once sat amid the Anne Arundel County farmlands, when the produce harvest was launched from the bugeyes off Sprigg's Landing. The Spriggs-Lamb house boasts "sweeping views over to Little, Dobbins and Gibson Island." It ensconces poignant memories of the various farm gatherings, such as the Spriggs, Lamb, and Lynch families, complete with meals of Aberdeen Angus roast of beef as well as Chesapeake seafood. The evolution from farm to modern community suburbs of this area occurred when William Dixon bought the land and developed it into *Ulmstead Estates* in the 1960's.[8]

Deep Creek

The history of Deep Creek is intimately connected with that of Annapolis or "Providence," as it was called in 1649. According to a resident historian, Bob Johnson, "the first settlers of Deep Creek were pioneers and farmers who came as exiles from Nancemond, Virginia. They were known as Separatists or Independents because they refused to pay homage to the Anglican Church as the Jamestown authorities demanded. . . ."[9]

From Providence they spread out across the Broadneck Peninsula. The first white settler of Deep Creek was probably Richard Moss. His great-grandson, James, relates the story of Deep Creek, placing family history in perspective with historical events of early Annapolis. A written account from "Ye Lost Towne at Severn," describes the modest Deep Creek settlement of 1652:

> *On Deep Creek we find Richard Young and near him Ralph Hawkins who seals his will with his arms and who owns much land. Focus the glass carefully. The moving object is the Hawkins cow 'Nancy.' In Deep Creek is anchored the* Golden Wheat Sheaf *out of London, Captain James Connaway. . . John Sanford as his mate. The Captain owns a plantation on Deep Creek. West of Deep Creek, Edward Lloyd's "Swan Neck" and "The Addition" of Richard Moss. On top of 'The*

Deep Creek calms and charms me. There's romance to the old ways. There's a good feeling of worth and work attached to it. There are some strong, hard-working families along that creek. They live more like the first settlers than the rest of us—more independent, more self-reliant, living more in harmony with the tides and the seasons.

—Bob Johnson

Mountains of Magothy' (Gibson Island), farthest north of the Settlement—James Homewood, James Orrick and Richard Moss.[10]

Early land plats show that six properties, originally adjacent to one another at the juncture of a stream bed at the head of Deep Creek, formed the first community. Other patented farm holdings were "Moss' Purchase," belonging to Richard Moss II, and "Deep Creek," owned by William Slayd, who was once an indentured servant of Richard Moss. "In those times indentured servants served seven years under contract, then were given five barrels of corn, a shooting iron, and 50 acres of land."[11] Johnson notes that the entire properties were referred to in the records as "Richard Moss' Quarter," which meant that this formed a kind of headquarters or a base of operations for defense purposes. The placement of this early community was "close enough to tidewater for transportation, and right on the fresh water for their drinking."[12]

The Cape St. Claire pier at Deep Creek, 1963. (photo by Joan B. Machinchick)

Remnants of a mill which processed grain grown on the peninsula farms, including Whitehall, date to the mid-1700s and are still visible on Deep Creek. According to a land grant, when the *"mill washed away in a storm,"* all of the farms were hard pressed, for the only other mill was owned by John Brice (near Whitehall). After several attempts were made to divert water to a mill built at Whitehall, a dam was built on Cat Branch Creek at the headwaters of Little Magothy Creek and carried by canal to Whitehall. The dam spillway is still in existence.[13]

Focused, hard work and determination were displayed by pioneers of the Magothy. Charlie Haas, an early settler of Deep Creek, known as the "first perma-nent resident along the creek in our era [post-Depression Years]," remembers a vigorous life of the riverfront: "When we got here in '32, we worked an 18-hour day. We built all this ourselves. Back then there were two piers on the Cape St. Claire side, Richardson's and Tate's (See Map, p. 126), used for shipping farm produce to Baltimore. The sailboats used to pull right up beside the pier and load up for their produce." Haas, fondly known as "Buck" recalls watching the fox hunter on horse-back on the opposite shore. "And at night all you seen was coon hunters and their lanterns." He adds the inevitable comment so commonly expressed by people of the Magothy in the thirties: "We used to get 25-30 dozen soft crabs just dipping around the shore. Back in '33 they cost maybe 35 cents a dozen."[14]

Glen Walters, Centerville waterman, unloading on Deep Creek, 1997. (photo by Michael Dulisse)

Buck Haas relates that before World War II there were about ten waterfront families on Deep Creek. "Now [about 1933] there's just the two Haas families, and charter-boat Captain Gil Pumphrey at Fairwinds Marina. Captain Gil still lives there to this day." Captain John Haas, Sr. adds a juicy note connected with the Creek, as he points across towards Cape St. Claire: "There were no homes when I came here, only farms. And bootleggers. There were plenty of stills back in those

Top: An unpaved road in Cape St. Claire in 1967, during its early days of development. Bottom: Deep Creek, looking toward the Magothy River and Gibson Island, 1998. (photos by Joan B. Machinchick)

woods. In them days there were plenty of stills everywhere. People used to make sour-mash in the bathtub."

Much of the property of this area of the Cape later was amassed by Dr. Hugh H. Young and his wife, Bessie Colston Young. In the early 1920s, the Youngs had intended to develop this area into a community for the elite of Washington, just as Gibson island was for the elite of Baltimore, with a ferry connecting the two communities. Land records reveal that Dr. Young purchased property near the entrance to Gibson Island. A ferry route was established between the "south bank of the Magothy River and Gibson Island. One resident notes that "with ferry service between this point and the Island the old motor route to Washington is shortened by approximately twenty-one miles."[15]

It was said that the crash of 1929 ended Dr. Young's hopes of developing Cape St. Claire as he had dreamed, for "certainly the elite were as hard hit, if not more so, than the farmers."[16] He then tried to rid himself of lands on the Cape side and asked Mr. King of the Gibson Island Company to try to sell it off in large tracts, an endeavor which proved unsuccessful. Later, in 1938, the River Bay Land Company was established to transfer the land. They platted the community of what is now Cape St. Claire.

During the 1920s, Magothy waterfront owners, like those of the 1800s, owned farms concurrently in various locations all over the river. Farther northeast between Forked Creek and Deep Creek were lands owned by H. Chairs. Of the lands bordering Deep Creek, and extending to the Little Magothy Creek, the Albert Pettebones and the Rawlings owned huge tracts, along with the Redgrave and the Baldwin families.

On the south side of the Magothy exist two lovely lakes of clear fresh water. These support hiding haunts for the Great Blue Heron, and the private grounds for a prolific goose and duck population. Wild grasses and some marshes, so essential to the river's ecology, surround the lakes. Lake Claire, on the east side of Deep Creek, and Lake Placid on the west side continue to offer meditative refuges for nearby residents. A resident near Lake Claire, Joan Machinchick, reports that in the 1960s, "huge snapping turtles would appear from the water to lay their eggs in the sand." She also remembers the "wonderful families of quail marching in little lines, emerging from the underbrush around the lake." She notes that the lake still draws the community to its edges with small ice-skating parties, gathering there "when the ice is good."

Ice-skating on Lake Claire, 1997.
(photo by Joan B. Machinchick)

Little Magothy River

This pristine creek now known as the Little Magothy River was labeled, "Magothy Creek" (*G.M. Hopkins Map, 1878*). Reaching deep into the Broadneck Peninsula, it harbors pristine marshes and serene small coves. Captain Thomas Homewood amassed nearly 2,000 acres, patented as Homewood's Lott, an area extending from the east shore of Little Magothy Creek to Sandy Point and south to Whitehall Creek. To the west of Homewood's Lott lay 260 acres which had been patented to Richard Pettibone in 1650. By 1653 a part of this land was re-patented as "Leonard's Neck," a major part of what is now Cape St. Claire. This land connected with another piece patented to Richard Bayley in May of 1685, designated as *Betty's Point*, located on the northeastern tip of Leonard's Neck and is bordered to the east by Little Magothy Creek.

Two historic houses remain on both the east and west sides of the Little Magothy River, sentinels of its colonial life. On the east side is *Pettibone's Rest,* or "Bayhead"; on the west is the historic *Persimmon Point House* and farm, also called the "River Bay House." The Persimmon Point House still graces the edges of the Little Magothy River. William Stinchcomb had owned the house in the 1860s and 1870s, but its oldest original section dates to about 1735. This house remained in the Stinchcomb family until the death of Sarah Stinchcomb in 1945. The current owners, Thomas and Margaret Howard, have faithfully restored it, keeping its history alive. They have raised their nine children there who know every secret hiding

Above: Persimmon Point House in Cape St. Claire near the Little Magothy River, now owned by the Thomas Howard family. Right: remnants of the ice house on the grounds of the Persimmon Point House. (photos by Joan B. Machinchick)

place. The original brick kitchen still exudes an aura of the congenial presence of families gathered around the table for stories and laughter. Soft pine floors and gracious stone fireplaces contribute an aura of intrigue, its dense walls holding secrets of Little Magothy history. A chronicle relating to this house reads:

> Here [in the tiny loft bedroom, insulated with corn cobs] the roof is close over the head, and the sounds of night—the ducks and a lone crane settling to rest in Little Magothy Creek, the rain and wind of the northeasters that gather strength sweeping across the Chesapeake—are close too. And the fog is close, and you can feel it, and you imagine that you can reach out the window and touch the ships calling lost. I wonder who was the first child to know these sounds, snug and warm under heavy quilts; and how many others have since.[17]

A few feet away the thick foundations of the ice house remain, but the original corn crib, slave quarters and carriage house are gone. However, a single stone chimney from the slaves' quarters was found in close proximity to the front of the house by Thomas Howard. Mrs. Howard claims that its location afforded an easy vigil for the proprietors to guard against runaways. Evidently in this house most of its slaves remained with the original families, for reportedly many slaves are buried behind it where the corn crib once stood. The ground in the approximate area swells and dips with the regularity of closely spaced graves, notes Mr. Howard.

Pettibone's Rest, on the east side of the Little Magothy Creek, is presently owned by the extended Stinchcomb family and is listed as the *Alfred Stinchcomb House* in the National Register. The new section was

Pettibone's Rest, the home of Alfred Asbury Stinchcomb and his family, including daughter, Masonetta Stinchcomb Waring. Shown here in 1992 is Masonetta's great nephew, Walter Stinchcomb II. (photo by Sara Anne Stinchcomb)

built in approximately 1882, but an older house once existing on the property has been recorded. A journal written in 1953 by Masonetta Stinchcomb Waring goes back to the history:

Stinchcomb family cemetery adjacent to the Persimmon Point House property. (photo by Joan B. Machinchick)

> *In 1881/82 the Pettibone Farm was sold. It had been in that family since l656. Grandfather bought this place [Pettibone's Rest] for $6,000 and gave it to his son Alfred. . . . The house there was very old with a brick floor in the kitchen. Alfred started the new house at once. . . . A larger house was now in order to suit the family (This house still stands). . . . Along with the house was built a new ice house, . . . a real shop was built here and fully equipped. There the horses were shod, the wagons built, the kitchen tin re-soldered, the shoes half-soled, the gum boots patched, the furniture mended, the farm implements repaired—and tiny coffins made for many negroes.*[18]

There, the slave quarters are still intact, as well as a family cemetery. From Pettibone's Rest come detailed diaries and letters of the life during the latter 1800s and turn of the century which provide accounts of everyday Magothy farm life.

1. Marie Angel Durner, Fred M. Fetrow, eds., *Anne Arundel County History Notes,* (from Herbert Drucker's collection: "The Stinchcomb Family from Here to Now"), p. 3.

2. *Anne Arundel County History Notes,* Roger White, "Saturday Night at the Dance Hall," Vol. XXI, No. 1, p. 3.

3. *Maryland Historical Trust Worksheet,* Nomination Form for the National Register of Historic Places, National Parks Service. (AA-17-W-a [133]). Map 16.

4. *Broadneck, Maryland's Historic Peninsula,* (Annapolis: Broadneck Jaycees, Fishergate Publishing Company, Inc., 1976), p. 54.

5. *Anne Arundel County History Notes,* p. 2.

6. *Broadneck,* p. 55.

7. "Inventory Form for State Historic Sites Survey," Maryland Historical Trust, (AA-305) pp. 1-4.

8. *Broadneck,* pp. 9-29.

9. Bob Johnson, "Deep Creek," in *Broadneck Hundred, Life and Times Between the Severn and the Magothy*, (Bowen Marine Construction, Winter 1975, 76. Vol. 1, Number 1), p. 2.

10. Johnson, p. 3.

11. Ibid.

12. Johnson, p. 5.

13. Ibid. p. 13.

14. Ibid.

15. Warren Wilmer Brown, *Gibson Island, An Appreciative Description*, Baltimore: Gibson Island Company, p. 6.

16. *Long Before the Good Old Days,* author unknown, who quotes from an excerpt from Dr. Radoff, 1976. (Published by the Cape St. Claire Improvement Association in celebration of the silver anniversary of the Cape St. Claire Strawberry Festival, May 1983.)

17. From an original manuscript by Paul Cramer in the possession of Mr. & Mrs. Thomas Howard: "The River Bay House."

18. Masonetta "Macie" Stinchcomb Waring, "A Record," Jan., 1953.

STRAWBERRY TIME

Strawberry time in the fields of home
Strawberries under the clover foam;
Down to Arundel the pickers go,
Women and children from row to row
Dew of the morning, and birds in rhyme
Chattering, chattering, strawberry time!

Dawn on the patches with cheeks ripe and red
So the cheeks of berries amid the bed;
Delicate, dainty and fragrant gleam
Of the red-ripe glow of the strawberry dream;
Strawberry, Strawberry, Strawberry time,
Down in the dells of the strawberry clime!

"Tubbs" and "Gandy" and "Sharpless" array
To the good green world where the patches lay,
Bloomy and boundless and deep with sweet
Of the honey of dew in the noon-day heat;
Robin and Thrush in a song sublime,
Chanting the coming of strawberry time.
— by Folger McKinsey, The "Bentztown Bard"

CHAPTER 7

Farm Life on the Magothy: A Time Capsule

Magothy whispers tales of farm life and the rigors of living on the waterfront when the land was still the viable source of life-blood and the waterways formed the gateway to mobility and marketability. The waterfront farms operated in harmony with the river, effecting a purposeful and useful existence for its inhabitants.

Before the Civil War, all the land from the Bodkin to the Magothy was cleared for farming. But with the advent of the railroad in 1908, produce from the large Virginia farms could reach Baltimore and Annapolis earlier than could be supplied by small farmers from the Magothy. However, the slow process of land division there began to occur steadily by the mid 1920s.

Farm life on the Magothy in the late 1800s, and into the early 1920s, flourished and centered around crop planting and harvesting. When strawberry season began each May, the produce "pickers," many of them of Polish descent, would come from Southeast Baltimore to work on the farms. Although many of the younger men had regular work as stevadores at the nearby docks, the older men, women and children eagerly took jobs on the farms.

Strawberry season in May was the time they would eagerly await for the hay-filled wagons to transport them from Baltimore to points in Anne Arundel

I only meant for this book to be a life of my Mothers, to go down to her descendants that may know a time foreign to even those now.

—Aunt Masonetta
Stinchcomb Waring

County, including Magothy waterside farms. In spite of rather meager housing in shanties, and simple bedding made of hay, farm people had pleasant experiences, baking fresh crusty breads and rolls in outdoor brick ovens and picnicking outdoors for most meals. The spirit of merging work and play was evident on farms of the early 1900s with country dancing, polkas, and songs drifting through the river dusk.

When the day's work was complete, the workers took their produce to be counted in exchange for "picker's checks," marked with the initials of the resident farmer. These coins were most often round or octagonal and each contained a number of quarts or bushels that had been checked. The tokens were accepted at nearby grocery stores instead of cash and were exchanged for money at banks when needed. At the end of each picking season each employer redeemed all checks bearing his own initials.[1]

For the Magothy farmer, riverside farms yielded plenteous supplies of melons, strawberries, peaches, peas, beans and corn. Alongside the farms, the river and coves provided rich sources of oysters, crabs, and fowl for family tables. Masses of seaweed which heaped upon beaches fertilized the earth; in winter the river provided deep ice for storage in ice-houses. The chunks of ice would be carved from the river by the farmers and hauled by horse or mule to the ice-house.

Through a vivid account written by Mrs. Masonetta May Stinchcomb Waring, a woman of vision who lived on both the north and south sides of the Magothy, we are whisked into a miniscule time capsule of mid-nineteenth and early twentieth century farm life on the Magothy River. "Aunt Macie," as she was fondly named by her relatives, decided that "the life of the people from 1844 to 1932 felt many changes, just a bit more than any other century." In January of 1953 she wrote a journal of the life of her ancestors as she remembered them in order to record a way of life fast changing: She states, "The wholesome ways of the great middle class is foreign to many now, so I place here these custums that must have been right or else our country would not have lived in such perfect Peace. . . ."[2]

She refers to the life of her maternal grandparents, Sophia Johnson and Thomas Welch Adams, who farmed in Anne Arundel County in the 1800s. Although some of the early farmlands were inland, gradually Sophia moved to waterfront farms. In her journal Aunt Macie also recalls her own parents, Sarah Adams Stinchcomb and Alfred Stinchcomb, who were river-front farmers in the mid to late 1800s. Characterizing them as well as other river residents, she states,"The inhabitants were deep rooted. Such strength permitted solid growth, just as the iceberg is balanced by what we do not see."

She relates vignettes rich with intimate domestic detail as well as practical information about farm management, the importance of Magothy mills, slave life and river wharves. She speaks of the rigorous life of her maternal grandmother of the early 1800's, Sophia Johnson who had married Thomas Welch Adams:

Sophia's husband, [Masonetta's grandfather] did not take any part in management of the farm, she did. The slaves came to her by inheritance as well as the farm. The negroes were named Pack. Some of the Pack family live along the section from Jones. . . to Elvaton. The produce on this farm was hauled to a neighbor's wharf on the Magothy River, where sail boats made regular trips (to Baltimore) taking and bringing necessities. The old grist mill at Waterford Pond (at the head of the Magothy River) was the center of the section served—I recall it in working order in 1895 or there about. The corn was shelled at home, two big sacks were loaded across the back of a horse and then off to the mill. The meal was brought home and was the source of good eating—corn pone, cakes, mush, dumplings, in sprouts, hoe cakes, ash cakes (the batter dough was put on cabbage leaves, packed in hot ashes until tender). Flour was bought but little used. It was for company and Sunday bread.[3]

All vegetables that were used were home grown. What could not be used immediately were dried or packed in salt. Root crops were banked in kilns. Cabbage was packed in a furrow, covered with pine branches. Canning was not in full swing. Glass jars with sealing wax poured on the top was very effective.

• • •

No farm family lacked a balanced diet even tho we only had green things only in summer. Tomatoes were grown only in flower gardens for their beauty in the early 'forties'.

• • •

Herbs were grown and dried—also many weeds—they were hung from the rafters in the attic. Brew was made [from these] for many ills and I expect recovery results were about the same as the stuff we pour from a vial—to the tune of many dollars. . . .

• • •

[It was so cold] in the early 1850s that railroad tracks were laid down on ice on the Susquehanna River and many took trains over for six weeks. The meat kept then as if in deep freeze of today. Fish and game were abundant and in summers when the meat was [too] salty, then poultry [sufficed, along]with crabs and fish. The tables of the rich and poor were full. . . .

• • •

A few weeks before our produce came on in spring, sail boats would bring things up from Virginia but perishable things could not be shipped by sail boats.

When Sophia's husband, Thomas Welch Adams, died in 1846, ". . . things went on as usual. Kind neighbors lending a hand at butchering time or any other need. After several years of widowhood, [in 1855] Sophia married Thomas Heath in Magothy Church Section. He took her to his home, her children and her slaves too." Thomas Heath died a few years later, ". . . so she now rented a home on the Magothy river as a wharf on the place saved much hauling." (On the north side of Magothy Narrows was said to be a vegetable and produce landing where the Walgeon Farm is now.)

A microcosm of domestic Magothy farm life emerges through the eyes of Aunt Macie:

> Sophia's mother, Aarah Johnson. . . helped with the sewing. The sewing machine had been invented, but few families had them at this time. All sewing was done by hand, and much of that by candlelight. Children were kept busy adding bits of light wood, fat pine, to the fire. The bright blaze aiding vision, as those long seams were back stitched. . . . Maria Pack was the cook, and a good one too. The work all done by an open fire. Baking of bread, meal, pies, cakes was possible because of flat iron lids fit on iron pans (on legs). A shovel of coals on the lid cooked the top as did the hot coals under the pan. One had to have experience to know how much. . . . Johnny cakes were patted on thin boards and set in front of the fire. Not until about 1860, when Sarah went to Harrisburg Pa. did she see a layer cake. Meat was roasted on a spit, an iron bar.

This reference to Maria Pack relates to a well-known slave family, the Packs, who were highly regarded by Magothy River families. The Pack family slaves chose to stay with their original families after emancipation. They were a viable part of river front farm life.[4] Later, many of these former slaves owned farms of their own in Anne Arundel County; however, some chose to stay. Masonetta

notes: "Maria Pack remained in this family many years after slaves were freed. She helped with many things. An expert in wool. This required so much work before it was sent to the mill on the South River to be woven into blankets and cloth. . ." Macie looks at some domestic details of river life, referring to another revered former slave who moved with them to Pettibone's Rest on the south side of the Magothy:

> *The last child Lanona was born September 23, 1885, just about the finish of the building program. Fortunately there was always a colored girl living in besides "Aunt" Harriet Carr who came to do the laundry and all the extra things. She could stay nights for baby sitting. Mother went to church and its activities. Also to Piney Grove and Magothy. They knew all the people but no strangers, only the young descendants. [Aunt Harriet Carr was a former slave.]*

Life for the Magothy slaves was harsh with a relentless schedule of work planting, cultivating and preparing the tobacco crop so prolific on river plantations of the seventeenth and eighteenth centuries. The section of land known as the Magothy Hundred on the Broadneck Peninsula (lands which bordered the Magothy), had more residents and more slaveholders than those of the Broadneck Hundred (lands which bordered the Bay). Forty-one slaves resided on the Magothy Hundred. Knowing that he or she would have to serve in bondage for a lifetime, Magothy slaves lived minimally with food, clothing and shelter, barely even adequate.[4]

Large farm or small, waterfront or inland, the treatment slaves received depended on the temperament of the master or mistress. Several slaves commented on their fear of the "nine-ninety-nine," meaning a severe whipping which lasted until the slave collapsed. Others told of good masters, but harsh mistresses. Slaves who could congregate after work, attend services at their own church on Sunday, enjoy the same holidays whites celebrated, hunt and fish and not feel afraid of being sold to a dealer considered their masters as good persons.[5]

At the close of the eighteenth century, a slight swing of attitude occurred. "A growing feeling on the part of many whites that slavery was wrong, spread from the Eastern Shore westward and triggered a sizeable manumission movement throughout the state."[6] As a result, by 1860 at least 50,000 blacks had received their freedom, creating the nucleus that made Maryland the state with the largest free black population in the entire nation."

River plantations shared in this movement, and many planters released some or all of their slaves. However, some owners hesitated to free their chattels in the belief that their slaves would not be able to succeed on their own. Actually, most of the freed slaves from Magothy farms adjusted well and prospered, setting up small rural farms which still exist today around Anne Arundel County. Most maintained their own homes or lived in facilities still under the jurisdiction of whites—in some cases their former masters. The most common occupations of the free slaves by 1860 near the eve of the Civil War, were farm hand, laborer, independent farmer and servant. They also became washerwomen, carpenters and sailors—a meagre beginning for a free population of African Americans.

The contribution of African Americans as pioneers and groundskeepers of the land surrounding the Magothy and the Bay is tremendous; many became artisans, craftsmen, lumbermen, sailors, boat-builders, watermen, preachers, doctors, architects, statesmen and centers of households which still reach into scars of a sorrowful past.

The mid-1800s formed an era when river time was spent growing, preserving, and preparing crops for Baltimore and Annapolis markets. The life was vigorous, intimate, self-sufficient, sometimes grueling. Masonetta writes, "Not many carriages were about at this time, roads were so muddy. It was better to ride horse back so that was the mode of travel among these people." But when travel by horse was prohibitive, due to horse epidemics or such, furniture was moved by schooner to the wharves. Once, "when the furniture was finally moved to the wharf and loaded, the schooner caught fire and half of the things were destroyed."

The Magothy River was also the backdrop for jolly times—riverside was the place to be! Celebrations and parties formed the silver lining of everyday existence, even if sometimes the going became a feat of endurance. First, one had to get there! Masonetta records:

One night a party was on, the sleigh was broken. . . . Alfred went out to the barn, took the broken basket off the sleigh, nailed up two strawberry crates on platforms of sleigh, padded it with lap robes, hooked up a spirited horse 'Jackson' and drove up to the front door. . . .

Christmas parties on the river were continual:

At Christmas Sarah made dozens of cakes. When I say cakes I mean just that. Not "cookies," that name was not used. But two bushels of sugar and ginger cakes were made, usually cut out with a biscuit cutter. Then many times more would have to be made. The table was spread for refreshments, just after the noon meal. It was fixed company fashion, every day neighbors came and went. This was done in all homes then. No supper during the holidays, you just ate all the time. It was "open house."

Anne Worthington, great-niece of Aunt Masonetta Stinchcomb Waring, relates:

When party time came, Aunt Macie would hang a sheet way up on the porch near the roof of her house so that all the river people would know and be reminded that a party was in the making. Then almost everyone would paddle over from the north side of the Magothy including those from "Gibson Isle" to the house for a whole day of picnicking and fun. Everyone brought food.

But life intermittently surfaced into hard-core farm living. Masonetta recalls the cold winters "when winter was really winter." During that time of year the ice house became central to river life. Only then could fresh meat be stored from early November until March. Masonetta relates that the ice-house was one of the most important buildings on a river-front farm: Of the Stinchcomb house in Manhattan Beach between Cypress and Dividing Creek, she writes:

Alfred built first thing a fine ice house, a huge brick circular pit that held ice for him and his neighbors through the entire summer. It was of brick too. Kept ice from ice to ice. It was filled from a pond, now extinct, near the Bay. Neighbors helped to fill it and were welcome to get ice anytime. The filling of the ice house was done in a day. Mother would have a dozen to dinner, usually four in the kitchen. The meal was a hearty one. Cutting and tossing ice was a man sized job." (Ice houses were completely underground, covered by a roof.)

Ice was usually found when filling time came again. Ice cream was had often but no iced tea. People did not know ice tea, only hot! . . . these are the ways of the inhabitants of Anne Arundel County. I never saw iced tea until 1900.

Life was community oriented; however, each farm became a complete unit of self-sufficiency. Each farm compound contained a stable, barns, slave quarters, an ice-house, a milk house, and even a blacksmith shop. Masonetta notes that she was paid five cents an hour to pump the old bellows used to blow the red hot iron for tools and horse shoes.

Most of the early farmhouses were small and practical with the emphasis upon building a large barn and outbuildings for supplies. But gradually, the larger farmhouses of the Magothy were built as families became more established: When the Stinchcombs moved to *Pettibone's Rest* at Bay Head, Masonetta writes of new home building on the south side of the Magothy: "A larger house was now in order to suit the family. . . Three children, hired men, nurse girl, governess etc. and a spare room was a must in those times."

The following account has become an integral part of the living history of what is now Bay Head. In 1882 Masonetta's grandfather, George Stinchcomb, bought the Pettibone farm and gave it to his son, Alfred A. Stinchcomb [Masonetta's father], who at that time resided at Manhattan Beach with his wife, Sarah. This new property was located near the mouth of the Magothy on Magothy Creek, now called the Little Magothy River. Masonetta describes the land there in 1882 and 1883, formerly owned by the Pettebones: "[The Pettibone farm] had been in that family since 1656. Grandfather bought this place for $6,000 and gave it to his son Alfred." She describes this homesite where she spent her childhood:

> Three hundred acres almost square. It was divided in four fields by two long fence rows of cedars. It took some years to grub [remove] them all. The task was slow. Two of the trees were left and lived on and on. . . . The house was very old with a brick floor in the kitchen. Alfred started the new house at once. . . .

The original house on that farm was torn down and George Stinchcomb built a new one, still called *Pettibone's Rest*.

Now there would be enough room for the houseguests, so endemic to river-front life: Aunt Macie writes of the formalities of hospitality in the late 1800s: "Folks wrote of their intention to visit. . . . Met at the station [Jones Station] and the visit usually lasted two weeks. . . ."

She speaks fondly of the rainy days when river-front community was in full swing:
> . . . the shop would be full of neighbors. They brought all sorts of things to be mended. On such days it was a happy crowd, all busy at the work bench or forge. Such fellowship was so wholesome, swapping experience, yarns and crop plans. No house in this section [of Anne Arundel County] ever had such magnetic power as that old shop. (It was still standing in 1953).

A unique use of the waterways is noted:
> The two boys started to school—St. Margarets, as soon as they landed [in the new house]. The Duvalls lived on the next farm. The boys would later row up Little

Magothy Creek to go out to school with their cousins. It was a long walk over muddy
roads for little folks on bad days.

• • •

. . . No bridge across the Severn at this time. The journey to Annapolis was far more
glamorous than now. Taking the Ferry boat over. To go to Baltimore, one went by
way of junction—Old Elkridge R. R. Not too long after this the bridge was built, also
the rail road was run up through the country. Its passing was a lament to many.

She recalls the era of ship and steamboat and top buggy:

Another [way of travel] was to Baltimore by steamboat, coming to Annapolis twice a
week. It was much easier for my people to drive to Baltimore. By this time we had a
"top" buggy and always a pair of driving horses. (descendants of Gov. Sharpe's stable).

When the new electric short-line railroad came through, Macie comments that
even more house-guests would arrive: "About 1886 the Short Line came through.
Arnold Station was near and Mr. Arnold generously took care of the horses. Two
trains in the A.M., two in the P.M. each way took care of traffic. . ." Later when
the Bay Bridge opened connecting the Eastern with the Western Shore, the house-
guest population grew:

The new Bay Bridge was opened this summer (1952). In six months, 1 and 1/2 mil-
lion [dollars] has been spent in tolls. Never heard of a "week end." Folks came,
brought their trunk! Each family or group came for a two week stay, plenty of fried
chicken, fresh vegetables, home cured meat, foams of curd floating in cream, home
made bread. Such a spread was enjoyed by city cousins.

A list of house guests on the south side, who came via train or horse and
buggy or waterway were:

. . . Sallie and Cora Stinchcomb, Bessie Duvall, Minnie Pettibone, Mag Duvall
(Ridout), Maria Duvall, Sadie and Maggie Anderson, Sadie and Nettie Spriggs,
Lou, Nettie and Lizzie Cox, Ida and Ella Waring with their beaus."

She recalls the intimate domestic details forming the rhythm of farm life:

It was not the custom to cook on Sundays, that was done on Saturdays. A cake was
made, ham was cooked. In that ham broth, vegetables were boiled. Pies, usually fruit
ones, were baked. When I say pies, I mean pies. Nine meat pies, usually ten in winter

and half of those our own mince meat. She laments, *Now adays a pie must be made an hour before dinner.*

No picture of farm life on the Magothy could be complete without the grocery list of 1911 which "came on the *Emma Giles* to Sprankly Wharf below Sandy Point:"

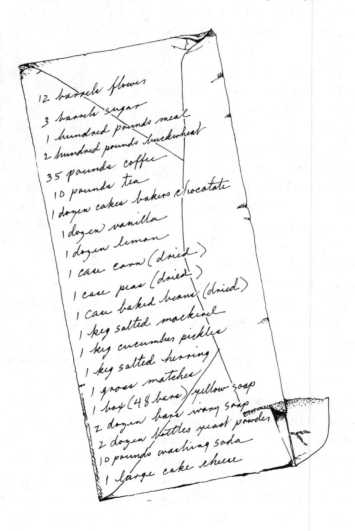

12 barrels flower
3 barrels sugar
1 hundred pounds meal
2 hundred pounds buckwheat
35 pounds coffee
10 pounds tea
1 dozen cakes bakers chocolate
1 dozen vanilla
1 dozen lemon
1 case corn (dried)
1 case peas (dried)
1 case baked beans (dried)
1 keg salted mackerel
1 keg cucumber pickles
1 keg salted herring
1 gross matches
1 box (48 bars) yellow soap
2 dozen bars ivory soap
2 dozen bottles yeast powder
10 pounds washing soda
1 large cake cheese

Rich detail about the logistics of getting the peaches onto the pungies in the river are found in Masonetta's journal:

Peaches being loaded for the Baltimore market in 1911. From left: Alfred Adams, a deck hand, Alfred Asbury Stinchcomb, J. Everett Waring (Masonetta's husband) and another deck hand. (photo courtesy of Sara Anne Stinchcomb)

> *Father had by this time put out many peach trees. Orchards covered these hundred acres. To see them all in bloom was worth while. He built two large row boats — 40 foot long to take the peaches out to the 'pungy' boat lying at anchor in deep water. His own home built peach wagons were loaded, driven out in water to the horses' stomachs. The row boats came up between the wagons, and loading went on from each wagon at the same time. While the drivers returned to the field for more, the row boats were rowed out to the 'pungy'. About 1200 baskets a day were sent to Baltimore at a price of about 17 cents a basket, sometimes lower. I have know[n] a trip to run in the red.*

• • •

> *Weather was a great question on this bleak shore. Those farms in the river had a wharf. When I first recall, peaches were shipped in boxes, similar to orange crates. The material came flat. These were assembled in the barn in winter. The smell of those pine boxes I'll never forget. I still have the stencil "A.A.S." used to mark the peach boxes. Each farmer had his own crates returned. One farmer could not read, so he had a horse above his initials so he could know his own.*

Produce from the Stinchcomb farms was shipped to the Marsh Market between Pratt and Light Streets in Baltimore, and sometimes sold right off the boat. According to John Smith, elder—a farmer of Anne Arundel County, strawberries commanded five cents per quart in the 1920s and tobacco, six or seven cents per pound.

Life on the farm included its hunting forays:

> *Father's hunting season was in the cold weather. He kept rabbits and birds for the sons to shoot. He liked swan and geese as his target across the creek (Cape St. Claire).*

A Stinchcomb family gathering in March 1954. Left to right: Nona Stinchcomb Ridout, Walter Mansfield Stinchcomb and Masonetta Stinchcomb Waring. In back is Bertha Johnson Stinchcomb. (photo courtesy of Sara Anne Stinchcomb)

Grandfather had a row of nails along the north end of the house that were strung with frozen water fowl. When a neighbor came in, one was handed out. . . . The winters then were all <u>deep freeze.</u> Long single or double barrel guns were used. Powder was measured, then shot. The loading was an event for us kids. . . . the wild geese fed on celery grass on the creek. At dawn they arose and flew out to the bay, always head to the wind. (The Wright brothers borrowed that trick at Kitty Hawk). Our men would stand on the sand bar, if the wind was east, on the creek bank if south. The swan was a different game set up. They would feed in close enough to shore to be reached by a Winchester rifle. Usually a trip through drift ice in one's birthday suit was in order to retrieve the birds. Oh, they were best when all roasted.

• • •

Mother picked the water fowl carefully. Her own feather beds were choice. Not like the lumpy sacks some folks called feather beds. Making them up required skill. Our beds looked like Beauty Rest Mattresses when made.

• • •

Mother raised ducks and geese, solely for feathers, but her big flock of turkeys were sold off each year to keep us in things other than necessities. . . .

Of the depression she writes that "these years took their toll upon the family. Some of the land was sold at that time." Many of these large 500 acre farms began to be split at this precarious time in the country's history.

However, farm life still carried the river-pace of relaxation mingled with hard work, just as it does today. A small glimpse into the social river-front life on the south shore of the Magothy reveals a way of life which still exists:

Along about 1920 a Social Club was started [The Saturday Night Club]. Orlando Ridout Jr. was the first president, then Dick Duvall. We offered them this home (Pettibone's Rest) every July 4th. The place was filled. Each brought a basket of food, it was put on one big table, served buffet style. After dinner, about 4 P.M. the ice cream cake that followed the same path, with choice cake to go with it. Then we were ready to watch the fire works. The display at that time was great. From every quarter, Bay Head, Gibson Isle, Tolchester, Lone Point, Annapolis, even Baltimore saw the sky light up. . . .

Masonetta's magnificent account of river life in the mid 1800s through to the mid-1950s ends with a marvelous poem written by Folger McKinsey, a frequent guest at the fourth of July parties on the Magothy and a member of the "Social Club:"

PETTIBONE'S REST

An old house resting in the trees
that looks across the Bay and sees
the ships go up, the ships go down
the freighter bound for foreign town
the sloops, the bugeyes and the yawls
when summer to the whole wings calls.

Green lawns, old maples, lovely flowers
and here, thru all the sun much hours
the soft waves of the Chesapeake speak
a language of strange romance
and yonder Gibson Isle slopes green
to wooded shores of dreams serene.

A Boston steamer moves along,
a tropic fruiter passes by,
an old tramp of the oceans song
is silhouetted against the sky,
in fall the oyster fleet, and then
the storms of winds beat again.

Here rest the Pettebones of old,
and ancient family lean and bold,
here sits the dwelling by the shore
to watch the light of Baltimore
and here the Warings make you feel
a hospitality that is real.

—by "Benztown Bard,"
Folger McKinsey

Masonetta ends part of her account with modest words which carry river tradition through the spirit of Magothy women: *"I only meant for this book to be a life of my Mothers, to go down to her descendants that may know a time foreign to even those now."*

This property remains in the Stinchcomb family. The tombstones which include many Stinchcomb family members still lie there at Pettibone's Rest as reminders of a river life, now past, a gentle time when farming was a family endeavor, and when communal sharing of food, crops, farm implements, hunted game and fowl provided subsistence. The roots of Magothy historic families still lie deep within its soil at water's edge. Masonetta Stinchcomb Waring reminds us that the value of ourselves as river people lies in knowing our traditions: *". . . and remember, Reader, tradition has always been considered as correct as the written word."*

1.   Isabel Shipley Cunningham, "The Pickers of Anne Arundel County," Anne Arrundell County Historical Society, Inc., pp. 1-4.

2.   All quoted material of mid-nineteenth century farm life is taken from a personal account by Masonetta May Stinchcomb Waring, entitled, "A Record," dedicated to Capt. Harry W. Stinchcomb, New Orleans, La., Jan. 1953.

3.   Masonetta M. Stinchcomb, [This particular reference to the grist mill verifies the existence of an important mill on Lake Waterford.]

4.   *Broadneck Hundred*, p. 34. (issue, author, name of article, date, etc.)

5.   Richard Walsh, William Lloyd Fox, *Maryland: A History: 1632-1974*, (Baltimore?, Maryland Historical Society, 1974), p. 227.

6.   *Broadneck Hundred*, p. 34

PART III

Of Old Boats
and Stories to Tell

My river speaks of a time remembered, but not lost. It speaks of a time when Magothy memories mark the life-threads of small moments. Her stories are told with mixtures of chuckles, guffaws, tears and quiet tones of reverie. The common weave reveals a strength and a pride of place in the story-teller, voicing small shreds of life, logged in memory forever.

CHAPTER 8

Ye Boats of Old

Intimately connected with the waters of the Chesapeake live the memories of its old boats logged in the minds and hearts of Magothy's captains and watermen. Boats are the soul of the Chesapeake's experiences of hard work and livelihood as well as intimacy, fun and reverie. The river-stories told around crab feasts center on forays into sailing, motoring, canoeing, fishing, crabbing, sculling, cruising or just boat-watching. Paramount to the Chesapeake fisherman is last week's eighteen-pound rockfish story. To the competitive racer, it's the two hour lull in the Wednesday Night races. Long conversations center around what kind of chum is best, or the quality of picked crab meat of last week's catch.

Because of this nostalgia and reverence for historical boats, Chesapeake people place them among their fondest recollections. According to Robert H. Burgess, people of the Chesapeake seemed to cling to the "old maritime ways long after they had been displaced elsewhere."[1] Along with the pleasurable side of boating, Magothites also consider the particular function of a boat to be of primary importance. Thus, historically, the log canoe, pungy, bugeye, skipjack, ram and brogan were first built to "suit the trade in which they were to engage and the waters in which they were to sail."[2]

. . . these vessels remind us of places to embark and to enter the world of river dreams. . .

Log canoe, 1922 (photo by Milton Oler, courtesy of Howard W. Schindler)

Beginning with the late 1700s, the boats of the Magothy and all Western Shore tributaries were a lifeline into commerce, forming connections with markets and trade, as well as the sources for primary transportation. The historic boats of the Magothy, from the mid-seventeenth century and the eighteenth, through to the mid-nineteenth century, were work boats of trade; the lumber barges, the brogans used for dredging oysters, the buy boats or "runners" which stood in deep waters, ready for pick-up of produce and fish from shallow landings, the steamship excursion boats bringing people to the shores, and the bugeye schooners which hauled produce and fish from landings to the buy boats. Many of these boats evolved as the need arose.

Native Americans of the Chesapeake crafted log canoes out of a single log by burning down a tree trunk and hollowing it with fire and with stone implements. Colonial boat builders borrowed and improved upon these dugout canoes by adding two more logs fastened with drifts and shaped them with axe and adze. Later, rib and plank methods evolved, using more logs to make wider craft. Evolving from the early dug-out canoes of Native Americans, the log canoes were two-masted sailing vessels which were more swift and facile than their counterparts, and used efficiently as working boats for fishing and hauling. Gradually log canoes used for racing were developed. These craft sported the graceful line of a long sprit over clipper bow and carved trail boards. With flexible and unstayed double masts, the racing log canoe has a club at the clew to increase sail area. These historic boats can be seen racing on special festival days in the Chesapeake, their crew hiking out on "springboards." Their working counterparts, more stable with wider beams and lack of bowsprit and jib, are now in museums or rotting on mud banks.

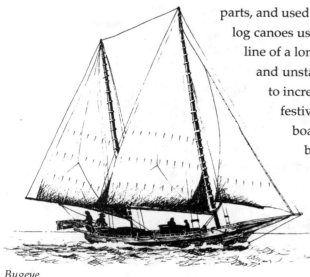

Bugeye

The colonists set up boat yards on Kent Island as early as 1634 and progressed to the building of larger craft for carrying trade goods. Quickly the boat yards expanded to Baltimore and to the Magothy River. The bugeye evolved from the log canoe. Originally these craft were also of log construction, were completely native to the Chesapeake, and were designed as oyster dredgers. Ketch-rigged, the main mast is stepped forward of the shorter mizzen. She carries leg-of-mutton sails with a single large jib. A patent stern, in some boats extends abaft the rudder post, the added length made the mast appear short and the boat under-rigged. The bugeye, historically seen so often in Magothy waters, lacked the grace of the log canoe, pungy and schooner.

Schooners were developed early, both for Bay use and for the high seas. The ocean-going Baltimore Clipper was derived from a fast Bermuda design. Normally a schooner or a topsail schooner, the clipper was sometimes rigged as a brig with square sails on both masts. Fast sailors, they were a favorite of slavers, privateers, and other seafarers whose fortunes depended on speed. Many a colonial boat-watcher admired the beauty of these craft as they were viewed from Gibson Island, Cape St. Claire or North Ferry Point on the Magothy.

The brogan was an enlarged design of the old log canoe, making trips to market more profitable. Thirty feet in length, the brogan had a fixed bow-sprit, a jib with two raked masts, and a narrow open deck. Gradually, larger boats such as the 60- to 80-foot pungies were built to handle larger loads of fish and produce for the demanding markets of a developing new country. Out of these evolved the gracious clipper ships designed for pleasure and profit.

Many lumber rams entered the Magothy to pick up logs in Blackhole Creek. These rams were specialized schooners, having a shallow draft with a centerboard which Bay schooners featured. Delaware-built, the ram stepped three baldheaded masts in a slab-sided, flat-bottomed hull. The main

Lumber ram

Pungy

mast was off-center to one side of the centerboard case. A donkey engine helped hoist the sails with their heavy gaffs, and a yawl boat pushed from astern when the wind died. Operating as freighters, they carried produce and bulk cargo as far north as Delaware Bay and as far south as Currituck Sound. A few operated outside the Virginia Capes in the Atlantic coastal trade. Small crew and negligible fuel costs allowed them to offer cheap freight rates, and they were able to compete with railroads and trucks until the late 1940s.

Another two-master was the pungy. Like most Bay boats, she had a shallow draft, full bow, and broad beam. A sharply-raked stem, masts raked abaft, and a broad dark stripe around the hull gave the pungy a handsome yacht-like appearance. The sharpie was another bay boat, used for taking oysters and terrapin, and the cat-rigged crab scraper was a type of boat which pulled in many crabs of the Bay.

From this evolution of historic Bay craft comes the skipjack, the last of the sailboats in the United States Fishing Fleet. Developed in the 1880s for dredging oysters, the skipjack design has not changed. It is a V-bottomed centerboard sloop with a single mast stepped far forward to provide a clear deck. The boom extends well over the stern. The mast is sharply raked and bowed abaft as with so many Bay boats, and a long bowsprit with trail boards adorns the clipper bow. The single jib is club footed and a com-

Skipjack

plicated system of lazy jacks facilitates reefing. The rudder is outboard; beyond it extend davits for a yawl boat, the only propulsion engine permitted by Maryland law. A scuttle just abaft the mast provides access to the forecastle berthing. Abaft the scuttle is an open deck for dumping and carrying oysters. A fence arrangement on each side keeps the piles of oysters aboard. Aft of the hold is a house and a donkey engine for hoisting the dredge, then a deckhouse for captain and mate. The boats need not be weatherly for dredging. They tack back and forth across the beds, often reefed, towing the dredge over the side. The beaminess and the hard chine provide the stiffness necessary for such work. A few of these historic craft still operate the beds for a limited season.[3]

Beacons of the Magothy

Imagine a dark Magothy night when the waves lap fiercely against shorelands and high winds scream through the funnel of water between Broadneck Peninsula on the south side and the Town Neck Hundred peninsula of the north side. A faithful old ferry needs protection and glides swiftly into the river. High on a hill overlooking what is now Camp Whippoorwill shines a beacon light glowing through the wind, both a welcome and a respite for incoming boats and ferries.

In an account written about Camp Whippoorwill, the Girl Scout Camp, the light is documented:

> 'The Little House' or 'Emmie's House' was built for Mr. Whitby and the site of the present day 'Big House' or main building was originally a large three-story farmhouse owned by Captain Robinson, who farmed the land. The Captain's House stood on a hill surrounded by trees and fields and served as a landmark for the country folk for miles around. It is said that Captain Robinson kept a light burning in the third-floor window to guide the large produce boats and ships that sailed up and down the river.[4]

Another known beacon light, the Bodkin Lighthouse, was located at the head of the Bodkin, lighting the way to the Magothy peninsula of the Western Shore. [See Chapter 4]

Steamboats, Excursions and Ferries

Steamboats of old on the minuscule Magothy? Of course! These nostalgic boats glided along the Chesapeake Bay, clustering into the Baltimore Harbor, not far from the Magothy. Sometimes one would slip into the Magothy to drop off passengers for a day of solitude. These venerable steamboats were the primary means of transportation during the mid-1800s, connecting the ports of Baltimore with those of Annapolis, Washington, the Eastern Shore and Virginia.

One such steamboat, the *Louise,* was reported to be seen in Magothy waters by Mr. Hugh Zeichner, a resident of Dividing Creek. He recalls that his grandfather told him about the *Louise* when he was a young boy and how it used to drop off

Side wheeler steamboat, B. S. Ford, passing a lumber schooner as they entered Gratitude harbor, August 1922. Such vessels frequently entered the Magothy River. (photo by Milton Oler, courtesy of Howard W. Schindler)

people at a landing on the south side of Dividing Creek. This landing connected with a pavilion and a small inn which was used as a kind of early hotel for overnighters. This particular place has been traced to the old manor house formerly owned by Dr. Michael and Nancy Saarlas on the south side of Dividing Creek opposite what is now South Ferry Point Marina.

Robert H. Burgess, historian of Bay boats, informs that the *Louise,* which he calls the "Belle of the Bay," was built in Wilmington, Delaware, in 1864. Her original owner was Charles Morgan, who named it after his daughter. The *Louise* had a long history as a magnificent excursion boat on Western Shore waters; however, many people do not know that she also was used during the Civil War. She was chartered by the United States Government from December 1864 until after the close of the Civil War. Later, in 1874, she was purchased by the Baltimore, Chesapeake and Richmond Steamboat Company to carry freight and passengers between Baltimore and West Point on the York River in Virginia.

When the Tolchester Company acquired the *Louise* to take care of their expanding business in 1885, she was rebuilt and emerged as an excursion steamer with a capacity of 2,500 persons. "Year after year the *Louise* served as a sure sign of spring around the Baltimore waterfront as she was overhauled to transport thousands across the Bay for another season."[5] She had a reputation for playing a prominent part in the courtships of several generations of Baltimoreans.

Endearing side-wheeler steam ferries such as the *Louise* made short stops at Magothy area landings as well as other river landings on the Severn and on Tolchester Beach. Boat-watchers of Ulmstead Point, Gibson Island, Chestneck Point, Broad Creek, North Ferry Point could probably see the old steamers plying near the mouth of the Magothy as they graciously and slowly entered into view. Ferry boat passengers of the late 1880s and early 1900s enjoyed school and church picnics, lunch and club outings. Gradually these early pavilions developed into the "amusement parks" of the twenties which sported wooden roller-coasters, merry-go-rounds, spaces for picnics and barbecues and swimming beaches. The excursion boats would ferry passengers on the Magothy to such places as Crystal Beach, Mago Vista Beach, Royal Beach, and the picnic pavilion at North Ferry Point.

During the thirties and forties, transportation to the smaller beaches such as Beachwood Park, Sunset Knoll Beach and Magothy Bridge Beach were accomplished by motor launches or by rental boats from Mago Vista. One such launch was called *Maid of the Mist* which plied the waters between a point "outside Gibson Island to Mago Vista Beach."[6]

Another launch which performed her tasks of carrying people from one side of the river to the other was the *Diana*, the motor launch used by the girl scouts to travel from the south side to Camp Whippoorwill. Even the very small boats were plentiful and revered. Beale's Boat Yard near Magothy Beach rented out

Maid of the Mist, 1920. (photo by John Gass)

hand-made rowboats, crafted carefully by Mr. **Beall** for the purpose of lazily drifting along the upper Magothy River.

A typical steamboat trip is described by Robert H. Burgess in the book, *This Was Chesapeake Bay*. He describes "the days when a steamboat trip to Fairview Beach, on Rock Creek was the event of the summer." What follows is an account of a typical annual Sunday School picnic, an event reported nostalgically by people of the Severn as well as the Magothy. Burgess recalls:

. . . the whole family . . . took off for the day. For several days prior to the outing, Mother would be occupied with preparing the perfect picnic lunch basket.

. . . The object was to get aboard (the pier at Broadway and also at Pier 6, Light Street,) . . . as early as possible in order to get the choicest deck space because the trip down the harbor and the Patapsco was always interesting. In a little more than an hour, the steamer would enter Rock Creek. . . . Her whistle would resound throughout the countryside announcing her approach. That landing smacked of all the atmosphere once found around tidewater steamboat wharves —just a few pilings, roughly planked wharf, and shed. Long before the steamer's lines had been heaved to the wharf, the boys would crowd around the gangway, anxious to get off and race for the most suitable lunch tables—those with roofs. A full day of swimming, rowing, or enjoying various games and sports events followed. . . . Having discharged her early-morning passengers, the steamer would cast off for Baltimore to bring down the afternoon crowd.[7]

One such steamer, named after its owner, was the excursion boat from Baltimore, the *William Linthicum*, which stopped at the picnic pavilion made of chestnut at North Ferry Point.[8] Another side-winder ferry made its way into Magothy waters. Donated by the Bethlehem Steel Corporation, the *S.W.Smith* ended her days by becoming the barracks for the boys at Camp Milbur in a cove near Long Point. [See Chapter 4.]

Working Craft   An endangered species, the venerable skipjack of the Chesapeake, has found its way north into Magothy waters. Historically, the working oyster dredger of the Chesapeake, seen so often by elder residents of the Bay in their youths, was a symbol of the bursting natural life of the waters, the provider of plentiful oysters for the entire East coast. Now because oyster production has reached historic lows, the last fleet that harvests seafood under sail has found its way to the Magothy waters, working near the mouth of the Magothy and slightly north. Captain Wadey Murphy has the oldest working skipjack in the diminishing United States fleet, the *Rebecca T. Ruark.* Built in 1886, she dredges out of Rock Hall, as well as points north of Deep Creek in the Magothy, where she sometimes harbors for the fall and winter. She is wooden, weighing about 40 tons with a broad beam nearly a third of its 45 foot length, its huge mainsail designed more for torque to plow the bay bottom than for grace or nimbleness. A practiced Captain knows when the dredge is on barren mud or oysters and can even tell whether they are live oysters or just shell deposits.

In the 1800s the skipjacks plied completely under sail; now, a small auxiliary motor helps with maneuverability. The crew dredges and culls the dead shellfish from the live ones, piling the good oysters onto mounds on board. Knowing how the tides and winds affect her, the captain licks across the oyster bed, with the wind filling her sails. She comes about smartly and licks again. She is a piece of living Magothy history, as she plies out of Deep Creek on a bristling, windy fall day, or gentles her sails after a long slow afternoon of oystering. The *Rebecca* continues her 110 year old tradition of dredging oysters. Now that the oyster habitat is greatly reduced, the skipjacks have become an "endangered species." Tom Horton, noted conservationist of the Bay states: "Today's bay has less than half the habitat for oysters than it did a century ago, simply from physical destruction of the reefs by dredging and hydraulic tonging. . . . The shellfish beds that remain are so flattened as to be more susceptible to smothering by sediment."[9]

Magothy stories are told of bugeyes such as the *Florence,* which reportedly stopped at landings at Wilson's Wharf in Deep Creek and Spriggs landing, Mill Creek Landing, Pea-Patch Point Landing, Cornfield Creek Landing, and Black

A boat used for oyster dredging docked at the pier by Deep Creek Restaurant, 1998. (photo by Joan B. Machinchick)

Hole Creek to pick up melons, fruits and vegetables for Baltimore markets. The *Florence* was owned by John F. Dougherty, the grandfather of Herbert Dougherty of Magothy Bridge. Herbert recalls that the *Florence* "would come into the Magothy and pick up the hogsheads and other items for trade." They would be loaded from the landings and hauled to the nearby ports of Baltimore, Chestertown, Annapolis, Alexandria and Norfolk. Less speedy than the Baltimore Clipper, this type of schooner, the *Florence,* was a smaller, slower, rather full-bodied boat, designed for carrying cargo, freight trade, as well as passengers. Schooners such as this venerable craft were shoal-keeled, common on the Bay and used for shallow tributaries as well.[10] These craft were between forty and fifty feet in length with a jib, leg-of-mutton foresail and a large mainsail. They were round-stemmed and gaff-rigged.

Another venerable schooner, the *Nancy,* was owned by Colonel Elijah Robeson (Robinson) whose father, Oneal Robeson, had it built in the mid-1700s. Found on an old tax list of 1767, it harbored in Cattail Creek along with her *"riggin," two batteaus and some old sails.*[11] She was used to deliver the produce to Baltimore from the large farms along Old Man and Cattail Creeks, and probably the melons from what is now Sunset Knoll, Riverdale and the farms of the upper Magothy. Schooners of this type were reported to land at Dividing Creek Landing in the mid-1800s. Mrs. Renoff, from the south side of the Magothy keenly awaited her grandmother's stories of the big schooners which would load and unload vegetables and farm products from "a landing at South Ferry Point."[12] This landing became the county wharf in Anne Arundel County in the mid 1900s.

The Marley Creek Schooner, *Maine,* used for lumber-hauling, was a two-masted schooner that freighted Carolina and Virginia lumber up the bay. This boat was built in New England, and through frequent coastal trade common among Western Shore Rivers, was brought to these Western Shore waters in 1886, one of the thousands of similar vessels to be used here. The Bay waters were considered a "haven where they [schooners] were to ply under sail for many years." Robert H. Burgess informs that the *Maine* was "a handsome vessel in her unique way. Her solid, chunky appearance differed completely from the sleeker Chesapeake-built schooner . . . She had been built by shipwrights accustomed to turning out huge deepwater ships."[13]

This schooner, the *Maine,* was sighted in 1908 on the Magothy by Milton Oler, former resident and early historian of the Magothy.[14] Robert Burgess adds that like thousands of similar vessels built like this one, they were to be used with "one thought in mind—that of making a dollar."

Of course, the early lumber mills provided the *modus operandis* for the Magothy lumber-jacks. The presence of the Johnson Lumber Mill surrounding the lands of Black Hole Creek as well as many other lumber mills on Marley Creek, on points of the Patapsco as well as the Severn and South Rivers, provided the sources of chestnut and pine needed for colonizing and developing a nation which was fast emerging as the most powerful and productive in the world. Pragmatically, some of the early pleasure craft designed for carrying passengers were utilized and modified to become lumber barges. One such transformation took place on the *William Linthicum.*

In fact, lumber was brought by boat in 1932 to the Colonel Howard Schindler property at the convergence of Cockey Creek and the Magothy. Also, lumber for the "big house" on Blackhole Creek owned by the Dr. Paul Watson family was also barged. Built in 1894 at Church Creek, Maryland, the *William Linthicum,* a three-masted schooner, had a long career on the Bay. This was a lumber ram which had its work to do—the loading and unloading of logs—a natural resource which unwittingly was now beginning to be a great commodity for the building of the entire East Coast.

From the early dug-out log canoes of the Indians, graduating into pinnaces or single-masted sailing canoes, to the pungy, the skipjack and the ram—boats built with a productive, pragmatic purpose—all Western Shore boats and their owners had an integrity of purpose and a goal. Bay waters were being utilized realistically; yet at this point they were not sources of pollution because there were relatively few of them.

Magothy seniors report that their grandfathers talked of the pungies which sailed into the Magothy. Mr. Milton Fick of Cornfield Creek, whose family has been on the Magothy since the early 1800s, reminisces how his grandfather relied on the pungies to carry his vegetables as well as Mr. Henry Alfred Cook's produce over to Baltimore and even sometimes to Annapolis. Franklin B. Spriggs, the Postmaster-General at Arnold, Maryland and Harry L. Spriggs, farmers at Ulmstead Point Farms in the early 1900s, would haul peaches, tomatoes and watermelons to Forked Creek out to a two-masted bugeye which sailed to Baltimore to be sold by commission merchants on a percentage basis at the dock.[15]

Howard W. Hammerbacher of Cape Sable on the north side of the Magothy recalls the bugeyes coming into Pea-Patch Point from the city. "They would haul watermelons and beautiful peaches, produce like corn and beans and strawberries. As a little boy I would watch them come in . . ." This was done on a daily basis. At the height of each crop, an average of 1,000 baskets of tomatoes, 1,000 baskets of peaches and 3,000 watermelons were dispatched by hauling down to Forked Creek by farm wagons and ferrying by boat to the bugeye sloops.

Milton Oler, a member of the Maryland Historical Society and a team member of the first archeological dig on the Magothy in the early 1900s, documents the occurrence of particular bugeyes in the Magothy: In a letter to Colonel and Mrs. Schindler of Cockey's Creek, he states:

> I took the photo dated 1922 when some friends and I were on a cruise around
> the upper part of the Bay. The pictures of the bugeye were taken sometime in the

late 30s in the Magothy between Shoreacres and (Dutch Ship) Dobbins Island. The first photo was taken in the afternoon as she went to pick up watermelons at Spriggs farm on Olmstead Point [known as Sprigg's Landing]. The rest were taken the following morning on her return trip. I think the Bugeye was named the Edith M. Todd. *Some years later Frank Spriggs told me that the masts fell out of her while she was tied up to a wharf.*[16]

If one were to look out over Magothy waters on a misty summer morning, a vision of a bugeye glides into view with soft, gentle flap of canvas sail reaching into the next puff of wind. Perhaps it could be one of those historic boats piercing a time warp and entering the cusp of the twenty-first century. But no! It is the *Heather II*, a classic bugeye, built as a pleasure yacht in 1915, now owned by Captain Jerry Smith of Pea Patch Point on the Magothy.

Whether they are a classic original Trumpy (built by Trumpy Boatyard in Annapolis) or a refurbished double-masted bugeye schooner, the historic boats dwell among the mists and fogs of the Magothy as they swirl in the minds of senior Magothy people. The sparkle of good times runs through the river stories like silver seams along the coarse fabric of weathered sails. Everyone took time from the labor-intensive farming and lumbering to have fun. When the schooners had collected watermelons and produce, entire families would board ship and go to market where, enlivened by the harvest, they would picnic on the long docks at Baltimore's Market Place near Lombard Street. August and September were the months for watermelon festivals and homemade ice cream. These vessels helped to transform the Magothy and the upper Western Shore from a pulsating, pragmatic waterfront into a place for the pleasure of reclaiming solitude, joy, and simple fun.

Accounts by seniors of the Magothy detail how some of these Western Shore water craft operated: Mr. William G. Rothamel, a caretaker who worked with his father, William H. Rothamel, on many Magothy farms, recalls how "the pungies

Top: the bugeye Edith M. Todd *entering the Magothy in 1922. (photo by Milton Oler, courtesy of Howard W. Schindler)*
Bottom: the bugeye yacht, Heather II. *(photo courtesy of Jerry Smith)*

would carry gravel onto the landings. There would be a pulley on the mast, fastened to half a barrel. A mule would be attached to the pulley and haul its cargo half way up the beach." At that point, helpers would carry the gravel by wheelbarrows. He remembers the "bountiful produce of peaches, strawberries, corn, tomatoes, melons which were carried from landing on the rivers by old schooners to the markets." Dan Vivi, nephew of the J. Gordon Rileys, early conservationists of the Magothy, recalls Deep Creek's Landing. "There were so many skipjacks anchored in the creek, I could not get out till they left." He adds an interesting note: "The lumber-jacks would split the hickory for the eel pots we made when I was a young boy." Sometimes the boats of the Magothy were used for more macabre purposes. Rothamel recalls his dad's stories of "how the dead from the Battle of Severn Run would be taken by barge to Cockey's Creek to Linstead's Burial Ground. . . . the only consecrated ground in these parts for burial!"

Boats of the 30s and 40s

Less colorful, but more efficient power craft were developed in the late forties to perform the chores of yesterday's sailboats. Two distinctive designs, developed in this area of the Bay, were the deadrise and the Hooper Islander. The deadrise, used quite often on the Magothy, is a long narrow launch with a small house forward and a long open deck abaft. Usually from thirty-five to forty feet long, it has a shallow "V" bottom. There are two steering arrangements, a conventional wheel in the deckhouse and a vertical pivoted lever in the waist coupled to the steering cables. From the after position, one man alone can control the boat while he works his trotline or crab pots. The Hooper Islander, with its large hull sylishly designed, is more distinctive in shape, but less efficient as a working oyster-dredger. Developed at Hooper Island, she too could have been viewed in Magothy waters. With her small house built forward in the craft, and painted white, she was a beauty.

In the late thirties, forties and fifties, small launches and crabbing boats performed the working tasks of the Magothy. The *Lucy H,* a 34-foot deadrise was owned by William Hammerbacher and used for crabbing. "Crabbing was so

excellent then. We'd get fifty cents a dozen, thirty-five cents a dozen for soup crabs," notes Frank, his son. Captain John Haas owned the bayboat, *Shenoock,* which he used heavily for gill-netting and trot-lining for crabs. People of the Grachur Club talk of the *Lucy H.* also as a ferry which was used to take them from the south side of the Magothy to the north side. Other craft used as ferry launches were the *Emma I* and *Emma II,* originally owned by George Hammerbacher. In

Buy boats receiving the day's oyster harvest from skipjacks near the mouth of the Magothy River, 1969. (photo by Marion E. Warren, courtesy of Maryland State Archives)

the thirties and forties, the larger Trumpy boats made their way into the Magothy, gracious yachts, forty to fifty feet in length, pridefully slipping in and out of Magothy coves, holding parties of people on the open decks sipping mint-juleps and watching the sun set over Cypress Creek.

One of the early small pleasure sail-craft, reported by Mr. Schindler of Cockey's Creek, was a specially rigged sailboat: "Royal Brumwell had one of the first small sailboats I've seen . . . a rowboat made of cypress—an old tree mast with a pillowcase for a sail and an oar for a rudder. . . " Other small pleasure craft were the hand-made rowboats, the little skiffs, and the graceful small canoes seen running between the north and south side of the Magothy. People paddled every-where in those days between the twenties and the forties. They attended parties, held rowing contests, jousted for prizes on small craft, and held picnic rendezvous and courting sessions in quiet coves. A few of the children even rowed to school and to church! (See Chapter 4).

Shipwrecks of the Magothy

The reverse side of long slow after-noons gliding along Western Shore bays, inlets and rivers, are the treacherous, unpredictable and sometimes violent storms of these waters. Unfortunately, some of these venerable ships sank into watery graves of the Magothy. The earliest recorded ship to have sunk off the Magothy is the *Gazelle.* This steamboat of unknown type foundered and sunk off the mouth of the Magothy on June 11, 1884. The *George Lewis,* a schooner, foundered and sank on August 12, 1905, and *Laura A. Muir,* a schooner, sank on December 6, 1918. The *Maryland* was another ship which yielded to the demons of the Magothy River of quick mood reversals and shifting shoals. A steam side-wheeler, she happened to be the first steamer built for the Baltimore and Annapolis Railway Corporation and was placed on the Pocomoke River route. Unfortunately, she was burned off the Magothy River on January 22, 1915.[17]

Other boats whose graves form a part of the Magothy History are the *Edith,* a steamboat which burned off Gibson Island on October 4, 1909; the *Anna Camp,* a schooner which burned and sank on November 19, 1926, the *Quo Vadis,* a gas screw skipjack, burned and sunk on August 9, 1934 off Sillery Bay; the *Sterling Sisters*, another gas screw skipjack, sunk on April 10, 1953 off Gibson Island. On September 19, 1955, the *My Shadow Hill*, a gas screw Skipjack, burned off Mago Vista, ending the litany of bad-luck news of Magothy's old ships. Earlier documented sunken ships on the Bodkin are an old unidentified schooner ferry on October 7, 1746, an unidentified schooner on Bodkin Point on December 15, 1806, and the *Albert Sydney*, a schooner, which sank off Bodkin Point on March 12, 1888.

Captain John Haas, of Mill Creek, reports that the derelict tugboats used for building the Baltimore Light were purposefully sunk behind Gibson Island. Also, behind Dobbins Island was a place for "the boat people" to harbor during the depression. They could not afford houses, so they stayed there.

The Excursion—Renewal and Rest

Not far from Magothy waters, places to which yachts and water craft clustered for disembarking, developed into centers for recreation. A typical activity grew all over the Chesapeake—the excursion—an afternoon or a whole day of waterfront renewal and relaxation.

The institution known as "landings," provided a place for the excursion boat to disembark and to enter the universe of river-dreams. This was the world of floating on inner tubes, quietly paddling on rented row boats, eating under the picnic awnings to celebrate mild Chesapeake springs, of experiencing sweltering summers and the smooth, delicate breezes which slip into the hottest days, then to luxuriate in the cool whip of a breeze sneaking into a hazy fall river-day on the Western Shore.

Known recreational landings of the Magothy operating from 1850 to 1930 were at South Ferry Point, North Ferry Point, Cape St. Claire, and Mountain Point (Gibson Island). Beach landings at Mago Vista Beach, Royal Beach, and Magothy Beach came into high vogue in the twenties and thirties. Nearby landings such as those at Fairview Beach in Rock Creek, and at Colonial Beach, Fox Point, Jenkin's Club House at the head of Rock Creek, Stony Beach Landing, Thomas' Altoona Beach, Weedon's Beach at the head of Stony Creek—all of these were neighbors and a part of the huge complex system of recreational places for Baltimoreans and Washingtonians to visit.

Along with this recreational transformation, as landings grew into larger piers, small clubs evolved into boating centers, which later became the yacht clubs of the Chesapeake. The Maryland Yacht Club leased the area around Fairview and Rock Creek in 1945. Slips for yachts were built out into Wall Cove; a former hotel nearby served as a clubhouse; in the same manner, small yacht clubs were formed on the Magothy.

Captains of the Magothy

The Captains of the Magothy and the Western Shore rivers carry with them shared memories of nostalgic schooners, sloops, skip-jacks, pungies, buy boats, and side-winder ferries which plied Chesapeake waters. Many of the captains were descendants of the early colonial families and even civil war families, veterans of an era when the river was the primary work-center of their worlds. The collective consciousness of the draw of water and river bear their weight and their pleasure upon the minds and hearts of many.

One such person, Captain Gil Pumphrey, better known as "Captain Gil" of Fairwinds Marina at the head of Deep Creek, recalls the "old days" at Stinchcomb's Boat Yard (now Ferry Point Yacht Basin). Captain Gil or "Buddy," a descendent of the Turpins of West Virginia, an old Chesapeake Bay family, worked there at Mill Creek from 1935 to 1948. He recalls that this area in the Magothy boasted "the best pike fish in the state. . . . Also you could get plenty of yellow perch . . . so good tasting . . . in those days." He remembers that a lot of people drowned in the Magothy in the twenties, thirties, and forties, probably because they used the river more for transportation and for getting a meal. He would "take a boat up and down the area" to report or find drownings. He adds, "We worked hard, then, building and repairing boats. . . . But you couldn't work on Sundays. . . . Currently Captain Gil owns the *Fairwinds Lady,* which he charters for boating parties for rockfishing or sport fishing. Optimistically, he reports that "more rock are coming in now in masses—undersized, but in large schools. . ." He owns one of the last of the charter boats on the Magothy. The *Fairwinds Lady*, forty feet long, was preceded by the thirty-two-foot *Helen H.* "In those days from the thirties to the sixties, we caught fish all the time in droves. The water of the Magothy was blue-green and you could see the turtles down deep." He remembers one particular old house called "Magothy Manor," the home of Folger McKinsey, the famous writer and poet of the Magothy. "The beautiful house burned down," he added, "and the Magothy lost something great."

Captain Clyde McGowan of Deep Creek, former owner of "Captain Clyde's" [now turned into Deep Creek Restaurant], a well known dining and docking place for Western Shore boaters, has had a thirty-eight-year tenure as Magothy River Boat Captain. Late fall and all winter on the Magothy, one can revisit the past by peering at the five old skipjacks docked in front of the restaurant. Captain Clyde remembers the old Ogle farms on the Magothy which grew tobacco. Sadly, he recalls the demise of the ferries at Tolchester Point in 1952, but quickly regains his optimism when he discusses the rockfish comeback on the Magothy and in the Bay during 1993. He reports that the spring of '93 was a good rock season and beams when he says, "the river is cleaner now than it has been for 20 years . . . yes, I see a cleaner, clearer wake now." He adds that increased fines for raw sewage discharged in the river from boats can run up to $2,500. Captain Clyde encourages the building and use of more pumping stations, a strategy included

A skipjack docked at the pier by Deep Creek Restaurant, 1998. (photo by Joan B. Machinchick)

for the nineties in the recommendations stated in the *Magothy River Comprehensive Vessel Management Plan.*

Another renowned captain of the Magothy, Captain Nathaniel Kenney, was founder of the Junior Fleet of Gibson Island. At that time Captain Kenney used what they called "Kidboats" to initiate the children of Gibson Island into the fine art of sailing. This kind of spirit and insistence upon discipline, fun, and responsibility, so fostered by many Captains and Commodores of the Magothy, becomes the more subtle, transformative power of river life. The determination and focus at Captain Kenney's call, "Don't give up the ship!," has produced captains of fine sailing ability who have excelled not only on the Bay, but all over the world. Various students of the Captain, such as Tommy Nelson, won the first Chesapeake Bay Junior Championship. Later, Harry Primrose and Richard (Juddy) Henderson sailed their yachts across the Atlantic in 1975.[18]

A seasoned Magothy skipper, Captain Robert Joy, recalls the days of good spirits and high expectations for excellent fishing, both in Magothy waters as well as in the Bay, aboard his forty-foot charter boat, the *El Joy,* named after his wife, Elvira Lusby Joy. A waterman of Manhattan Beach, he fished mainly for the prize rockfish of the area, went out seven days a week on charters in the forties with good results and repeat business. The *El Joy* is still in the water at Cypress Marina, once a shipyard in the area; it remains an emblem of historical memory, cared for and loved as a gentle reminder of days long gone.

Captain John E. MacLeoud, known as "Mac" to river people, still owns the first yacht built by the Trumpy Boat Yard in Annapolis for the Chesapeake Bay. Built in 1947, this forty-eight-foot Annapolis design "Trumpy," named the *Mimosa,* has been lovingly renovated and cared for by Mac, who spends his full time with the boat, winter and summer, harbored now in Swan Cove under an old covered dock. He talks about the river in the era between the thirties and the fifties: "We really used the river and the beaches, back then. The women would be on the beach every afternoon. . . . Swimming in the river was the sport of the day. Why, Tudi [his late wife], and Beverly [Luper], after a long afternoon of swimming and sunning, would wait for us to come in by boat. . . . Then we'd join on board and have cocktails far into the evening." Mac recalls that even up to fifteen years ago there were only 3,300 boats on the river. " Gee. . . . Look at it now!"

The tradition of fishing excursions for pleasure and fun continues on the Magothy and all Western Shore rivers. Several Bay Captains still reside on the Magothy and take out fishing parties. They include Captain Don Brogley of Magothy Marina, Captain Bob Spore who writes for the *Baltimore Sun* on fishing topics, Captain Ronald Meadows, Captain Bob Gibson of Snow Hill and Captain John Collison. Fishing charter boats became entangled with the livelihood of these Captains, providing a challenge each day of facing the elements and becoming a part of real Bay living.

Captain Collison, Magothy fisherman for fifteen years, recalls longingly the days when the river was clear, and the seaweed high. He would take out the *Mary Emma I* and *Mary Emma II*, Chesapeake Bay deadrises, with great success. His hopes are high now that the days of sport fishing will return. Captain Collison reports that in the spring of 1993, the surge of rockfish came in with catches up to thirty-six inches long. Captain Bob Gibson, now living in Snowhill, recalls the days of haul-seining for rockfish off Mountain Point, as it was called in the forties. He claims, "We would back a wagon onto a level place to haul mounds of rockfish to Baltimore."

A commercial crabber leaving the north shore early on a summer morning.
(photo by author)

Yacht Clubs and Recreational Boating Clubs

Along with the increasing private ownership of boats in the late 30s and 40s, harbors and clubs were developed for centralizing and mobilizing the myriad activities connected with boating. Yacht clubs such as *The Gibson Island Yacht Squadron*, the *Potapskut Sailing Association*, and associations connected with the river, such as the *Magothy River Sailing Association* gradually developed as sources of commu-

Yachts at the pier and moorings at Potapskut Sailing Association on Blackhole Creek. (photo by author)

nity camaraderie, fostering keen competition among boaters. Sailing regattas, races, cruises, and educational opportunities for young upcoming generations of boaters now flourish on the Magothy.

First commodore of the Potapskut Sailing Association (P.S.A.), Marshall Duer, remembers the early days of the Association. Although the club was formed by John Rogers at Rock Creek, with room there for about ten or twelve boats, it moved to Black Hole Creek in 1946 and the clubhouse was built in 1947. Fostering camaraderie and family fun, proficiency in sailing and yachting, this early institution of the Magothy still continues in its strong traditions of educating and engendering its people, both young and old, in the traditions of Chesapeake boating. Potapskut Sailing Association sponsors lovely small regattas, races, and youth competitions. It started the early Delta class and has a concentration of Flying Scotts, Force Fives, and the little El Toros. Little Cedar Island perches near

Spinnaker training at the Potapskut Sailing Association junior summer sailing program (photo by author)

the mouth of the cove and acts as a buffer for it. Although most of the giant cedar trees are gone, it houses the area's resident ospreys and great blue heron, and serves as a nesting place for the bufflehead and mallards.

The Magothy River Sailing Association [M.R.S.A.] perpetuates the rigor, friendship, and skill-building usually associated with teaching the youth of the Magothy to sail. Included in their activities are a summer sailing school for area youth, with much junior day-sailing activity, cruising handicap racing and frequent unorganized individual river sailing.

A prominent writer and sailor, Richard Henderson of Gibson Island, relates the history of The Gibson Island Yacht Squadron, still carrying on its traditions. In "A Brief History of the Gibson Island Yacht Squadron," Henderson writes:

> *The present Gibson Island Yacht Squadron elected its first Commodore, Dr. Hugh Young, in 1932. Prior to that date, yachting activities were managed by the*

Star Fleet, Gibson Island, 1938. Left to right: Willis Margus, _____, Oliver Reeder, Randy Fisher, Ralph Bulgeano, Jake Rogers, Payne Thomas, Meluin Grosvenor, David Dunigan, Marge Hughson, Jim Wolfe, Veasy Graycroft, Dick Orrick, _____, Bobby Miller, Hank Strong, Eddie Novak, Tommy Lee, Helen Grosvenor, _____, Walter Hughson, Nancy Wolfe. (photo courtesy of Gibson Island Historical Society)

Water Committee of the Gibson Island Club. Early projects included purchasing a fleet of one-design boats known as the Fisher's Island Class and in 1923 organizing the Chesapeake Bay's first Star Class Fleet. Under the leadership of such colorful sailors as J. Rulon Miller, Nathaniel "Cap" Kenney, Sifford Pearce, and later Harold Smith the fleet grew to 26 boats and it gained some national respect when Miller won the Lipton Cup in 1926. But the greatest victory for Gibson Island's "Rainbow Fleet" (so called because every early boat was a different color) came in 1929 when Graham and Lowndes Johnson won the Star Internationals in 1930 and again in 1951. Another yacht squadron member, James Allsopp, took the world title when he won the Internationals in 1976. Carrying on with the Star boat tradition, Gibson Island continues to host the popular Miller Series held annually in part to memorialize Rulon Miller who was called by Yachting *magazine, "The*

LJ-22s of Gibson Island. (photos courtesy of Gibson Island Historical Society)

father of yachting at Gibson Island." In 1990, Gibson Island hosted the J-22 World Championship Regatta.

• • •

The development of the big boat cruising fleet did not lag far behind, for in l925 Gibson Island's harbor was graced by Miller's schooner Harpon, *The Henderson brothers' yawl* Vega, *Sam Thomsen's bugeye* Applejack, *and Lawrence Bailliere's skipjack* Pelican. *The Club sponsored an ocean race from Cape May to Gibson Island in l927 and a longer race from New London to Gibson Island two years later. . . . In the latter event three new sister yawls belonging to members William Henderson, Ellis Ellicott, and Este Fisher finished within a space of 15 minutes. Other New London to Gibson Island races were held in 1933 and 1937, but later the Annapolis Yacht Club took over running the event, and now it has become the* Annapolis-Newport Race. *A prominent ocean racing member of the early period was William McMillan whose famous schooner,* Water Gypsy, *sailed in the 1931 Transatlantic and Fastnet races and did exceeding well in the 1932 and 1934 Bermuda Races. During World War II, a number of Gibson Island yachts were volunteered to serve with the "Corsair Fleet" on Atlantic coast anti-submarine patrol. Corrin Strong's cutter* Narada, *was sunk off Cape Henry while on that particular duty. For many years the Gibson Island Yacht Squadron has sponsored four major Chesapeake Bay Yacht Racing Association events annually. The Narada Trophy is the coveted prize for these events. The high-point scoring Yacht Squadron skipper in these events wins the coveted Narada Trophy given by Commodore Strong in memory of his yacht. . . .*

• • •

The Junior sailing program known as the Junior Fleet . . . was organized in 1924 by Cap Kenney with six active members who sailed various small boats such as Kidboats, Barnegat Sneakboxes and later LJs (designed especially for Gibson Island by Lownedes Johnson), Comets, and Penguins. Today the program supports fifty children sailing Optimists, Lasers and 420s. The Juniors race in Chesapeake Bay Yacht Racing Association regattas which draw young people from the entire Bay area.This program is capped off at the season's end with a gala awards banquet. Years ago Cap Kenney insisted that all award winners, including even the six year olds, give a little acceptance speech. This provided a lot of fun for all but the poor award winners. . . .[19]

The advent of the original Yacht Clubs and River Associations led to the proliferation of neighborhood docks. In the 1950s and 1960s, small boating docks began to house their community boats. As people moved to the river's edge more permanently, boat ownership increased. The docks gradually were made larger to harbor the influx of personal water craft. The transition of the Magothy as a working river to a recreational river was complete by the mid-fifties.

The junior fleet of the Cape St. Claire Yacht Club sail training program, conducted by the Chesapeake Bay Yacht Racing Association, 1993. Right: setting out from the Lake Claire beach (Fairwinds Marina in background); bottom left: sailing practice in light winds, under the direction and watchful eye of an instructor in a powerboat; center: stepping masts on the fleet of 420s at the beginning of the season; lower right: many hands make light work as the students launch one of the boats. (photos by Joan B. Machinchick)

Recreational boating on the Magothy. Top:"Reelentless" ready for a fishing expedition (left to right: first mate, Rachel Taylor, Captain Timothy Rinehart and Robert Taylor); right: a pair of early morning scullers. (photos by author)

Many communities along the Magothy continue to foster the spirit of sail and water sports through their frequent inter-club regattas, sailing schools of instruction, and club sponsored in-class navigation such as the Whitehurst Club, the Cape Arthur Community Club and the Cape St. Claire Yacht Club. The sailing school of the Potapskut Sailing Association [PSA] brings the Juniors all the way from Seaman to Racing Skipper throughout consecutive summer programs with an intense summer camp. Races out of Blackhole Creek are held during weekday evenings, and lovely picnic suppers follow at the club, sponsored by the mothers of the group.

Wednesday nights on the Magothy are the special race nights with all classes from all yachting centers coming out for the competition. One gazes out to a scene of sailboats dancing in the wind, sporting a gala of multi-colored spinnakers. All classes of boats, from various clubs come out in the spirit of River-Sail. Of course, there are also the quiet races with flat, lazy sails, floating on calm waters. But, fast or slow—no matter what—the Wednesday night races continue into the millenium.

1.   Robert Burgess, *This Was Chesapeake Bay,* (Cambridge, MD: Tidewater Publishers, 1963), p. ix.

2.   Ibid. p. 107.

3.   Carvel Hall Blair and Willits Dyer Ansel, *Chesapeake Bay Notes and Sketches,* (Cambridge, MD: Tidewater Publishers, 1970), pp. 129-136.

4.   *Maryland Living,* (July 7, 1968), p. 3.

5.   R. H. Burgess, pp. 89, 90.

6.   Oral history, reported by Mrs. Catherine Helm, Nov. 3, 1995.

7.   R. H. Burgess, p. 89.

8.   William G. Rothamel, oral history account, as was reported to him by his father William H. Rothamel in 1901 [account related to author in June, 1993].

9.   Tom Horton, *The New York Times Magazine,* (June 13, 1993), pp. 32-35. [All specific information on dredging is obtained from this article.].

10. R. H. Burgess, *Chesapeake Sailing Craft, Part I* (Cambridge, MD: Tidewater Publishers, 1975), p. 104.

11. Dr. Stephen Hittle, in tax records of Colonel Elijah Roboson, 1767.

12. Mrs. Paul Renoff, as oral history to author (June, 1983), reporting of her grandmother's records, 1883.

13. R. H. Burgess, *Chesapeake Sailing Craft,* p. 127.

14. Milton T. Oler, in letter to Colonel Schindler, May 29, 2987. reported to author, June, 1993.

15. Franklin B. Spriggs, in a letter entitled "To Whom it May Concern," copies 2/14/67.

16. Letter, M. Oler to Howard Schindler and Mrs. Schindler, May 29, 1987.

17. Donald G. Shomette,*Maritime Disasters on Chesapeake Bay and its Tributaries, 1608-1978,* (Centreville, MD: Tidewater Publishers, 1982), p. 267.

18. Louisa B. Reynolds, *Hearsay,* p. 17.

19. Gibson Island Yacht Squadron, 1994 Handbook, Gibson Island, Maryland. [The history which I use is taked from the "Foreword" of the handbook, entitled, "A Brief History of the Gibson Island Yacht Squadron," written by Richard Henderson.]

CHAPTER 9

I've Heard Tell

The stories which follow are told by Magothy River people in their own words. Some are shaped tall; others small. Some speak quietly; others can be boisterous. All of them, however, are a part of the richness of Magothy lore.

"Broad Neck Hundred" — (Vol. 9, No. 1, Winter 1975,1976), Bob Johnson, ed.[1]

Captain Clyde's tavern collects the people and the stories that make up much of the recent history of Deep Creek. Bob Acord, who started coming down to the creek from Baltimore 30 years ago to go pike and yellow perch fishing, remembers when R. L. Baker "ran a real small place" there. Some of the old-timers remember when "pigs and chickens used to walk through here." Then Bill Becker owned it, and now Brenda and Clyde McGowan own it.

• • •

Rudy Lerp, Sr. has been coming down to the Creek since '32. Waterfront lots were selling for $400 in '32. . . "Years ago the oyster boats used to come in here—oysters 50 cents a barrel—they'd come in to get water at the spring in the late 30s, and others came here for harbor."

• • •

Rudy Lerp Jr. tells the best stories. If you're going over to Clyde's for a draft and some crab soup, and Rudy, Jr. is there, ask him about Mary's nickname and ask him about the woman who used to sober up by jumping drunk into the water and floating on her back in the creek unconscious all night. "You never could be sure. You might find her floating asleep under your pier Sunday morning."

• • •

A lot of fishermen spend time at Clyde's. . . . Be prepared for a lie or two. A friend of Otis Meadows puts it a little stronger, "Mr. Otis and I have been coming here three years now and all I ever hear is lies. But what I'm going to tell you now is the gospel truth. You can ask Bill Morris about it. He was with me. It was about a half an hour after sunrise toward the end of April this year (1975). Bill and I were near the navigable head of the creek in my canoe, sitting still, enjoying the peace of nature's early morning way. The water surface was as smooth as glass. Suddenly near the shore in a cove we saw the water begin to ripple. It looked as if a short, thick log were rolling around on its own, disturbing the water. We paddled closer. How does a log roll itself? As we approached it, we both remember feeling more and more confused as to what it could be. Then we were right on top of two gigantic snapping turtles—mating. Make a circle with your arms and touch your fingers. That's how big their shells were. They were as surprised by us as we were by them. I'll never forget how that look on the face of that top turtle changed from indignation to panic as he bent his long neck around to see what on God's earth was so crudely interfering with his private life."

Later at Clyde's, we told Luke about it. "Oh Yeah," he said, "There's turtles up there all right." Then he told us how one of the women on the creek makes turtle soup. "First you have to kill the turtle. You put a gaffing hook in its mouth and pull the head and neck out—it'll come out about a foot—cut it off, then hang the carcass up by the tail to drain the blood out. When you take the gaffing hook out of the mouth be sure to throw that head far away or bury it, because those jaws can still bite you bad until after sundown." [It's been said that the heart keeps beating for two days.]

Items from St. Margarets *– December 29th, 1886*

Mrs. Ridout remembers when there was but a simple oyster shell road into Annapolis. A mill trough from the stream stood at the head of the Little Magothy running fresh water

MY RIVER SPEAKS

to the Ridout farm [St. Margaret's] where this wild intersection stands today. [The old Route 50 and Cape St. Claire Road intersection]

• • •

This neighborhood is and has been exceedingly lively. The people here are having a genuine good time. Surprise parties are quite numerous and very pleasant. There will be a party at J.J. Tate's (South side of Magothy) on the 20th of Dec. and another on the 31st of Dec. at the residence of James Ridout. A large crowd and a grand sociable time is expected!

• • •

Most of the farms have filled their ice houses. Game is plentiful. . .

The Mysterious Grave Opened – January 14th, 1887

Yesterday, Justice Phillip Pettibone acting under the instructions of the State's Attorney summoned the following jury of inquest: Henry Tydings, foreman; A.A. Stinchcomb, Frank Ridout, H. S. Ridout, F. Simon, Jas. Warren, John Stallings, E. Tydings, T. Y. Tolson, and Wm. Tolson and proceeded to the shore of Mr. Wm. Stinchcomb on Magothy River where was reported to be two mysterious graves. Instead of two, only one was found and there was no placard as has been reported over the grave with the precaution, "small pox" upon it or anything else to mark the grave. The grave was near the river shore. . . When the body was reached, it was found wrapped in an old army blanket and clad in a coarse under shirt and drawers. . . . a long bruise was found across the breast indicating that the deceased had been struck by the main boom of a vessel or by a blow from a heavy club. . . . The jury rendered a verdict that the deceased came to his death by some cause unknown to them but were of the opinion that the deceased had been fouly dealt with by some dredge boat captain and his body taken ashore and buried for concealment. The matter will be thoroughly investigated by the authorities. The body was put into a plain coffin and buried on the shore near where it was found. [This practice, called "paying off by the main boom," was common among some unscrupulous oyster dredge captains during the oyster wars of the last century. After a season of oystering, the skipper would jibe while the unsuspecting crew member was on deck, killing him with a blow from the main boom, thus avoiding paying the deck hand for his winter's work.]

A Ramble Through Peach Orchards – *Third District (1885)*

Reader: Do you love to make short journeys? Have you ever visited Egypt—that country just across the Severn River—better known as Broad Neck? But why the Annapolitans call us Egyptians, we are at a loss to comprehend. We do not build pyramids, we may, perhaps, have a few mummies, nor do we cover up and try to hide the lovely faces of our beautiful women. Then why do they call us Egyptians? A sweet school girl, leaning on my shoulder as I write, perhaps answers the question: "Is not Egypt just across from Arabia?" [This is the only explanation given surrounding the mysterious name, "Egypt" for Magothy's south side.]. . . . Well, well, come along, we don't care what they call us.

• • •

Let us turn off here to the left and go down on the Magothy flats, and take a ramble through some of the peach orchards. . . . This is the beginning of Mr. H. A. Tydings's orchard. Look what a strange trade mark is on these boxes. It is a hat—what has a hat got to do with peaches? . . . Why, can't you see, the initials of his name spell hat. . . . Yes, yes, so they do; but just look at the peaches on the ground–did you ever see anything like it? What a waste! Why it is enough to give the poor man the "indigo fiends." We shall hardly hear glad tidings this afternoon. Hush! hush! there come HAT now through the trees. . . . Good afternoon, Mr. Tydings, what in the world is the matter with your peaches, that they are dropping from the trees in such large numbers? . . . I cannot tell you, sir. I judge there are at least 2,000 boxes on the ground rotting; but it don't make much difference, they hardly pay to ship them. . . . First, the trees were too full, consequently the fruit was very small; and then again, we had so much rain it destroyed the flavor of the fruit, so much so it was hardly fit for table use. . . . Secondly, the packers are putting up comparatively few peaches on account of the condition of labor. They know not what moment a strike may be upon them, therefore they have made but few contracts.

Mr. Tydings has about seven thousand bearing trees and three thousand more to set out this fall. He has shipped three thousand boxes and has more to ship. His trees are young and thriving. Everything about his place shows brain as well as muscle. The farm is situated on the bay near the mouth of the Magothy River.

Winter Sports in Old Egypt – *January 6th, 1887*

. . . *On Saturday, New Year's night, the residence of Mrs. S.H. Anderson was visited by a large party of young people in the neighborhood [St. Margaret's] and taken by surprise and a pleasant time spent.*

• • •

Skating parties have also been formed and on Mon. afternoon, a number of ladies and gentlemen started from the residence of Mr. S. H. Anderson for the creek near by when several hours were spent in this beautiful exhilarating sport. . . .

• • •

On Tuesday night a hop was given at the residence of Mr. O. Pettibone when the young folks tripped it on the light fantastic until a later hour. If there is any other section of the county where more pleasure and enjoyment abounds at this season of the year, we would like to hear from it.

Mencken, Beer, Music on a Waterfront Farm – *Mary McKinsey Ridout*[2]

My father (Folger McKinsey) was a friend and lifelong admirer of Walt Whitman, but he also greatly admired and respected H. L. Mencken, with whom he worked for many years at "The Sun" and knew socially when both were members of the famous Saturday Night Club. . . . [He] invited members of the club to outings at our property on the Magothy River. . . . The "place," as Mr. Mencken called it, was a 500-acre farm my father bought soon after he started working at The Sun in 1906. . . . My father wanted a farm, though, and as soon as he had enough money saved for a down payment, he bought the one on the Magothy. He paid $8,000 for the land and six miles of waterfront! My brother Jamie just sold the last waterfront lot for almost a hundred times the amount my father paid for the entire farm. My father never farmed the land himself. He had a tenant farmer who did it. But he loved to walk the land, and many of his columns in "The Sun" were about things he saw on his walks—the first robin of spring, wild blueberries growing on a hill, a summer storm. . . . He enjoyed catching and steaming crabs and he absolutely loved growing his own lima beans. . . . He considered the lima bean "the king of all vegetables" and fried chicken, pot roast and peach pie "among the finest Maryland dishes." That, in fact, is usually what we served the members of the Saturday Night Club on their *outings to the farm—fried chicken, corn pudding, fresh lima beans and either peach or pumpkin pie, all prepared by my mother.*

• • •

The men used to come out on Sunday. My father would drive the mile or so to Robinson's Station in Severna Park and meet their train and drive them back to the farm in a farm wagon. He always had a new zinc tub on the lawn filled with ice and bottles of beer. They would sit and talk and drink beer and eventually they would get their instruments out and start playing. We used to bring the piano outside on a tile patio for Mr. Mencken to play. I always thought he was a very good piano player. . . . We loved listening to them while we were cooking. They played classical music until we served dinner, usually around mid-afternoon, and then they sat around and talked and drank more beer or wandered down to the river and sat by the wharf. They would all be a little tight when it was over. Some time in the late afternoon or early evening, my father would load them in the farm wagon and drive them to the station in time to catch the train back to Baltimore. . . . They were always properly dressed when they arrived, but by the time they left many of them had their ties off and their coats slung over their arms.

• • •

The members of the Saturday Night Club gradually stopped coming out to the farm a few years after my father's 50th birthday in 1916, although I believe they continued to play together into the 1940s.

The Turtle Race: a Day of Reckoning on Blackhole Creek
— by Spencer Rowe[3]

I don't know how many people have ever seen a turtle race. I suppose they are not very common any more, but when I was growing up on Blackhole Creek, turtle racing was an important part of my life, and I was a witness, at the age of 10, to perhaps the most amazing turtle race of all time. . . . It's funny how one event in a day can make us remember the detail of the whole day. That summer's picnic is clear to me still. It was held as usual on a farm that overlooked the mile-wide Magothy River. . . . It was a windy day, and the breeze came off the river to spin the freshly-cut grass into little eddies that swirled all about us. I remember how the wind shook the crab and beer tents, and how it carried the laughter of the adults across the whole wide field. . . . To a child of nine it was a magical sort of day that reminded me of the old English fairs I had seen in the movies. I could imag-

ine jugglers wandering through the crowd. I could almost hear the fanfare of trumpets and see knights jousting in the distance. . . . [of the race:] One of the great things about turtle races was how much time they took and how much time there was to cheer and scream and plead. In all past races the lead changed dozens of times and most people thought their turtles, at some point in the race, had a chance. . . . But now none of this was true. This was not even a race. It was a blowout, a blitzkrieg. . . . That little turtle of Brian's [the author's brother] went into action the instant he saw daylight. I don't know how his little legs got him so high off the ground. His head and neck pointed straight ahead, and as he took off, his long tail streamed aft. He never hesitated. He never looked left; he never looked right. He never zig-zagged and he never stopped. . . . He crossed the line, flew across a patch of grass and disappeared into the woods before any of us could take a second breath. Nobody moved. We stood there, mouths open, dumb-founded, staring at the place where he entered the woods. It was the quickest turtle race you could ever imagine. . . . Brian nodded, "I won, I won. . . ." Something came over me. "Oh, shut up," I snarled. I stalked away but he kept on. . . . "Nah, nah, nah-nah. . . You think you know everything, but you don't know anything. . . ." He added, "it was your arrogance that hurt you." I am still afflicted with a large dose of that same arrogance, but now, when I find myself being narrow-minded and smug, I often hear my brother's sing-songy voice echoing over the decades. . . . I guess most people learn the important lessons of life in church or in school or in the home, but my church was Black Hole Creek and my teacher, on that day, was a little turtle.

Beach Walking *– reported by Ann Cravens of Magothy Beach*

Back in the 50s and 60s, we did a lot of beach walking from the shores of Magothy Beach to Cockey's Creek looking for tadpoles and snakes across the marshes. We were always afraid of Mrs. Shindler who always shouted at us because she was afraid we would fall and drown. One day when we were near her house, an alligator, two feet long slithered near the shore. . . were we scared! Then it disappeared into the marshes, never to be seen again. Later, we found that a pet alligator had escaped from a neighbor's house from a community back of Magothy Beach.

While walking the beaches at Mago Vista, I can remember the curly-headed rams running through the briars there behind the beach. . . .

A human "totem pole" of friends at Camp Milbur in 1930. (photo by John Gass)

While on the beach near Dougherty's Bridge [Magothy Bridge], we'd throw in a line to catch giant carp there. . . also to swim from the shores of Magothy Beach to the store called "Towne Hall" [Riverdale]. . . . How great a cold soda tasted and the ice-cream bars were so smoooth! There [by Riverdale] were big old 'sunny holes' [for catching sun-fish]. . . . We could lean over with an old rag and catch 'em.

Of Civil War Cannonballs – reported by Pamela Drain

At the end of Cattail Creek, several muskets and cannonballs which date back to the Civil War were found there by a man named McNamara. . . . Our family used to own 600 acres around the Laurel Acres area and parts of Camp Whippoorwill and the arrowheading near the shores was spectacular. We found pottery shards and pipes and our shelves are loaded with arrowheads. Of course, now our children arrowhead with us, and the "points" are few and far between.

Of the Little Emma – reported by William Howard

We had happy summer days coming over to the Magothy from Baltimore on the W.B.A. Railroad, getting off at Jones Station and walking to Dividing Creek Landing. . . When I took The Little Emma *over—a launch named after Fred Hammerbacher's wife, I thought I was in heaven, gliding along that clear, green river. There were few roads so the launches and the railroad would get us around.*

Oh Where, Oh Where Have the Bloomer Girls Gone?
– reported by Gail R. Blaisdell[4]

Singing camp songs around a flickering fire, eating hamburgers cooked on buddy-burners, and making sit-upons in crafts class are as much of a tradition at Girl Scout Camp today [1968] as they were when girls wore bloomers and middie blouses. Time has passsed at Camp Whippoorwill, a building project of a hand-carved totem pole has become a landmark and the trees have grown and more darkly shaded on the 19-acre camp on the Magothy River–but the thrill of camping and the spirit of scouting has not been altered since the Girl Scout camp was started in 1928.

• • •

The camp uniform of the late 20s consisted of bloomers (a black pair for formal dress), a white middie blouse, a black tie, knee stockings and low-heeled shoes with rounded toes.

The rules stipulated that short socks were not allowed at camp and that no silk stockings were to be brought. Bathing suits of the two-piece variety were in order and long pants did not appear on the list of items for campers. . .

• • •

When the Girl Scouts took over the area, they too were able to sit on the porch of the handsome farmhouse [Captain Robinson's old farmhouse high on a hill] and watch the river traffic. But in 1939, the Girl Scout "Leaders Club" held its annual meeting at camp and the roof of the farmhouse caught fire, and despite a strong bucket brigade, the majestic farmhouse burned flat.

• • •

The colorful totem pole at Camp Whipporwill [a replica still stands] was made in the summers of 1934 and 1935. Two senior girls worked daily on the once naked log which now stands on a bluff near the large campfire circle at the camp. The old chestnut tree tells the story of camp activities from the beginning.

Starting from the top, the trefoil signifies that the camp is of the Girl Scouts. The pine tree represents the junior unit which is still called, "Peter Pan's Pines." Robin Hood's horn represents the "Robin Hood Unit" which was in Sherwood Forest and is now known as "Shernano." The skull and crossbones is a symbol of the seniors "Treasure Island," now "Holly Hill." A profile of an Indian signifies the pioneer unit where the girls lived a primitive session in Adirondack tents and cooked all their meals out in the open. The chestnut leaf stands for the nature program while the bowl tells the story of the arts and crafts done at camp. Clay used for pottery is still taken from the banks of the Magothy. The crossed tennis rackets recognize sports and games and the carved fish reminds girls of the waterfront. The final symbol, the sunset, shows the flight of a wild goose into the setting sun and wishes "Peace and Goodwill."

Camp Whippoorwill Reunion
– from an article in the "Baltimore Sun", October 1, 1995

"I was just absolutely moved. I remembered every smell, every texture, every kind of tree," said Jackie Anderson Mattfeld, 70, upon seeing Camp Whippoorwill again. Ms. Mattfeld was president of Barnard College from 1975 to 1981 and now teaches at Northwestern Illinois University in Chicago.

"I really believe that being at this camp was the place where I felt most completely myself," Ms. Mattfeld said. "We found soul mates here—other young women in love with the outdoors." The former Girl Scouts indulged in two favorite camp activities—eating and talking.

The Old Log Cabin – reported by Sue Miller[5]

William H. Rothamel, Lake Shore's "Grandpa Moses" paints what has brought him the most pleasure in his full 93 years—the country and the water. . . The Magothy River. . . has played an important part in Rothamel's life. On Pea Patch Point, a promontory overlooking the Magothy. . . he built a three-story 17-room log house reputed to be one of the largest of its kind east of the Mississippi River. . . He built the house during the winters of 1920, 1921 with just a few tools. . . the logs were of the Anne Arundel County bull pine variety. The famous log cabin started out to be a play house, but Dr. and Mrs. Guy L. Hunner [who later bought the house] turn[ed] it into their home. [The hand-hewn log house still stands as a proud testament to the "hard work and love of riverfront of Mr. Rothamel.]

Of the Old Magothy Bridge – reported by Colonel Howard Schindler

The old Magothy Bridge was about one and a half miles from our summer cabin. When I was a small boy, we'd come to the Magothy from Baltimore, take off our shoes and never put them on again until fall. Of course, we stayed the whole summer. When we heard the planks rattling on the bridge with its old steel framework, we would say, "So and so" is on their way. After we heard the sound we knew that it would take one half hour to get to our cabin [Cockey's Creek]. It was an event to have people come over. . . There used to be an island near the Magothy Bridge called Hale's Island. It has now disappeared. . . The Johnson family farm used to be near the Magothy Bridge. The original deed to the farm read, "no negro or oriental could live there, but could be hired as day workers. . ." We had one of the first hunting lodges on the Magothy. Hunting was big back in the early twenties, and those shacks seemed like the cat's meow to be able to be quiet in them and to get away from it all. [The lodge is now a part of their living room]. . . I remember when Mountain Road was a single file dirt road and Magothy Beach Road, an old oyster road. . . We'd park the old Franklin and had to walk through the woods to the lodge. . . . There were no roads on the north side of the Magothy in the early twenties. . . . We paddled everywhere, especially loved paddling to the Grachur Club. By 1923 the large farms began to break up, and more people bought land to come to the Magothy shores.

Ferry Point Yacht Basin – reported by Mrs. M. Warren

In 1908 there were only three boats in the original boat yard at Ferry Point Yacht Basin. The triangle there, in front of the yard, was planted in watermelons. The Ogles owned much of the land around the original South Ferry Point. . . Our Magothy was known for its safe harbors.

Cape Sable – reported by Howard William Hammerbacher

My grandfather had the launch, The **Little Emma**, named after my grandmother. It would be used to pick up people on the other side [south side of Magothy], to take them to Grachur or to camps on the north side here. . . I remember that before 1938, only trot lines were used for crabbing. Crab traps were invented by a man in Harryhogan, Virginia. The crabbing was so good. How we'd haul 'em in. We'd get 50 cents a dozen for the jumbos and 35 cents a dozen for the soup crabs. One day when we were crabbing early in the morning, we heard a thump, thump against the boat—scared us silly—The small motor we had, bumped into a huge clump of bananas probably from some boat off the bay . . . I also remember the high tide of 1933 and all the docks floating away. What damage the hurricane did to the old Mago Vista Beach Club! Some people's summer "shacks" just blew to pieces . . . Our boat, the **Lucy H.** was a 34-foot deadrise which we used for trot lining . . . When we first came here in the early twenties, we'd get well water from Natalie Leach. There were very few dug wells because of lack of equipment. . . There was an old Electrical Plant at Chest Neck Point in 1923. We'd call it the "Plant," and it held 16 batteries of 2 volts each.

• • •

There used to be back-ups for two and one-half hours at Lippin's Corner [Old Annapolis Blvd. and Mountain Road]. There was a tavern there, and people would get out of their model "T's" and have a few while they had to wait. . . . the roads were abominable. . . dirt and shell. . . and the cars slow. But they all made it to the river, sometimes stopping at the bridge [Magothy Bridge] for a swim. Everybody had bathhouses back then.

Senior Counselors at Camp Milbur, 1930. Above: Frederick Kircher sails in front of the camp; below:Frederick Kircher and John Gass. (photos courtesy of John Gass)

The Watermelon Jump at Mago Vista – told by Eileen Schaeffer

A lot of the fellows would do a watermelon jump from the high dive at Mago Vista just to get all the people wet who would be near the railing which edged the pier. They'd lean over the railing to look at fish and the guys would do a cannonball off the dive. My, would they get splashed–all in their picnic finery.

• • •

The life-guards at Mago Vista were really kinda' cute. We'd all love to take swimming lessons there. When you could swim from one side of the river to the other, then you really "made it. . ."

• • •

Sometimes the Maryland Yacht Club would rendezvous at Mago Vista and when we were out in our canoes, all we had to do was to wave the end of a rope and we'd get a tow home.

• • •

I remember the fire at Mago-Vista. The firemen went to the fire in rowboats from the B. and A. Boulevard. They think it was electrical, coming from the big ball of mirrors in the middle of the dance floor, catching the crepe paper on fire, which dangled from the center of the ball.

First Date on the Magothy – told by Mrs. Paul Renoff

My husband and I had our first date on a rowboat on the Magothy. The full August moon was out and you could hear the music floating in the air from Mago Vista. We rowed over to the Bittisen's rental house on North Ferry Point. It used to be right near the water, but they had it moved because the kitchen looked right into a hill. . . But that was a special time back then (1930s). The river was alive with lots of paddlers. It was the real place to be. That night I knew I was going to marry him [Paul Renoff] and live on this river. . . . Nothing like it.

I Was Never Anywhere Else – told by Beverly Luper

In the early 1900s my parents and their friends journeyed to the south side of the Magothy where they were picked up in a launch by Jake Steedman. They vacationed in a two room cottage on Steedman Point owned by George Yost and Annie Steedman Yost.

Girls on one side and boys on another! Then when I was a small child, my parents rent-ed a cottage there every summer and later built a place next to the point. It is here that I have my happiest childhood memories of close friends, swimming, paddling, and picking huckleberries. All summer I was never anywhere else. Later, my husband and I moved to his parent's home on Eagle Hill all year round.

Hide-and-Go-Seek at Camp Milbur — told by Mrs. Evelyn Kansler Gass

We girls used to play hide-and-go-seek on weekends—we had a lot of fun with games back then (1920s when the girls would be invited to the camp for ethe entire weekend). We'd hide in the woods around the camp which was about twenty-six acres of places to get away from the boys. One time we nearly fooled them. We had our bathing suits on under our clothes and we swam out fifty yards to a swim ramp where we hid around the back side of the platform. It was a very long time before those boys actually found us . . . that was a good joke on them since they usually found us right away. . . .

• • •

I remember those long swims in those days. . . . We swam for miles. . . . Once we were out on the swim raft, we'd have the boys scoop the sea nettles out of the water with a crab net before we plunged in.

Beach beauties at Camp Milbur in 1930. (photo by John Gass)

The Railroad Tracks in the Middle of the Magothy
— told by Oliver Snyder, III

The Waterbury Inn on East Cockey's Creek used to be a grocery store at first, selling vittles to boaters who needed supplies and later sold meats and produce as neighborhoods sprung up around it. My dad bought the inn in the 1960s. . . . Here, the locals come and tell the stories about the railroad tracks of Magothy Beach and how the short-line used to haul produce from the farms on this side to the other side. [apparently from the Magothy side to the Severna Park side where it could be sent to Baltimore or Annapolis.] Peaches were big on this side of the river for some reason. . . I guess the open lands and mild cli-mate. . . . I remember when one small group of people came here from the old dirt road which is now the Ritchie Highway and they asked to see the "Indians." "What Indians," I asked. they said, "We came all the way from Baltimore to see 'Indian Village' and the artifacts there." We had a lot of laughs over our beer since all we could see there were cot-tages and small houses. . . .

Royal Exhibit at the Smithsonian
— exerpt from the "Baltimore Sun," June 12, 1972

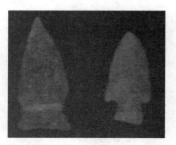

A pair of arrowheads presented to Queen Elizabeth by Governor McKeldin in 1959 and loaned by her to The Smithsonian Institution for exhibit in 1972.

Queen Elizabeth II of England is lending royal memorabilia from her own collection to the Smithonian's National Museum of History and Technology for an exhibit called "Silver Jubilee." [The Exhibit] shows how members of the royal family have interacted, at first with early American settlers and later with inventors and presidents. . . . In 1957 Governor [Millard] Tawes presented these [picture of artifacts shown] arrowheads to Queen Elizabeth. . . . the smaller [one] is from an Indian village site on the Magothy near Annapolis. . . .

Waterfront Property for Sale . . . of the Clear, Green Magothy
— told by William H. Rothamel

On the north side of the Magothy the Swift Packing Company sold large parcels of land [in the early 1920s] for between 50 cents to $2 per acre. The country was wild and not easy to get to. . . . Before the Alleghenies took shape, there was a mountain range in the area. Big rocks are still left at Lake Shore Volunteer and the crystal rocks show that they were in existence before the Alleghenies formed. That's why Pasadena means passage between the mountains. . . . In the Magothy during the early twenties you could see eight feet down and there was a lot of seaweed. . . . I remember that William Hammerbacher used to run a launch between sides of the Magothy and used a foghorn to announce his departure and arrival. . . In the winter we used to cut ice off the cove at Bittisen's at North Ferry Point and use the ice house near the cove where the Taylors live now.

Babe Ruth Lived Here *— told by Phil Beigel*

Babe Ruth's family had a summer home behind Jeff's property [area near Camp Whippoorwill and the Grachur Club at the conjunction of Cockey's Creek and the Magothy.] This was their place to cool off from the city and the famous guy was just a kid then. . . . We haven't found any baseballs, though. . . .

Farmhouse—Complete with Ghosts – told by Peg Howard

Our house [at Persimmon Point] was advertised as "Old Farm House complete with ghosts." We laughed and bought the house anyway, but the previous owners verified that there were ghosts which roamed the house at night. . . Well, I know that they are here, because one night I heard some rattling sounds and thought it was the boards creaking in the old house (dates from the 1700s). The next morning, several picture frames were turned upside down and a mirror was taken off the mantel and placed against a wall across from its original place. . . every once in a while things are gently moved. . . Even my husband [Tom] who is not a believer in any of this . . . admits to our house-ghosts. . . They are nice ghosts, though. . . never do any real harm and we all love waterfront life together. . . .

While on the Subject of Ghosts . . .
– told by Marianne Taylor and Nellie Watson

When we bought Ferry Point in 1974 there was the old farmhouse [1845] which we barely renovated, but rented out to those who loved old houses. Each renter would sheepishly admit to me that the house had ghosts. One renter, after having several mischievous pranks done to her such as hiding her coke bottles and moving and re-arranging her kitchen appliances. . . consulted a medium. The renter had refinished all the floors, but one spot would not accept any varnish. The varnish formed a complete circle of dry wood where no surface finish could be applied. The medium said that a body was buried under the house in that spot. She said it was a man who was pushed down the stairs [very steep ones] who hit his head. . . That renter left, and the next one claimed that there was a ghost who loved to rattle kitchen things. . . She would hear sounds of water in the middle of the night. . . One night she saw a ghost with a dark sort of cape or mantle over his shoulders. She said it was not an evil ghost. . . a nice ghost whom she could live with. When she was transferred to Utah, she said I should know all about it. . . She loved the house and hated to move. . . even if there were ghosts.

Same Ghost . . . Different Slant
– the following is Nellie's story connected with the same farmhouse

In the twenties when the MacDowells owned Ferry Point [north side of the Magothy] they had a spinster sister we called Miss Stein. She kept cows which made wonderful milk and butter and many people would row over to buy their milk and butter. The caretaker there was John Schools. When Miss Stein got really old [she lived in the old farmhouse on the property], John took care of her. . . It was rumored that she fell in love with him. . . but she never married. . . She found out that he had another woman. . . Come to think of it, no-one ever knew what became of him. . .

• • •

I have never experienced the ghost myself, as I gather the history of the Magothy in the upper room of the very same farmhouse, but when I heard Nellie Watson's story about Miss Stein, I began to look. . . and to believe. . . [M.T].

Ice Skating to Music – told by Kathleen Giddings Hankins

We've been in Cape Arthur since 1948, and the river and some of its coves always seemed to freeze more back then. I remember when some of the people in Cape Arthur would play their radios loudly and provide music for the skaters. . . . I remember the old lovely Magothy Hall where Folger McKinsey lived. . . The story was that someone broke into the house to steal its furnace and in the process, it burnt down. . . Furnaces were a rare item in those days.

The Magothy in solid ice, winter of 1977. Above: Sherry Schindler; below: an anonymous Volkswagon going to dinner at Riverdale Restaurant across the ice. (photos by Howard Schindler)

The Old House on Dobbins Island
– told by Milton T. Oler [Mr. Oler was a member of the first team of archaeologists who dug for artifacts on Ulmstead Point.]

I can remember a big rambling waterfront house on Dobbin's Island. At one time it was owned by the Palmer family and called "Palmer's Island" by everybody here. They'd hold big river-parties and people would be "carriaged" over by horse to attend. . . always something going on there in the summer. We lived on Ulmstead and I always remember all the Indian artifacts and arrowheads in the waters at low tide. We'd tie a rope around a colored boy so he'd be safe and he'd go looking for us. Also he'd find plenty of soft-

shelled crabs that way. . . I also remember Dr. Bull from Cape Sable coming over here to do a huge research project on mosquitoes on Sprigg's Pond.

The Weddings at Riverdale – told by Brad and Rose Kelly

Oh! Riverdale in the old days was the center of our social lives. We'd celebrate weddings, 50th and 75th anniversaries and would also have most of our New Year's parties there. . . . The children were always welcomed there. . . it had such a family atmosphere. [It still does.]

Rum Runners and Mill Creek – told by Bill Gilbert

Stories were told to me about the rum-runners during prohibition and how they'd hide in the Magothy. In fact one of them sunk right at the head of Mill Creek. Mill Creek's Landing always was supposed to sell the best corn, melons and produce. . . .

"The Maid of the Mist" – told by Catherine Helm

I was a volunteer nurse in the Army and when we had a party, everybody would come. My parents would stay overnight in the old side-winder ferry boat [H.S. Smith], which was donated by the City of Baltimore to the Magothy. I also remember the The Maid of the Mist. It was the boat launch from Gibson Island to Mago Vista. I think they motorized it after the motor was invented. . . It was a huge old thing. . .

• • •

During the First World War the Women's Land Army lived at Camp Milbur . . . on the old ferry boat. Farmers of the area would send their trucks down there loaded with produce for "the cause." But the last camp there was in 1942 or '43. [The State of Maryland also housed women there in the 40s from the University of Maryland.]

• • •

Back in those days when my parents had a river party, everybody came. . . I grew up with Alice Shulz, and Marie Angel Durner was my grandmother. . . Before 1926 there was no gate on Gibson. . . only a poor dirt sand road. . . The whole river was invited to parties there when everybody knew everybody else.

A Bridge at Anchor's Away – told by Kimberly Groebel

My grandfather said that at one time there was a bridge which connected the house, "Anchor's Away" with a point on Steedman's Point. . .

Park Creek—a Mite of History – told by William J. Stallings

John F. Ellison used to farm the lands there. In the 1800s the Smiths owned all of the land at Park Creek and the cantaloupes and produce from there were the best anywhere.

The Maryland Anti-Pollution Association of the Magothy
– told by M. Daubert

Oh, yes indeed, we had back then, from 1969 to 1989, a group of people from around here who were very interested in what terrible effects pollution was having on our river. We called it the Maryland Anti-Pollution Association. . . Somehow the group just petered out in '89 from lack of interest, I guess. . . The fish back in the early days? Tons of them. . . Back in the 40s you caught so many you could hardly get rid of them. . . Someone told me that the word "Magothy" in Indian meant "Mad-Waters. . . ."

Of Secret Tunnels and the Underground Railroad
– compiled by Blodwin Shipley Potee[6]

Yes, there is a lure of mystery about the island, [Gibson Island] particularly a secret tunnel which was used during the Civil War as part of the "Underground Railroad." This tunnel has been closed these many, many years.

• • •

The old restored stone house [formerly of Elmer l. Palmer] built in 1924 . . . had a jail, a chapel, and an ice house. . . its early inhabitants had grown homesick for the red soil of England. They had some of the soil brought here and placed near the back door of the home. The family graveyard had used sandstone to mark the graves of their loved ones and the dates of their demise were carved on holly trees.

• • •

There was a barn "at the top" of the island and a big tree where an early countian is supposed to have hung himself.

The Causeway at Gibson Island – B. S. Potee[7]

The present causeway was built by J. Rulon Miller of the Empire Construction Company of New York [shortly after 1924]. He came, as many do, to the island as a summer resident and loved it so much that he made it his permanent home. (Before the causeway was built, residents of the area had to traverse the sand spit which connected it to the mainland at low tide. . . the island really never was an island. . . just a peninsula. . . .) 'Tis true–many of the residents are descendants of old Maryland families, but all they and their ancestors have wanted is solitude and privacy. Wasn't it Thomas Lincoln who would move his family "on" when the smoke from his neighbor's chimney could be seen?

Grachur Club—Back in the 1930s – told by Phil Beigel

Back in the 30s one of the best larks was when a small group of Grachur Clubbers found a deal. . . from Mago Vista Club. . . Somehow they bought a complete set of cast iron table and chairs for "nothing." But nobody knew how in the world they would get it back across the Magothy. They decided that it was such a short distance, they could paddle them across the river. How they got such a really heavy set back in that small boat, no one knew. . . They just kept telling that story of what a "lark" it was.

Moonlight Sail – [article in "County Chronicle," Fall 1948] told by Tommy Nelson

Tommy Nelson, a previous commodore of the Gibson Island Junior Fleet, tells of the time at the races when the moon finally came out, and the wind was totally dead, "They [the Fleet] finished in the order in which they were picked up. . . . "

Gibson Island—President Taft's Summer Home?
– [accumulated lore of Gibson Island Historical Society]

The story goes that at one time 1,000 acres of Gibson Island was considered as land for President Taft's summer home [He was president between 1909 and 1913]. . . . The Island was also suggested as the site of a fortification to protect Baltimore and Washington, but because of excellent facilities further down the Bay, and also Forts Carroll and Howard, the plan was abandoned.

An Autumn Ride – *from Gibson Island "Hearsay"*

With the coming of autumn, a crispness in the early morning air greets horses and riders out for a canter before breakfast.

A Treasure-Dig – *"News American," August 18, 1907*

A Baltimore man riddled with rheumatism and too poor to pay for doctors decided to dig for treasure rumored to be found on Gibson Island. He was penniless, but he thought that his finding would help him to bargain for a wagon to get to the steamboat wharf seven miles away. After waiting for the moon and stars to get in the right conjunction, he dug one night, but the moon getting behind a cloud, he was compelled to desist. The next night just as his shovel struck the strong box containing the valuables [rumored to be hidden there], he says the Spirit of Gibson appeared and told him to stop, and he could not let him have the money at that time. So, in the morning he returned the box to its grave and walked to the steamboat seven miles away.

End-Note – *told by Bill Hoshell*

Back in the 60s the river was very calming. . . I remember the clear blue-green water, it was so amazing to gaze down and see the grass shrimp and the dark green seaweed. . . I'd like to see the river get closer to what it was. . .

Above: a lone skater on Lake Claire. Opposite: a boat frozen in the ice near Cape St. Claire. (photos by Joan B. Machinchick)

"Magothy Winter"
– Anonymous: found in 1943 at the home of Christine Councill

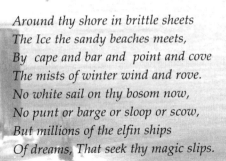

I look afar to Gibson Isle,
I see the waters gleam and smile.
I hear the surf beat on the shore,
My Magothy that I adore.
Sweet River of a thousand Dreams,
Blue Estuary of the Bay
And Winter now upon you gleams,
And all the birds have gone away.

Around thy shore in brittle sheets
The Ice the sandy beaches meets,
By cape and bar and point and cove
The mists of winter wind and rove.
No white sail on thy bosom now,
No punt or barge or sloop or scow,
But millions of the elfin ships
Of dreams, That seek thy magic slips.

Old homes of Anne Arundel peace,
Where orchards sleep and turmoils cease,
Dear Homes that in the winter spell
Have so much of dear love to tell.
My river of Chesapeake,
Where faeries play at hide and seek,
Where memories dance in mystic haze,
My Magothy of other days.

1.   Bob Johnson, ed. *Broad Neck Hundred: Life and Time Between the Severn and the Magothy,* Winter, 1975-76, Volume 1, Number 1, pp. 2-20. All material which follows is quoted directly from this work.

2.   Mary McKinsey Ridout, "Mencken, Beer, Music on a Waterfront Farm," *The Baltimore Sun* January 25, 1981.

3.   Spencer Rowe, "The Turtle Race: A Day of Reckoning on Black Hole Cree," Chesapeake Bay Magazine, April, 1992, pp. 48-50.

4.   Gail R. Blaisdell, "Maryland Living," July 7, 1968, pp. 4, 5.

5.   Sue Miller, "The Anne Arundel Star," March 21, 1957, p. 1.

6.   Blodwin Shipley Potee, *Quarterly News Bulletin of the Anne Arundell County Historical Society,* October, year, Vol. 5, No. 1.

7.   Ibid.

PART IV

The Contemporary Magothy

Although we cannot preserve Chesapeake Bay for future generations without laws and regulations, all the legislation we could imagine will not be enough without an ethic that defines an enduring and maturing relationship between humans and their environment

—Tom Horton, William Eichbaum, "Turning the Tide"

CHAPTER 10

Contemporary Life on the Magothy; Ecology and Transformation

All of the history of the Chesapeake Bay, including the fond visions of what the rivers used to be, cannot save it from the devastating effects of pollution. Recollections of the Magothy's layers of history can only express a vision of the past so essential to the understanding of the future. Our knowledge of and inter-action with the Bay now are keys to its turnaround, its transformation. The poignancy of its message to us, a contemporary river-people, marks the begin-ning of its resurgence of natural life forms.

Like all bay tributaries, the Magothy is vulnerable to over-population, human sewage, sediments from over-chemicalization, loss of forested buffer, run-off from farm fertilizers and animal wastes, dredging, global warming, toxic pollu-tants from industry, and air pollution. The Magothy speaks through its warning signals of reduced fish populations, its narrowing blue crab output, and its decline of striped bass and oyster populations. It shows stress from its reduced dissolved oxygen levels, decline of its waterfowl life, loss of water quality, and the reduction of its rare species of plant life.

Hope lies in the Bay's potential for change. As a tributary of the Chesapeake Bay, the Magothy reacts to variable conditions with extreme volatility. Being a tiny part of the huge estuary of the Bay, it changes significantly with the merging of its salt and fresh river water. Tom Horton, conservationist, writes that "being neither lake nor mere river, running in only one direction for all time, nor ocean which has a constant salty chemistry, the Bay is a part of a constant three-ring circus of motion, productivity and changeableness."[1]

Perhaps people do not know precisely where we stand ecologically as a tributary of the Bay and as part of the Western Shore. The Magothy River is termed a "recreational" river, as opposed to being a "scenic and wild" river because ninety percent of its shoreline is developed residentially. But the Natural Heritage Program ranks the Magothy River as a "significant" river because it still has a major share of natural resources, endangered species and archeological sites. The term, "highly significant" is its rank of importance in the scale of natural resources because of the presence of several rare and endangered species surrounding the Magothy, as well as its large percentage of natural bogs.

Gradually, the rare species are returning to the area, lending a note of hope to an otherwise grim picture. Several peregrine falcon families circle the remaining forested lands and coves, while the return of the bald eagle reported at North Ferry Point is a cause for celebration. The bald eagle has been removed from the Endangered Species list. Environmental studies of the Magothy are ongoing, but official reportage comes every ten years or so. In 1988 when the last *Maryland Rivers Study* was recorded, the Magothy had a population of 100 black duck and a population of 4,500 canvasback; in fact a 3,200 count of recreational hunting waterfowl population was recorded.[2] Two updated studies of the tributaries of the Chesapeake entitled, *Maryland Rivers Study,* June 1992,[3] and *The Magothy River Comprehensive Vessel Management Plan,* 1992,[4] offer specific current ecological and scientific data on the Magothy. From these studies, the environmental complexity of the Magothy and other tributaries becomes evident.

The Magothy River is tucked into the ecosystem known to scientists as the West Chesapeake Basin Drainage Area, better known as "the watershed." This encompasses 1.3 million acres in the Coastal Plain and Piedmont provinces, extending along the western shore from the mouth of the Susquehanna River to the Patuxent River basin. But all of the rain run-off from the land mass between North Carolina and Vermont, a sprawling 64,000 square miles, literally drains

bald eagle

canvasback duck

into the Bay. All pollution from this land heads bayward including every discharge from sewage pipes, industrial outfall, uncontained oil spills, and "every styrofoam cup casually tossed into a drainageway."[5]

Thus, as a small, but unique part of this basin, the Western Shore rivers become a throbbing part of the heartbeat of the Bay. Specifically, the basin comprises approximately twenty-five percent of the total Bay watershed and includes about twelve percent (276,000 acres) of Chesapeake Bay tidal and non-tidal wetlands. Land is distributed relatively evenly among forest (thirty-five percent), agricultural/pasture (thirty-three percent), and urban usage (thirty-two percent). This distribution reflects a three percent decrease in forested area and an equivalent increase in urban area since 1978. The 1980 population of the West Chesapeake basin was about 1.9 million and approximately fifteen percent of the Bay watershed population resides in the area. Baltimore is the largest city in this basin.[6]

As a part of nine Western Shore tributaries, which include the Bush, Middle, Back, Patapsco, Severn, South, Rhode and West Rivers, the Magothy has its own diverse and unique characteristics. This kind of heterogeneity is precisely what creates the environmental differences among these various West basin tributaries. For example, the more northern rivers, the Bush and Gunpowder, have major portions of the watersheds in the Piedmont province. Rivers to the south, including the Severn, Rhode, and West rivers are almost exclusively in the Coastal Plain. The northern rivers of the Piedmont appear buffeted against acidification, while the Coastal Plain rivers are subject to episodic acidification due to acid deposition.

The Magothy, which lies somewhere in between, thus acquires the characteristics of both areas. Being closer to the Patapsco, which is subject to water quality degradation, particularly from discharges of chemical contaminants from Baltimore City industries and urban runoff, the Magothy

black duck

certainly can be affected by these variables as well. But there is an upswing in benthic community recovery in the Baltimore Harbor, suggesting a general improvement in water quality.[7]

The Magothy River is a unique resource to its people because of its diversity of uses. However, problems arise if conflicting uses occur. For example, there is a conflict between heavy boating use and crabbing; another exists between waste discharge and swimming. Recreational uses of the river, including boating and sport fishing, come in conflict with overcrowding through traffic density and crowded marinas. Aesthetic appreciation of the Magothy conflicts with pressure for access to its shores, through density-building. Questions relevant to the Magothy's Natural Resources are: Are we at the maximum potential of the Magothy or are we well below it? What uses of the Magothy diminish its potential for natural wildlife and fishes to use it as habitat, spawning, and nursery ground? How are we to decide what degree of conflict from over-use can be tolerated? These ongoing questions continue to the present in the various studies being conducted.[8]

Fish Studies

In the main tributary, creeks and coves of the Magothy, another natural resource lurks beneath the shining crests of water—the fish of the Magothy. Fish are a small, but significant part of the Chesapeake Bay, the world's largest estuary. The Bay's richly concentrated reservoir of finfish and shellfish depend upon its diverse range of aquatic environments; the Magothy plays its role in the ecology of such life. Diverse habitats of fish that are in danger of extinction or rare in occurrence, need to be respected and protected, especially those habitats that provide reproductive shelter for certain fish.

The river captains of the Magothy report that the increase of the clarity of the water "might be one of the reasons that we have increasing amounts of good rock fishing and other sports varieties such as white perch, blue-fish, weakfish, spot, shad and croakers." The shellfish waters of the Magothy, which include environments for oysters, soft-shell clams, hard-shelled clams and Maryland blue crab, provide 5,393 acres of har-

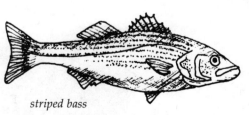

striped bass

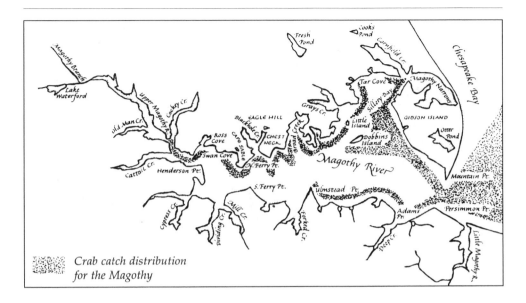

Crab catch distribution
for the Magothy

vesting waters. The king of all the shellfish, the blue crab, can be harvested in all
parts of the Magothy, but most of the commercial crab catches occur at the mouth
of the river.

Among the animals of the estuary, finfish rank as one of the most important.
Fish use the Magothy in four ways: as a spawning ground, as a nursery for small
fry, as a feeding area for adults, and as a staging area for fish to school before
they move to other waters. This takes place in Spring and Fall primarily by
the striped bass species. "It appears from college sponsored studies
that major species concentrate from Pea Patch Point, along the north
shore of the Magothy to Mountain Point including areas of Sillery
Bay, and on the south shore from Ulmstead Point to Persimmon
Point. During the Fall, high concentrations of sport fishes are found at
the mouth of the river in waters of twenty-five to thirty-five feet
deep. The reasons for the distinctly lower abundance of fish populations along major portions of the south shore are unclear, but
may perhaps be linked to water quality factors."[9] The Maryland
Department of Natural Resources (DNR)—Fish and Wildlife

blue crab

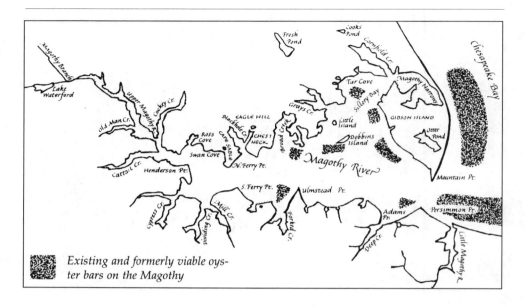

Existing and formerly viable oyster bars on the Magothy

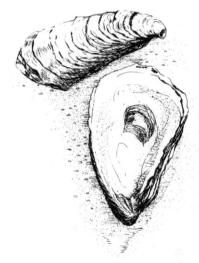

Services has conducted several species-specific studies, targeting yellow perch, white perch, and river herring on some of the basin's rivers in recent years. Data used and reported here are not totally inclusive, since the department has published only the best available data.

Striped bass, American shad, hickory shad, alewife and blueback herring, bay anchovy and white perch are the key species of fish covered by this particular "Living Resources Study." Yellow perch, spot, menhaden, hard clam, softshell clam, American oyster and blue crab also came under study. These studies reveal distinct degradation in numbers of spawning and living fish for the basin from the years 1972 through 1984. But more recent studies show some upgrading in the Severn, Magothy, and Western Basin, especially in the increased numbers of striped bass. "The upper western shore tributaries are [now] functioning as striped bass nurseries."[10]

One exception in the "Living Resources Status" is good news for

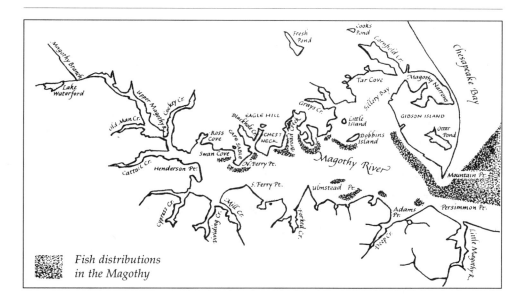

Fish distributions
in the Magothy

western shore fishermen and nature lovers. The white perch population is gradually increasing, peaking in 1962 to 120,000, and going to 100,000 in 1988. Also, yellow perch, one of the species of greatest commercial and recreational value within this basin, has increased markedly for the northern rivers during the 1980s. Levels have gone from less than 10,000 pounds annually during the late 1960s and early 1970s to nearly 40,000 pounds in 1988. But the stocks of yellow perch in the Severn, Magothy, Rhode, West and South Rivers have not fared as well as those in the northern rivers. Drastic reductions of yellow perch in the South, Severn and Magothy Rivers can be seen in the following data:

yellow perch

In 1978 in these rivers, 200 adult and juvenile yellow perch yielded to seining and trawling methods, while in 1987, a similar sampling program yielded only two adult yellow perch! Maryland DNR regulations of 1987 closed the West, South, Severn, Magothy and Patapsco Rivers to harvests of this species.[11]

white perch

Dissolved Oxygen Levels and Fish Studies

More recent DNR studies from 1989, 1990 and 1991 report a distinct association between dissolved oxygen levels (the amount of oxygen in water) and the number of species captured by the bottom trawl in the western basin. As potential indicators of environmental quality in the Chesapeake Bay, fish were recently sampled with seines and trawls in tidal segments of eight Maryland tributaries of which the Severn and the Magothy played an important role.

The startling news that the juvenile striped bass were found abundant in western shore tributaries north of the South River indicates that these areas may be important striped bass nurseries. Mean dissolved oxygen values (more oxygen levels in the water) show an increasing trend over the three years in the Severn River, South River, Magothy River, Wicomico River, and Mattawoman Creek. This is an indicator that some submerged aquatic vegetation (SAV) can be allowed to grow, although the increase is slow.

Studies revealed that a mixture of urban development and forest dominate and influence the ecology of the Magothy River and the Severn, but that the South River is mostly affected by forest, urban development and agriculture as well. Monitoring all of these rivers in terms of fish assemblages, the DNR found that these groupings of fish could be studied in terms of ecological stress in their respective aquatic systems. Thus an ongoing program of seining for fish samples is in progress on the Magothy.

The South, Severn and Magothy Rivers, which drain into highly urbanized watersheds in the Annapolis area of Anne Arundel County, are similar in salinity range. This report names the Magothy River as the most developed of the three, followed by the Severn River and the South River watersheds.

The methods used to conduct these fish studies in relation to dissolved oxygen levels were seining and trawling at various stations in each river. The results of the tests in the three western shore tributaries, the Magothy, Severn and South showed the same assemblage patterns, reflecting similarities in the fish community structure. The fish species were found to feed primarily on various forms of plankton; some feed on other fish or invertebrates; while others bottom feed. In

menhaden

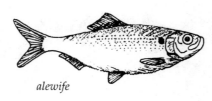

alewife

American shad

the Magothy, thirty-seven different species of fish were caught, while the Severn included thirty-six species and the South contained thirty-five species.

A plethora of unique names of fish such as the feather blenny and the tassellated darter, the naked goby and the gizzard shad or the fourspine stickleback, the hogchoker and the blueback herring—names which reveal the variegated marvels of nature, hidden from view, form a viable part of the natural world which strains to live under the stressed conditions of the Bay. Of the more familiar varieties, the official word according to these studies is that scientists "observed an increase in the CPUE [catch per unit effort is the amount of catch in a small measure of inches] of striped bass in the Severn River, Magothy River, and South River from 1989 to 1991." But the white perch (an important species), like the striped bass, were found to be extremely scarce. During this time frame, none were captured in Fishing Bay or the Severn, two notable places within the historic range of the species. However, currently (1998), fishermen are reporting a fine resurgence of white perch to be officially recorded in subsequent reports. (For more detailed information regarding the varieties of species and amounts of catch per river, consult the document, *"Fish Sampling in Eight Chesapeake Bay Tributaries."*)[12]

Water Quality

There was an indication of improved water quality conditions in some tributaries during the sample period, 1989 to 1991. Mean bottom dissolved oxygen values, so necessary for life support for fish and aquatic vegetation, revealed an increasing trend at many stations, including the Severn River, South River, Wicomico River, Curtis Creek and Mattawoman Creek. But the Magothy River apparently showed little or no increasing trend for oxygen level increase. Mean salinity values increased in the tributaries between 1989 and 1991.[13]

This valuable study has related changes in fish assemblages to land use. The Severn, South and Magothy Rivers and Rock Creek were termed, "urban impacted." This means that urban development, and excessive use of fertilizers along the shorelines directly influences the fish communities, even though the forested areas near the headwaters are present. One recent outcrop of Pfiesteria Piscicida, a fungus affecting the fish on the Pocomoke River, threatens to move to western shore rivers. Clearly, this type of degradation continues its course on the Bay.

The percent values of watershed acreage for each general land use is increasing at rapid rates. For example the Magothy River has 43.13 percent for urban use, 28.29 in forest, 5.13 for agriculture, 3.11 for commercial use, 19.96 of water area, and 0.0 is considered wetlands.[14]

The Magothy Aquifer

A unique formation which serves an important function in the Magothy River's watershed is what is known as the Magothy Aquifer. The north shore of the Magothy is the surface outcrop of the aquifer. According to a study of water quality issues of the Magothy by Anne Arundel Community College, "an aquifer is a porous sediment strata that allows water to migrate laterally, and serves as a storage reservoir suitable for tapping by means of wells. The Magothy Aquifer is a 30 to 60 meters (100-200 feet) thick layer of coarse sand, separated by impervious clay and silt."

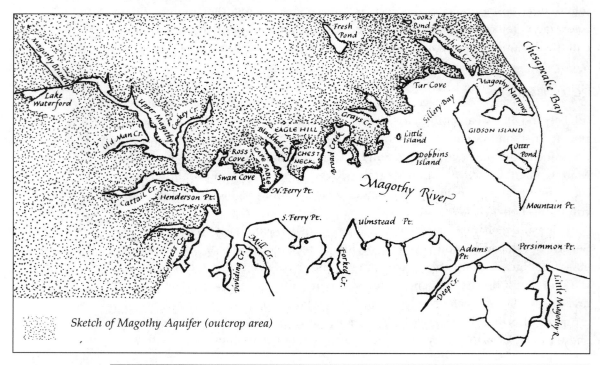

Sketch of Magothy Aquifer (outcrop area)

The important function of the aquifer's recharge area on the north side (see map) is that of supplying present and future water supplies. The interconnection of this key formation beneath the Magothy with water pollution issues, serves as a reminder that land use detrimental to Magothy River waters constitutes a threat to this key ground water supply. This report, states that development which created extensive"impervious areas" will reduce water input to the aquifer by reducing the amound of unpaved soils, altering stream flow and runoff patterns." The risk, also, of groundwater contamination by water-soluble pollutants is present with overdevelopment of Magothy River lands. [15]

In summary, these statistics are a reality check on recent trends which the concerned people of the Chesapeake already know. Trends do show positive signs of turnaround in the Bay. The juvenile striped bass catch in the upper western shore tributaries are a positive sign, both for the species and the tributaries. Although these tributaries show signs of degradation, they are still playing an important role in the reproductive success of this important species. But the dissolved oxygen (DO) is still quite low in the Severn, South, and Magothy Rivers and Rock Creek—a warning sign that the comeback of grasses and life which connects and feeds from this submerged aquatic vegetation is precarious, slow, and in need of strict conservation and environmental checks.[16]

Bird Studies

The United States Department of the Interior, Fish and Wildlife Service has conducted studies on the Magothy relating to its shifting bird population. For example, the National Audubon Society Christmas bird count site at Gibson Island reports the following species observed there from 1961 to 1988: black duck, redhead, canvasback, wood duck, great blue heron, green-backed heron, and bald eagle. However, key species such as the black-crowned night heron, American egret, snowy egret, little blue heron, and osprey were not observed from 1961 to 1988. The Maryland DNR mid-

great blue heron

osprey

winter waterfowl survey data, collected in cooperation with the U. S. Fish and Wildlife Service, provided wintertime abundance estimates in this West Chesapeake basin for black ducks, canvasbacks, and redheads from 1956 to 1990. A specific waterfowl survey (from 1967 to 1985) provided data with an index of springtime wood duck abundance in the West Chesapeake basin.

News from the U.S. Department of Fish and Wildlife Service is that, of the colonial waterbirds included in the list of key species, only the great blue herons and black-crowned night herons were observed in the 1988 data. Thus, some of these reports include species not included in other studies, such as the black-crowned night heron.

Wetlands

The percentage of wetlands considered "significant," are the transitional lands between terrestrial and aquatic ecosystems where the water table is usually at or near the surface or covering the land with shallow water.

Wetlands are critical to the unique set of ecosystems in the Chesapeake Bay tributaries for wildlife and plant community habitat, also for water-quality and natural flood control. Thus it is essential that we preserve the remaining pools of life on the Magothy, its natural areas of wetlands. The *Maryland Rivers Study* of 1988 states that "Our wetlands provide essential breeding, resting, and feeding habitat as well as sanctuary for many of our remaining species of wildlife, waterfowl and shore-birds." The study notes that essential habitat, cover, and food reservoirs for many fish and shellfish species are created when certain vegetation and water flow patterns coexist.

Tidal wetlands of the Magothy exist throughout the river with the common occurrence at the headwaters of its tributaries. The primary wetland vegetation types include meadow cordgrass; spike grass, cattail smooth cordgrasses, and common reed. According to *The Magothy Comprehensive Vessel Management Plan,*

black crowned
night heron

prepared by the Maryland Department of Natural Resources Boating Administration, 1992, submerged aquatic vegetation have many valuable ecological functions. Many parts of the plants are ingested by ducks, geese, and swans. SAV also serves as habitat and nursery areas for various species of fish, blue crab and invertebrates. Other significant attributes of SAV are their capacity to absorb nutrients, such as nitrogen and phosphorous, and remove suspended sediments from the water column. They are generally located near the shoreline in close proximity to wetlands and bogs. Horned pondweed is the dominant species found in the Magothy River in the following locations: Broad Creek, Inner Harbor (Gibson Island), Redhouse Cove, Lake Claire, Forked Creek, Old Man Creek, Cove West of Windless Point and east shore area of the mouth to Forked Creek/Cool Spring Cove. The "significant" amount of wetlands on the Magothy is 10 percent. There is a large diversity of these wetland classes, as shown on the U.S. Fish and Wildlife Service National Wetland Inventory Maps; the number of wetland classifications is seventeen. Submerged aquatic vegetation which had dropped to zero in 1988 is now reportedly very slowly rebuilding.[17]

green heron

The upland vegetation on the Magothy, that is, the amount of remaining forested edge is only twenty percent, a poor average of untouched lands. Our surrounding agricultural lands are few with only thirteen percent of open space available in the 1988 study; in the 1992 study only twenty-eight to twenty-nine percent of all lands surrounding the watershed is forested.

Specific designated threatened species on our upland vegetation include the giant cane and the whorled water-pennywort. The old cliche, "a matter of life and death," applies to this river and its balance of land and water use right at this moment. If the wetlands continue to be compromised by land developers or personal home waterfront dwellers, with loop-holes and crevices in the Maryland Critical Area Laws, we have little chance of clearing our waters from the continual pollution and degradation which has been our history.

The Magothy River Association and the Magothy River Land Trust are two essential organizations which preserve, honor, and attend to crucial ecological river concerns.[18] The Magothy River Land Trust seeks available pockets of land for preservation, with the philosophy that it is never too late to preserve buffer zones to wetlands or bogs.

Magothy Bogs

pitcher plant

The Magothy watershed contains a number of small Coastal Plain bogs or bog-like openings, particularly on the edges of old ponds. Judith R. Modlin of the Maryland Department of Natural Resources describes bogs as "open, acidic, nutrient-poor wetlands with sphagnum moss, heath shrubs, wildflowers, and often with insect eating plants. Bogs form when a mat of vegetation, especially sphagnum moss and sedges, develops on the edge of a pond, lake, wetland, or slow-moving stream. As the pond dries out, the bog mat may eventually grow to cover the entire surface."

Reports from naturalists writing in the early part of this century suggest that Coastal Plain bogs, similar to the New Jersey pine bogs, were once more common in Maryland than they are today. In 1918, naturalist W.L. McAtee listed thirty-four lush "magnolia bogs" in Anne Arundel and Prince George's Counties that were similar in species composition to several sites on the Magothy today. These bogs were probably remnants of an ancient pinelands ecosystem—pines on the sand hills and sphagnum bogs in the low areas—that migrated back and forth across the sandy Maryland Coastal Plain as sea level rose and fell with fluctuating climates.

In the past, Chesapeake Bay people rarely considered bogs, swamps or other wetlands as attractive and gave scarcely any time to thinking about how these quiet places are connected with the health of Bay water. Today, more people understand the significance of wetlands as filters of

sun dew

nutrients and as important plant and wildlife habitats. Presently most of Maryland's original Coastal Plain bog sites have been obliterated, but small bogs and bog-like depressions develop where water conditions and soils support bog plants. Anne Arundel County has more Coastal Plain bogs than any other county in Maryland (roughly ten to twelve known sites), and the majority of those occur in the Magothy watershed. These special sites harbor several plants which have become rare in the state, and they deserve our appreciation and protection[18]

Historically, the world of the bog as it once existed was a secret, special place, delicate to the human tread, holding in its small pools, rare and lovely plant species, such as dense shrubs of highbrush blueberry, swamp azalea, and sweet pepperbush. The curving limbs of sweet bay magnolia arched overhead, bearing sweet-scented, creamy white blossoms. In their prime, bogs resembled a primeval landscape where ancesteral prehistoric Indians once roamed. Gradually, in time, tall lush cinnamon ferns grew among the thick, fallen leaves and darkened earth, black with degenerating plants.

With a few careful steps, one enters the Magothy bog, a remnant of the original Coastal Plain bog. Sunlight checkers upon patches of sphagnum moss, carpeting edges of low shrubs and sedge hummocks. Mazes of pools and open water channel through mats of vegetation; the splash of a frog as it enters the water is the only sound. Plump berries hang from tiny-leaved cranberry plants, arching over the cranberries, branches of sturdy leatherleaf shrubs bear a row of small urn-shaped flowers.

Venturing forth deeply into the bog, one spies strange low plants with a greenish-red cast on the leaves—the pitcher plant offers a watery grave to unwary insects. Opening their lacy lower blossoms, the yellow-fringed orchids surprise and delight.

While listening to the musical twittering of bird song, one notices tiny, yellow bladderwort flowers which emerge from the murky water. Dozens of dragonflies and smaller insects hover in the landscape, beckoning. The murky peat sucks one into the quagmire, and a hasty retreat into much surer ground of nearby woodland assures safety.

Many of the rare and endangered plant species of the Magothy are within the confines of the bogs. These include forms of sphagnum, the *northern pitcher plant, the round-leaved sun-dew, the *coastal sedge, some evergreen shrubs of the heath family, large cranberry, rose-begonia, *yellow-fringed orchid. Several lichen such as the *British soldier, are considered rare, but not endangered.[20]

Of paramount importance in bog pro-

sedge

tection is awareness that a bog is a delicate area which is quickly affected by urbanization. Development too close to a bog produces impervious surfaces such as parking lots and buildings that change flow patterns and the amount of water entering the bog. Some pollutants, such as herbicides can damage or kill bog plants directly, and others do so by changing the acidity of nutrient levels in the bog. If fertilizers or lime used to treat lawns reach the bog, increased nutrient levels and reduced acidity may allow vigorous growth of more common wetland pollutants that can deplete rare bog species.

The best insurance against changing the chemical composition and water flow into bogs is through the maintenance of an adequate forested buffer on the slopes surrounding the bogs. By not touching or picking bog plants and wild-flowers; by preserving the area of the bog through awareness of its important function in the eco-system, and by joining or calling the Magothy River Land Trust or the Maryland Cooperative Natural Areas Registry, one can become active in saving the Magothy.[21]

Water Management Studies

On a clear, shining day, the Magothy sports its numerous boats like a benevolent god, showering gleaming toys on its children. Sailboats dance and dart; motor craft whiz or putter; occasional sculls glide silently. A quiet canoe slips into a creek and a wind-surfer leans into the wind, cavorting with it in the sun. The tiny jet wave-runners whine and whir, while the classical crabbing work boats or the skipjacks out of Deep Creek recall a time in the distant past when the river was used for livelihood and for sustenance.

But along with all of these recreational pursuits, problems occur in connection with the Magothy's essential life and ecological health. High vessel speeds, congestion, noise, and shoreline erosion result from overcrowded waterways. The Maryland Boating Administration, aware of these problems, conducted seminars and public hearings which encompassed Magothy boaters and users of the river. A town meeting followed, held to an exchange of ideas, reports, and information regarding the boating activities, especially the problems facing this busy waterway. The result was the origin of the *Magothy River Comprehensive Vessel Management Plan, 1992*. The key issues of extensive speeding with the accompanying noise levels and safety issues were addressed. The following solutions were incorporated:

1. a maximum speed limit of six knots effective at all times or during the boating season in areas which are narrow or confined, have heavy cross traffic, include extensive slip and marina development, or have poor line of sight.

2. a maximum speed limit of six knots in areas where high speed activity is in conflict with traditional recreational uses such as swimming and anchoring.[22]

In the *Vessel Management Plan,* geographic areas are marked for active or passive activity. For example, the Little Magothy River is deemed for "passive" use such as bird watching, crabbing, small boat sailing, swimming, anchoring, fishing, canoeing or rowing. Forked Creek and Cool Spring Cove are protected areas; the convergence area of Cockey Creek, Cattail Creek and the Upper Magothy including a large shallow area off Focal Point, are used extensively as an anchorage area providing swimming and wading opportunities for boaters. Also within this area are a large private community marina, a sailing school and a Girl Scout Camp. Blackhole Creek and Broad Creek offer pleasing aesthetics and protection from adverse weather conditions. Boaters can enjoy picnicking, sunbathing and bird watching.

Ross Cove is almost land locked with a narrow, but deep entrance channel. There is a large community swimming beach and the area provides much opportunity for passive recreation. Long Cove is still a cove with minimal shoreline development. Gibson Island's Inner Harbor and Blackhole Creek have large numbers of moored vessels. Additionally, there are two registered group mooring areas in the Upper Magothy: one in Dividing Creek and one off Ulmstead Point.

Swim areas exist throughout the entire river system. Twenty-three community bathing beaches are located within twenty-nine private community facilities. No bathing beaches are open to the general public on the Magothy to this date, however swim areas for the general public include areas such as Dobbin's Island, Eagle Cove and an area within the Upper Magothy off Focal Point.

Cornfield Creek, Eagle Cove and Dobbin's Island are identified as traditional anchoring areas. These areas offer pleasing aesthetics, and protection from adverse weather conditions. Swimming, picnicking, sunbathing and bird watching are enjoyed here. Water skiing is also popular in Eagle Cove and near Dobbin's Island.

Although recreational water skiing and jet skiing are enjoyed in many places on the river, sites which are particularly popular include Sillery Bay, Eagle Cove, between Holland and Purdy Points, and the waters between Ferry Point and Pea Patch Point. During weekdays some areas are also open to skiers, such as the Little Magothy and the main stem of the Magothy. The *Vessel Management Study* warns that in times of heavy vessel traffic, particularly on weekends, concerns of safety and visibility of fallen skiers and jet-boaters can be a problem. Here is where personal responsibility and good judgment must come into play. Because of safety problems and shoreline erosion resulting from the Magothy's entire boating community, especially on the Little Magothy River, Cockey Creek, Dobbin's Island and Gibson Island, certain regulatory cautions were established by the Boating Administration which can be consulted in the study.

By recommending and incorporating minimum wake areas where boat traffic might have an impact on existing endangered or threatened plant species, the problem can be ameliorated. However, ignorance of precious resources and lack of real awareness are most insidious enemies of true restoration of the Magothy.[23]

In addressing the water quality of the Magothy, the *Vessel Management Plan* makes recommendations: the Boating Administration stresses the need for placing more marine sewage pump-out stations, as well as more educational workshops for citizens. It also recommends that programs be developed to encourage proper septic functioning by all homeowners on the river and the installation of nitrogen reducing septic systems in areas where appropriate. Progress is slowly being made. For example at Broadneck, construction is underway to modify the waste water treatment plant for elimination of nitrogen into the river. Still, the political reality is that pro-active

cordgrass

citizens must elect officials who support monies for the precise purpose of Chesapeake Bay clean-up.

The potential for uncovering more historic and archaeological resources in the Magothy is great; in fact, the Maryland Historic Trust recommends that systematic underwater surveys be conducted to identify submerged cultural resources. In summer, 1993, an underwater archaeological team entered the waters and discovered many submerged artifacts, clues to the mysterious past. Due to lack of personnel and funding, the project was discontinued. The Department of Archaeology reports the "findings remain scattered and not labeled." These include significant ship-wrecks, piers, bridges and landings for the old ferries which lie beneath these waters, waiting to be discovered.

Strategies for Transformation

A battery of aggressive strategies to transform the Magothy is now underway, thanks to the Magothy River Association, the DNR, the State Office of Planning, the Chesapeake Bay Foundation, the Alliance for the Chesapeake and the Maryland Department of the Environment (MDE). They are assessing and upgrading wastewater treatment plans, implementing erosion and sediment control and managing stormwater and developing educational programs to regulate septic use. The MDE also is working on accelerating the nutrient management program as well as programs for optimizing the use of nutrients in the bay. They are encouraging farmers and all planters to plant winter cover crops to absorb nutrients that remain in the soil, especially for post-harvesting times. Soil conservation and water quality programs are emphasized with plans for increasing the planting of trees and forests at the water's edge.[24]

Specific Magothy River Projects

A number of exciting Magothy River environmental projects are ongoing and reported in the *Magothy River Association Newsletter*, July, 1994.[25] They include a yellow perch project, a four-year stream survey, and an artificial oyster reef program.

The Artificial Oyster Reef Program

The Magothy River Oyster Program was begun early in 1959 when the Magothy River Association purchased oyster spat, which is spawn of the adult oyster, from a hatchery in the Patuxent. Six locations on the Magothy produced very fine results in oyster hatching, even though these first attempts were aborted due to vandalism. The MRA up to date has distributed over 400 oyster growing systems to Magothy River Residents and marinas. Individuals, pier owners and communities are encouraged to continue this interest. In winter, 1993 several MRA members established an oyster reef at Ulmstead Point. Reports are that it is 700 sq. ft. and seeded with 4,000 two-inch oysters. In the summer of 1994 dives were conducted to see signs of life and growth. An oyster hatchery is now underway at Sandy Point State Park. New spat continues to be available for all individuals or communities.

The Yellow Perch Project

With grants from Anne Arundel Community College and MRA, a project has been established for the return of the endangered yellow perch. In 1988, an effort to restock yellow perch from the Sassafras River resulted in vandalism, but the 1991 restocking effort, supported by the MRA, took effect. Fishermen taking yellow perch are asked to call MRA at 410-255-2006 for monitoring of location, time of catch, size, etc. The good news is that indeed, the yellow perch were seen in the river in 1993 and continue to rise in numbers to the present.

Stream Surveys

Other ongoing measures to improve water quality and natural life in the Magothy are connected with monitoring specific tributaries and streams for water quality and other detailed shoreline information; thirteen creeks were selected and shoreline wake and boat-level inpsections are underway. For Mill Creek, Dividing Creek and Cypress Creek, findings are completed and have already led to corrective measures of the severe bank erosion and extreme turbidity, especially in Dividing Creek due to the College Parkway run-off. Over-development has its hazards, and all developers need to be aware of and informed of their extremely important role in saving the Magothy and all other rivers and tributaries of the great Chesapeake Bay.

Problems can certainly be identified, but only with individual citizen awareness and aggressive intervention can plan implementation begin and solutions be found. Tom Horton capitulates a message of hope for all of us:

The Bay, damaged though it is, remains a system capable of enormous and rapid comebacks, once we reverse our current polluting behavior. Given a chance, it will no doubt amaze us with the bounty it can produce.[26]

1. Granted with permission from *Turning the Tide,* Tom Horton, William M. Eichbaum, © Chesapeake Bay Foundation, 1991. Published by Island Press, Washington, D.C. and Covelo, CA. p. 9.

2. *Maryland Rivers Study, Tributaries of the Chesapeake Bay,* National Park Service, Division of Park and Resource Planning, and Maryland Department of Natural Resources Scenic and Wild Rivers Program, 1988.

3. *Maryland Rivers Study, Tributaries of the Chesapeake Bay,* William A. Richkus, Paul Jacobson, Ann Ranasinghe, Anna Shaughnessy, Janis Chaillou, Paul Kazyak, Carol DeLisle Bersar, Inc. ESM Operations, Columbia, Maryland, et. al. and Richard Batiuk, U.S. Environmental Protection Agency, Annapolis, Maryland, September 1994. All subsequent references will be called "Living Resources Status Report." These include: "Fish Assemblages and Dissolved Oxygen Trends in Eight Chesapeake Bay Tributaries During the Summers of 1989-1991, A Data Report," John T. Carmichael, Brian M. Richardson, Margaret Roberts, Stephen J. Jordan. Maryland Department of Natural Resources, Annapolis, Maryland, November, 1992.

4. *The Magothy River Comprehensive Vessel Management Plan,* Maryland Department of Natural Resources Boating Administration, June 8, 1992, p. 21. All subsequent references will be referred to as "Vessel Management Plan."

5. Granted with permission from *Turning the Tide,* Tom Horton, William M. Eichbaum, © Chesapeake Bay Foundation, 1991. Published by Island Press, Washington, D.C. and Covelo, CA. p. 3.

6. *Living Resources Status,* p. 29.

7. Ibid.

8. *The Magothy River, A Summary of Available Information Relating to Water Quality Issues.* Environmental Center, Anne Arundel Community College, March, 1981, p. 13.

9. Ibid. pp. 15, 16. For a table of Freshwater and Estuarine Fishes of the Magothy, see pp. 14-15 of this study.

10. *Living Resources Status,* "Fish Assemblages and Dissolved Oxygen Trends," p. 31.

11. *Living Resources Status,* p. 34.

12. *Living Resources Status,* "Fish Sampling in Eight Chesapeake Bay Tributaries," p. 17. All of the above information is derived from this study.

13. Ibid. [See graphs of DO and overall mean salinity on p. 22].

14. Ibid. [See charts on p. 23].

15. *The Magothy River, A Summary of Available Information Relating to Water Quality Issues,* Environmental Center, Anne Arundel Community College, March 1981, p. 3

16. Ibid. pp. 22-27. [These are important findings of DO levels].

17. Ibid. pp. 12-18 All subsequent references to *Maryland Rivers Study* are obtained in this information gathered in 1988, unless specified.

18. *Maryland's Natural Heritage,* text by Judith R. Modlin, assisted by staff of the Maryland Natural Heritage Program.

19. *Maryland's Natural Heritage,* Bulletin of the Maryland Natural Heritage Program, Div. of the Forest, Park and Wildlife Service, Department of Natural Resources, No. 9, Oct., 1990.

20. *= endangered species.

21. [For information as to membership, etc. in the Magothy River Land Trust, call (410/974-0756) or (410/647-6254).]

22. *The Magothy River Comprehensive Vessel Management Plan,* Maryland Department of Natural Resources Boating Administration, June 8, 1992, p. 21. All subsequent references will be referred to as "Vessel Management Plan."

23. For reporting violators of Magothy waterways rules, call:
    [The Natural Resources Police Communication Center is 410-260-8888; the statewide 24-hour number is 1-800-635-6124].
    [For Catch-a-Poacher call 1-800-635-6124].

24. *Maryland Tributary Strategies,* prepared by Maryland Department of the Environment, Maryland Department of Natural Resources; April, 1994. [This can be ordered from Maryland Department of Natural Resources, free.]

25. Information acquired referring to Magothy programs and specific ongoing scientific studies can be found in *Magothy River Association Newsletter,* July, 1994.

26. Granted with permission from *Turning the Tide,* Tom Horton, William M. Eichbaum, © Chesapeake Bay Foundation, 1991. Published by Island Press, Washington, D.C. and Covelo, CA. p. 286.

When we gaze out from our small worlds onto the shimmer of the river at sunset, for a moment we experience peace and a calm which only the water gives—a moment of free gift. But what can we give back to this river, lender of life, freedom, play, work and momentary relief from busy lives?

For Bay transformation to occur, Western Shore river people must look to themselves to find their level of participation, whether it be joining conservation organizations, participating in citizen studies, leading youth to more awareness, or simply by observing boating regulations, speed limits, and all anti-pollution warnings.

Thus, the vision of comeback lies deeply within each lover of the earth and its waters. The bottom line for all Magothites and Bay people in creating an environmental ethic lies in the care, the love and the participation we have of the watershed. This awareness stems from a long memory of history, an instinctive stirring in the blood. It is a bond with the waters; not only of the Chesapeake Bay, but with all waterways of the world; not only with forebears of a prehistoric and historic past, but with our contemporary people. Such it is that the history and love of one river, the Magothy, underlies the history and lore of all rivers. So too, the care of one river extends to the care of all rivers.